PRAISE FOR *I AM*

"*I AM* is a powerful book about self-realization. Howard Falco offers a profound explanation of the nature of your own existence and an understanding of the life you are capable of creating."

—Marci Shimoff, number-one *New York Times*–bestselling author of *Happy for No Reason*

"This magical book is both powerful and empowering! Howard Falco has delivered an ancient wisdom with a practical modern-day application. Imagine unleashing your infinite potential. . . . With the wisdom of *I AM* you will connect to a passion and a purpose that will forever change the way you live. *I AM* will help awaken mass consciousness by leading a discovery of who we really are."

—Dr. Darren R. Weissman, author of *The Power of Infinite Love & Gratitude*

"Years ago I had a dream in which the wisdom of the Universe was downloaded to me in a split second. By the time I woke up the next day, all but a fleeting shadow of the dream had evaporated in the morning light. Howard Falco had a similar experience, and fortunately for all of us, he has remembered the download. His book offers clear, concise, and useful wisdom that provides a road map to discovering who we really are."

—Arielle Ford, author of *The Soulmate Secret*

"Howard Falco's *I AM* is an inspiring and insightful guide for personal transformation and empowerment. This breakthrough book empowers readers by expanding their awareness of who they truly are, and what they are truly capable of creating for themselves."

—Ernest D. Chu, leading organization and business coach, and author of *Soul Currency: Investing Your Inner Wealth for Fulfillment & Abundance*

I Am

I Am

The Power of Discovering
Who You Really Are

HOWARD FALCO

Jeremy P. Tarcher/Penguin
a member of Penguin Group (USA) Inc.
New York

JEREMY P. TARCHER/PENGUIN
Published by the Penguin Group
Penguin Group (USA) Inc., 375 Hudson Street, New York, New York 10014, USA •
Penguin Group (Canada), 90 Eglinton Avenue East, Suite 700, Toronto, Ontario M4P 2Y3,
Canada (a division of Pearson Penguin Canada Inc.) • Penguin Books Ltd, 80 Strand, London
WC2R 0RL, England • Penguin Ireland, 25 St Stephen's Green, Dublin 2, Ireland
(a division of Penguin Books Ltd) • Penguin Group (Australia), 250 Camberwell Road,
Camberwell, Victoria 3124, Australia (a division of Pearson Australia Group Pty Ltd) •
Penguin Books India Pvt Ltd, 11 Community Centre, Panchsheel Park, New Delhi–110 017,
India • Penguin Group (NZ), 67 Apollo Drive, Rosedale, North Shore 0632, New Zealand
(a division of Pearson New Zealand Ltd) • Penguin Books (South Africa) (Pty) Ltd,
24 Sturdee Avenue, Rosebank, Johannesburg 2196, South Africa

Penguin Books Ltd, Registered Offices: 80 Strand, London WC2R 0RL, England

Bible quotations are taken from the New International Version.

Most Tarcher/Penguin books are available at special quantity discounts for bulk purchase for sales
promotions, premiums, fund-raising, and educational needs. Special books or book excerpts also
can be created to fit specific needs. For details, write Penguin Group (USA) Inc. Special Markets,
375 Hudson Street, New York, NY 10014.

Library of Congress Cataloging-in-Publication Data

Falco, Howard.
I AM : the power of discovering who you really are / Howard Falco.
p.   cm.
ISBN 978-1-58542-798-7
1. Self-actualization (Psychology).   2. Self-consciousness (Awareness).
3. Self-perception.   I. Title.
BF637.S4F35   2010   2010015346
128—dc22

Printed in the United States of America
1   3   5   7   9   10   8   6   4   2

BOOK DESIGN BY AMANDA DEWEY

While the author has made every effort to provide accurate telephone numbers and Internet
addresses at the time of publication, neither the publisher nor the author assumes any responsibility
for errors, or for changes that occur after publication. Further, the publisher does not have any
control over and does not assume any responsibility for author or third-party websites or their
content.

You are an infinite essence revealed in a finite expression,
destined to experience the truth of all forms.
Continually prodded and nudged into a restless sense of movement,
forced to evolve by the winds of endless change.

To humanity,
know thyself.

Contents

PART FOUR. *Who You Can Be* Is Based On . . .

A Note from the Author

I t is with the deepest sense of honor and love that I present the material in this book to you. It is all the result of a startling experience of transformation that happened in 2002, culminating in the awareness of the very nature of creation, and the mechanics behind the ongoing evolution of the personal experience of life.

One of the biggest initial questions I had regarding this astonishing personal occurrence was "Why me?," which after much further contemplation became "Why not me?" Which leads to the most important question in this very moment, which is "Why not you?"

If I learned anything from what happened to me it is the undeniable fact that this same information is always here for you when you are truly ready for it. How far you take it, embrace it, and integrate it into your life to achieve your desires is yours to decide. However, when you are ready, this awareness will prove to be all that's been talked about over the centuries of time and more.

So I offer this wonderful information to you. Challenge and question all that you feel necessary along the way. You will know whether or not an understanding is right for you if it "vibes" with you, for your body is a great divining rod of truth. This feeling generally emanates from your heart, and when it happens you are being offered something significant that is above and beyond what your head may have been trying to tell you for years.

I hope you enjoy your revelations of awareness as much as I have enjoyed mine. You are about to embark on an amazing journey of self-discovery where your life and the way you look at it may be about to change forever. On this journey you will find your ability to understand life and what you're truly capable of manifesting within it to be as limitless as you dare to allow. May your creative experience in this lifetime become more peaceful and full of love because of it.

With endless gratitude and love,

Howard Falco

I Am

Introduction

The Transformation to a New You

Answers are not found, they are allowed.

The journey of self-awareness and self-creation is the very intent of life. The capability to understand your true nature, expand your consciousness, and "know thyself" is a birthright. You will not be denied in your search. If you feel denied, it is because in some way you have denied yourself—thereby stretching your experience of time. You can always choose to avoid what shows up and interpret the world the same way you did yesterday, or you can decide to open to new possibilities that offer you a new reality for today. Either way, life will continue to bring you an endless stream of information to support you on your quest. This moment and this book is one of them.

Life, its origin and purpose, is one of the greatest mysteries mankind has ever contemplated. Since the dawn of human consciousness, we have searched for the meaning of existence. Saints, sages, mystics, philosophers, scholars, and poets have sought the answers to such basic yet enormous questions as: Why are we here? Who or what has created us? What is our purpose? Why do we suffer? Why are some humans blessed with good fortune while others seem destined to endure misfortune and misery? What is our destiny? How does one achieve peace in life? Who am I?

While all of these questions are essential to the evolution of consciousness, the answer to one fundamental question is the key that opens the door to answering all of the others, and that question is "Who am I?" A true understanding of the self is the answer of all answers.

This book presents an entirely new and powerful way of looking at who you are and what you are truly capable of experiencing. By allowing yourself to open up to new information about why you are the distinct individual that you are, you will begin to see and believe in more of the infinite potential of who you can be in your lifetime. And it is this realization that will allow you to experience an endless source of peace that has always been and will always be accessible to you, because it is within you. Realizing your infinite potential will enable you to make choices from a calmer, clearer, and more certain state of mind. From this incredibly powerful state of mind, you are able to create the reality you ultimately desire to experience: the reality of your dreams.

In the pages that follow you will be offered a fresh understanding regarding the way you define yourself, and how that definition leads you as you create and experience life. This journey to an expanded state of consciousness can go as far as you desire it to go, as it is based solely on your level of intent to receive the answers to your unique questions about life. This material has been drawn to you by you. As its author, I have simply been the organizer and deliverer. Now is simply a moment of opportunity (as is every moment) for you to decide if you are ready to experience more of who you are.

The information imparted in this book came forth as a result of a massive personal expansion in awareness that I experienced during the latter half of 2002. This experience was very startling and totally unexpected, as I was not consciously seeking or looking for something like this to happen to me. I was simply living a regular everyday life. However, what immediately struck me about my awakening was the overwhelming insight that everyone has the same access to this life-changing knowledge. There is nothing to practice and it isn't necessary to follow any particular set of rules to come to this experience. All that is required is that you demonstrate the will to open your mind to more of the possibilities that are already available to you.

For me, this radical shift in consciousness occurred when I was thirty-five years old. I was married and living with my wife and two children, aged three and five at the time, in Scottsdale, Arizona. My marriage was as perfect as could be, and my job in the financial industry was providing a sufficient living. I hadn't undergone any life-or-death situation or a personal tragedy. I also had no experience\with any of the hard sciences. I had not studied physics. I had not worked in the field of psychology. I also had no knowledge of spirituality. I had spent no time in India and seen no gurus, and I knew nothing about meditation. I had no particular attachment to religion or much experience with religious texts, and had never studied theology. My total worldly education was simply my life of experiences and a college degree in business from Arizona State University. This is hardly the résumé or the situation that I had previously believed would produce a certain understanding or knowingness about the nature of all things. My awakening was simply a case of an ordinary human being having an extraordinary experience.

I believe that my story genuinely illustrates the unequivocal truth that this powerful liberating insight is not just for a chosen few, but for anyone who chooses it. The source of truth is ever present and ever patient, waiting for the day and the hour that you decide simply and earnestly to allow yourself to receive it. When your desire to know reaches a level where you are finally willing to drop what you think you know, which hasn't sufficed, the seemingly miraculous will occur. That is exactly what I did and it is what you are always given the opportunity to do as well. When you are truly ready, the answers will flood your experience from every direction, providing you with the choice to accept or reject the wisdom for which you have so earnestly asked.

Do you think this book showed up by accident? This is just one of a million ways you consistently bring yourself answers. If not for your questions and curiosity, you wouldn't be holding it in your hands.

Many of the world's great religions assert, "Ask and you shall receive." Science, too, tells us that "Nature abhors a vacuum and immediately seeks to fill it." So remember, anytime you sincerely ask a question, you are creating a space or an opening in your mind that immediately begins to draw in the answer. Your experience of the "filling" of this space will take place as quickly and as efficiently as you are willing to allow. As you let these answers in, you will see them come to you in every imaginable shape and form. You will see that the answers are right in front of you, as they always were and will continue to be.

The main issue as it relates to unanswered questions has never been one of whether or not answers are available or whether or not you have been asking for these answers. The issue has been in the fear-induced resistance to a change in your way of looking at, experiencing, and interacting with the world that these answers will bring.

My asking some of the bigger questions in life started in 1981 at the age of fourteen, while I was on a fishing trip with my uncle up in northern Minnesota. After a ten-hour car ride from Chicago, we reached our destination of Bear Island Lake, which sits just under a hundred miles from the Canadian border at the eastern tip of the state. It was just after dusk when we pulled up to our cabin, which sat at the lake's edge. After unloading the car and settling in, my uncle, aunt, and cousin, who were exhausted from the day's drive, went to sleep, while I decided to take a walk and explore my new surroundings. I headed straight down to the water, walked all the way to the end of the dock, and stood there, peering into the darkness.

The first thing that hit me was the complete and unfamiliar lack of sound. Since birth, sound had been a constant in my life, making this moment seem remarkably strange. Adding to the complete absence of sound, there also was not a single breath of wind. It was one of those August evenings when the air temperature is so perfect that if you close your eyes you cannot tell whether you are inside or outside. The stillness and silence felt surreal. As I looked down, I was astonished to see that the water in this huge lake was completely still as well. It was placid and motionless, like a giant sheet of glass, without as much as a tiny ripple.

That's when I started to see them: hundreds, if not thousands, of white lights shining up from underneath the surface of the water. Confused and slightly startled, I looked across the whole lake and saw these thousands of lights shining in every part of it. "What in the world is going on?" I wondered. "Am I delirious? Am I imagining things?"

In one instant, it all became clear. I completely understood what I really was seeing. Slowly but surely I lifted my chin and my eyes to the sky. My mouth immediately fell open and my eyes grew as wide as saucers. What I saw in that moment changed my view of life forever. There seemed to be more stars in the sky above me than there was space between them.

Looking up at the moonless, star-filled sky in the middle of nowhere was a completely overwhelming experience. I was awe-struck. Viewing these millions and millions of stars that I had never even known existed before was a galvanizing moment for me. It was like looking at a great painting or an incomprehensibly brilliant work of art. Lost in a moment of pure experience, I took in for the first time the vividness and clarity of the Milky Way, as the thick band and cluster of stars in our galaxy stretched from one end of the night sky to the other. I lay down on the dock, put my hands behind my head, and, for what seemed like forever, stared at the incredible magnificence before me.

On that night, in the middle of the wilderness, hundreds of sincere questions filled my mind about the nature of life and my existence within it. My amazement and wonder about the world I lived in were elevated to a whole new degree of intensity. I began asking many of the "big questions" about life, but I would have to wait over twenty years to be in a state of readiness to experience the answers.

Flash forward to two months after my thirty-fifth birthday. Life from that moment in my youth up until this time period had been considerably ordinary.

After graduating from high school I put myself through college in Arizona, earning a bachelor's degree in business. After college, I gravitated to a job in the financial industry, and a few years later I got married and had two children. I had worked very hard to make my way through life to a point where I thought I was supposed to feel a sense of contentment, and yet I felt just the opposite. The feelings of anxiety and stress were a constant part of my day. I found it puzzling that I had achieved the necessary things and undergone experiences that were supposed to produce peace, yet my life felt incomplete.

I loved my wife and kids dearly. I was content with my job. Nonetheless, I felt an inner unsettledness from a source that I couldn't put my finger on. It must have been obvious how I felt, because at least a couple of times a week different people would ask if I was okay and question why I looked so stressed. My wife said I looked like I had the weight of the world on my shoulders. She couldn't have been more accurate because physically, that's exactly how I felt.

Looking back now, I realize that I was endlessly seeking to experience an idea that I imagined of self-perfection. I was chasing a vision of achievement, completeness, and self-acceptance that I could never seem to catch. My life felt like a bottomless hole that, no matter how much stuff I put in, never felt full. And the futility of this continual exercise was draining the energy out of my life in a way that felt like it was slowly killing me.

One day in July 2002, as I was walking down a hallway in my house, it finally got to me. Why was I so discontented? What was missing? In the few years that led up to this particular time I had thought that it was money; however, what I realized more than ever in that moment was that I had many of the vital things in life that money could never buy. The last excuse or rationalization for my discontented state of mind was gone. For the first time in my life I was truly out of answers. At that moment, I threw my hands up to the sky and with a desire and longing I never knew before, asked, "What's next? What do I have to do to be happy? How do I achieve lasting peace and fulfillment?"

In the weeks following this intense questioning in my hallway, I became more and more aware of just how little I knew about the world around me as the answers to many of my questions suddenly began to appear. Looking back, I believe that a collection of conditions that had been building for over twenty years all came together at the right moment for me to undergo a miraculous transformation. The tipping point occurred a few weeks after that day in July during a seminar I attended for my job on developing the mind-set to become a highly successful trader in the financial markets. At one point during the seminar we were talking about the nature of beliefs. While the rest of the class was looking at how this information related to achieving what you wanted as a trader in the financial markets, I was looking at it from the perspective of life itself. I began to challenge many of the long-held beliefs that I had that greatly influenced my life. In the process, a new understanding of the creation of much of my current identity began to unveil itself. Every experience I had ever gone through suddenly started to make sense. I was now ready to see and embrace the truth about my life that I had longed to experience. In an instant, I experienced an entirely new way of looking at the world. Everything suddenly looked brighter and more vibrant. So much emotional weight was lifted from my shoulders that I literally felt as if I were floating.

In less than one second, many of the limiting beliefs I had held about myself since childhood dissolved. All of the woulda's, coulda's, and shoulda's that I had carried in my thoughts for years simply vanished. I no longer felt any regrets, and I no longer felt contempt for myself or for anyone else. As I let go of the ideas I had about who I should be, I let go of all my resistance to who I currently was—and suddenly I was free.

I remained in a state of intense bliss for over a week, after which time I began to research what had happened to me. For almost four months I went through life in a trancelike mind-set as I learned more about the nature of this new opening in consciousness. In the weeks that followed, even more insights were unveiled. The core intent of all things in my existence and the purpose of all of the action within my life became crystal clear to me. I could see nothing but the perfection of everything in my world. I felt an abundance of love as I became aware of my role and connection to the oneness of all that exists.

As a result of this incredible experience, I learned how to truly allow the answers to my questions to enter my awareness. At the beginning of this realization it took weeks for an answer to enter my consciousness, but soon enough it began to take only a day, and then only about an hour. By the beginning of December the speed of these revelations was down to a few minutes.

In the middle of the month, something incredible occurred. I was sitting in my office and all of a sudden, as fast as a flash of lightning, answers began entering my mind. This new information seemed to be coming out of nowhere and it was very startling. However, what was truly stunning about it was that each answer appeared to enter my mind before I had even asked the question!

It all started like the feeling of the first big raindrop that plops down and hits the crown of one's head right before it starts to really pour. First one, then several powerful drops more, then a complete downpour. I felt as if the top of my head was completely exposed and information was simply dropping straight into it. I decided to pick up a pen and put as much of it down on paper as I could, but the information was coming in faster than I could write. I had no idea what was happening. I wasn't scared or worried, just bewildered and overcome by the magnitude of it all. What I later came to realize had happened was that the experience of time had completely collapsed. I had opened to so much possibility that my questions and answers had merged into a simultaneous awareness. Thinking had dissipated. Knowing was all that was left.

The next thing I remember was having an urge to leave work, get into my car, and just drive. I had no idea where I was going. I simply trusted and followed the amazing feeling that was going through my mind and body.

Soon I ended up parked at the public library. My heart pounded in my throat as I got out of the car and followed my footsteps as if I were being led. I found myself in a section of the library devoted to psychology, philosophy, and religion. There, I simply pulled any book off the shelf that immediately resonated with me. These included books by or about Socrates, Jung, Freud, Plato, the Buddha, Confucius, Krishna, Lao Tzu, Christ, and others. I took a stack of books to a cubby in the back part of the room and began to thumb through each one.

What I found was astounding. No matter what book I opened or what line I read, I was in shock to see that I completely understood every word of it. Concepts that would have seemed like an unknown foreign language only weeks or days earlier were now entirely comprehensible. Even more unfathomable to me was that some of the notes I had jotted down hours earlier were printed word for word in the books I was reading. I had never before read more than a line or two of the teachings of Socrates, Confucius, the Buddha, or Christ, yet suddenly I understood almost every single word. I was completely overwhelmed. The more I read, the more emotional I became, until finally I broke down, fell to my knees, and sobbed. The grace I was experiencing was too much.

"Why me?" I asked, as the tears flowed. "How is this possible?" Each year of my life it seemed I had been learning progressively through my experiences about different pieces of the puzzle of life, when all of a sudden it was as if a giant hand had picked me up and held me over all of the pieces at once, allowing me to see the entire picture. Each piece fit into a perfect matrix of connection and unity. At first I thought that the universe had opened up for me. This was not the case. The universe is always open. It was I who had opened to the universe.

Sitting there on the floor of the library, surrounded by these many great books and this new breathtaking vision of life, was remarkably humbling. I felt an overwhelming sense of gratitude that was, and still is, beyond words. I would spend the next four years of my life fully accepting that this event occurred, embracing and integrating into my life what was unveiled, and beginning the work of honoring this beautiful awareness.

Each individual is on his or her own completely distinct path of expanding awareness and experiencing answers. The infinite river of understanding, collective unconscious, or field of unlimited awareness that I was experiencing is endlessly available to everyone who seeks it. **This information is not only for those who are in some way "special," but for anyone with true, earnest desire!** The universe has no favorites. What happened to me can happen to you, and this transformation can occur in any moment of your life.

My realization led to another breathtaking insight that changed my life forever. **We are not our past, but whomever we decide to be right now.** In a single instant, I realized that I already am, in this moment, the perfection that I had been searching for in all the past moments of my life.

Inspired not only by how much these insights have affected

my life positively, but by the beneficial effect they have had on those individuals in my life who have been ready to open to and experience them as well, I became determined to share them with a broader audience. Thus, I have spent the ensuing years recording all of the information I became aware of in the book you now hold in your hands. The more you understand who you are and why you are creating and experiencing the life that you live today, the greater your ability will be to use this power to create the experiences of life that you truly desire to know tomorrow.

A good analogy for the experience of self-inquiry is car ownership. A car's purpose is to take people where they want to go. The more the owner of the car understands how it works from the inside out, the more control and confidence they will have both to drive it and to fix it when they get stuck. If the owner learns exactly how every component of their car works, they'll never need anyone else's help when their car breaks down. They will be able to recognize the core of the issue and fix it themselves. This is what will allow them more freedom to get where they desire to go, and to get there in much less time.

In the same respect, the more you understand about yourself, the easier it will be for you to see the core of any perceived issue in your life and then take the correct actions toward "fixing" it. This will put you in much more control of the creation of your life. The more you know *what*, *how*, and *why* you are the person that you are, the more control you'll have over *who you can "be"* in the next moments of your life.

Up to this moment you have interpreted and reacted to the events in your life based on who you believed you were. This is how you have created your past—even as recently as one minute ago. How you interpret who you are in this moment is what is determining your present experience of life and what lays the seeds for your future. The vital questions are, Do you feel content with how you have defined yourself and with who you experience yourself to be every day? Are you at true peace with your life and your day-to-day state of mind?

If the answer to either of these questions is no, undoubtedly numerous other questions about your life have been sparked. These are questions you may have been asking for years—in your mind and through your heart—calling out to the universe, to your idea of God, to your higher self, or to anyone who would just listen for a response. Perhaps you are hoping one day to experience information so liberating and inspiring that its recognition could reconcile the millions of conflicting opinions and explanations people all over the planet have about the experience of life. Perhaps you are anticipating, just as I was at age thirty-five, one day finally receiving an answer to the eternal question *What is the key to everlasting peace and contentment in life?*

Millions of people ask this vital question every day, but simply aren't ready for how these answers will change their identity and view of life. Questions that you may have been asking for years about many things, including relationships, your career, money, your health, or the nature of life itself, have produced answers that are only waiting for you.

Your true nature is unlimited and so are the ways in which you can experience and create life. Whenever your life seems out of control or you feel like peace and fulfillment are out of reach, it is because the belief you hold in your true creative ability has been limited or denied. As you come to understand more of the truth of your endless potential, you simultaneously open

up to an amazing realization of the limitless possibilities available
to you. Your every fear will be diminished, your every question
will be answered, your every prayer will be acknowledged. This
realization has the effect of collapsing the time it takes to reach
the state of mind where you freely enjoy peace and harmony in
every moment. For me, this felt like finding the Holy Grail that
man has searched to uncover for centuries.

> **The only way your world changes is one person at a**
> **time—that one person is always You.**

The book you now hold in your hands will help you trace the
process by which you create and experience your life. As you
become increasingly aware of the degree to which you create
your experience of life *subconsciously*, it will guide you toward
claiming more of your innate power to create and determine
your experience of life *consciously*.

From one perspective you are a distinct and separate individual with a name, a personality, relationships, and a history.
From another perspective, at the most fundamental level, you
are made up of the same energy as everything in the universe
and therefore connected to it all. As you embrace more of this
realization of connectedness, more of the perfection and purpose of all the things in your life begins to surface. It is the acknowledgment of moment-to-moment perfection that inspires
you to effortlessly integrate with all of the life around you on
the path to your truest dreams and desires.

Just providing yourself with new information does not mean
you will believe it. Your state of readiness is dependent upon
you being intent and willing—on your own—to challenge and

embrace some new and different ideas about every aspect of life. Perhaps the utter simplicity of how it all works will encourage you. The evidence of this simplicity is what this book will provide. The single most important question right now is, Are you really ready to turn seeking into realizing?

Throughout the ages, we have been offered many ways to understand ourselves and our capabilities in life. Many people have traveled different roads of thought in order to understand our place in the universe and make sense of reality. In the world today, four major paradigms dominate these inquiries: the fields of science, philosophy, spirituality, and religion. Each system of thought has developed a distinct set of beliefs and methodologies that distinguish it, some of which you may have embraced. As you travel down the road of self-awareness, many of your ingrained and unchallenged beliefs related to one of these paradigms may be seen as the reason some of your questions have thus far remained unanswered.

Throughout history many have traveled a similar path to new and life-changing information. However, it is important to know that each individual's journey to the state of readiness and the avenue that brings the information is completely distinct and unique. What triggers *your* experience of the answers to *your* life's questions can come from anything you encounter on *your* unique journey and it can happen in any measure of time.

What is relevant, regardless of your path, is your will to let go of a certain limited idea of who you are, in order to make way for something much more expansive. An expanded awareness of who you are and what is possible for you in life is what turns despair and uncertainty into hope and opportunity. In this more peaceful and balanced state of mind, you're able to make new choices and take the actions that construct a much more fulfilling reality. This is the path to claiming more of the unlimited creative power that is within you.

> The essence of free will is choosing how you will perceive and react to your experience in every moment.

You are the exclusive author of your story. You—and only you—choose your interpretations of and reactions to your life experiences. If there is one single liberating understanding to take from this book, it is the realization that you are the creator of your experience called life. It is irrelevant whether you are rich or poor, diseased or healthy, free or in jail, happy or depressed, single or married, shy or confident. It is meaningless to the self-evident truth that from this moment forward, you are making it all what it is.

> Your life is based entirely on who you believe that you are.

Each and every experience that gets created arises from a multitude of conditions that intersect in the same moment. A seed does not become a flower just because it is lying on the ground. It must be embedded in fertile soil. It must get the proper amount of water. It must absorb the energy of the sun. The creation of your life is no different. You must cultivate your reality. For you to know life in a new way, you must orchestrate the necessary conditions. You must continually ask questions and be willing to embrace the new information that leads to new choices and actions. This is the process that will lead you to the manifestation of your desires.

This book offers the step-by-step process of how the creation of "You" unfolds. In order to effectively convey the following material, a framework must first be built. Thus, the book is broken down into four comprehensive segments. Each part builds on those that precede it and contains information that is integral to the overall process of self-realization. If you feel you have misunderstood a concept, simply return to an earlier section and refresh your understanding before moving on.

Part One, "What AM I?," offers a framework for understanding your material essence: what you and everything else in the universe are made up of, how matter influences you, and how you influence every other piece of matter in existence.

Part Two, "How AM I?," uses the framework from Part One to examine how you interpret and define yourself in relation to everything else in reality. It reveals how you view yourself and your experience in the universe and explains how this critical self-reflection results in your moment-to-moment state of mind.

Part Three, "Why AM I?," unites the concepts from Part One and Part Two to show you the core condition underlying all your behaviors, emotions, and decisions, which have come together to create your life up until this point. This section reveals why your life has yet to change, and exposes the uncreative and damaging side of fear. Here you will learn more of your true nature, and what it is that blocks you from the answers that will lead you to a fully creative life of peace.

Part Four, "Who You Can Be," draws on the earlier sections of the book to demonstrate that no matter who you have been until now, *who you can be* is based on who you choose to be and how you choose to act and react to your world in this very moment. Everything in your life can change in a single instant based on your ability to ask questions and receive the answers that bring you to more of the awareness of who you really are. This is what enables you to become more of a true master of your reality.

A few years ago my whole life changed in an instant because I asked questions and then opened to receive the answers that revealed more of what is *not* true about who I AM and at the same time unveiled more of what *is* true about who I AM. In that moment, I saw the unlimited possibilities of who I *could be* and the infinite possibilities for all of creation. Ever since then, my sole intent has been to honor this grace by offering these revelations to anyone who desires to expand their awareness and understand more about life.

This book is dedicated to you and your journey to more moments of fulfillment and peace in life. Each page that follows is devoted to passing on the insights and concepts that helped me to produce the condition of self-realization that led to a wonderful personal transformation. If your intent and desire are grand, and your will strong, with the concepts and reflections offered here, inner peace and a new powerful way of knowing, living, and creating life can be yours. All of this originates through the realization of self-declaration that is one of the shortest sentences in the written world but the most powerful in the universe: **I AM.**

Truth

Infinite presence or eternally present,
It matters not which way you embrace,
As long as one day, if your path does intend it,
Your soul is granted this wonderful grace.

Blocked all your life by a false sense of self
Kept at bay by the fear that defends,
Pain continues to fester within you
Until faith breaks with love and amends.

Born are new eyes and a sight changed forever
And a day is dawned that is new,
Bearing sounds that are pure and sights of bright colors
Wrapped in a magnificent hue.

This river forever flows and awaits one to drink of it,
Available to all on our earth,
From a love that never stops, originating beyond time,
Ensuring for all a rebirth.

Denied every day this universal gift,
As sleeping souls pass it by:
The key to waking from the original trance,
Destined to reveal the great lies.

PART ONE

What Am I?

Chapter 1

You Are Energy
and Matter

Your existence as matter is the self-evident truth that you matter.

Anything that occupies space and can be perceived by one or more of the physical senses is matter. Therefore, you are an individual piece of matter. It takes force for matter to occupy space, and the force behind your existence as matter is the same force that creates and sustains every other piece of matter in existence: energy. Behind every "thing" there is no "thing," except for energy.

For energy to hold something as matter there needs to be a certain force willing it to be. Therefore, intention or the will to exist is the force behind all of creation. This force is what turns the infinite supply of energy into the finite form of matter. It is the force that binds the wave of potentiality (energy) into the particle (matter) to be observed. Everything observable in the world has a self-expressed "will." The "will" is evident in the intention of the atoms that form the molecules that produce the form that any particular piece of matter has taken in the universe.

Everything from a mineral to a plant to an animal to a human being is constantly expressing its particular intention. If you don't think a boulder or rock has a will, try breaking one in half with your bare hands. Intention, it turns out, is the most powerful and creative force known to mankind. Einstein's famous formula $E = mc^2$ (energy equals mass times the speed of light squared) expresses this concept of the infinite cycle of the evolution of energy into matter.

Intention has combined with energy to form matter into an endless number of structures, systems, and patterns in the universe: stars and planets, and in fact entire solar systems and galaxies, have all been formed by a constant force of energy into matter. Each of these forms is unique. When we look at the planet we live on, we find it filled with an unending amount of distinct "things." Each one of these "things" on our planet has gone through its own particular, cumulative journey that has shaped it into the form it is currently representing. While no two paths are exactly alike, the self-evident intention of each "thing" is aligned in the will to exist.

All matter in the universe is set apart by one or more observable distinctions. For example, the fact that at last count there were over 1.8 million known different species on earth is a powerful display of the current manifested distinct forms of possibility that have emerged from a limitless potential of creation. While many of these individual "things" may look similar in shape and size from a distance, once you begin to observe more closely and in more detail, you start to see more and more distinctions and variations among the categories of things that first appeared to be similar. "A beetle is a beetle" might be your

conclusion from a casual glance. However, upon further in-
vestigation you will find that, remarkably, there are over three
hundred and fifty thousand distinct species of beetles on our
planet.

From a distance human beings all tend to look the same as
well. But of course upon closer inspection there are multiple
differences between each of us, beginning with physical appearance. We have distinct facial structures, heights, and eye and hair
colors. We also speak different languages and dialects, depending
on where we grow up. Not only are differences prevalent on
different continents, but within each continent. The inhabitants
of Europe, for instance, speak over two hundred different languages. In addition, our cultural habits, including our religious
rituals, our cuisines, and our styles of dress, serve to further clas-
sify us. In the United States there are at least as many different
languages, dialects, fashions, and lifestyles as there are areas of
the country. The phrase "How are you doing?" sounds very
different in Seattle from how it does in Jersey City.

The main point being offered is that all over the globe matter
has continually adapted and evolved into different creative
forms. Each form or expression of matter that exists today is the
result of millions of years of action and reaction between matter
and the environment. The changes that result from these actions
have occurred generation after generation because of a singular
collective intent. This continuous evolution is happening on a
moment-to-moment basis with everything in the universe in
the effort to harmonize with the environment to sustain the
experience of existing as intended: to survive.

Nature is always expressing this intent. For example, one of
the key ingredients in the survival of plant life is sunlight. That's
why everything from grass to trees ends up finding a way to

grow in the direction of the sun to harness as much energy for growth and survival as possible. Nature's constantly changing ecosystem is a perfect display of the continual effort to adapt and achieve harmonization and balance. Continual adaptation can be easily observed in things like the changing migratory patterns of birds, the shift in spawning locations for certain fish due to climate change, and the ability of many insects and lizards to change color and blend into their current environment to avoid being seen by predators. Adaptation in nature is a built-in instinctual process.

What is evident from changes in the behavior of different multicellular organisms is that the first intent of life is always to continue to exist. This occurs through an organism's successful harmonization with its environment. If an organism cannot find a way to harmonize with or adapt to the environment, it eventually will not be able to survive.

For organisms that survive by reproducing sexually, social harmonization is a key element to the survival of the species. Life for such species is dependent on being included in a group, herd, school, or pack. Being in a group where there is a collective intent to survive helps to increase the odds of it. The group shares the common intention to eat, to reproduce, and to be protected. Activities such as hunting prey are more likely to be a success when attempted with the strength of a group or pack, thus making social integration a critical component to life.

For human beings, once our environmental survival is not in doubt, social integration and acceptance becomes a predominant way to feel fulfilled and alive. As few as one hundred years ago, even in developed nations such as the United States, many people focused their days around hunting or fishing for food. Supermarkets and massive building supply chains were not around in great supply to provide what is needed for everyday survival. A couple hundred years ago people felt a good sense of fulfillment and contentment through the ability to achieve and experience primary human needs of food and shelter. In the modern, developed world, with the exception of those living in extreme poverty, these primary needs are no longer as much of a daily concern for survival. In today's world many individuals have become increasingly dependent on social acceptance to confirm that they are alive and matter in the world.

The priority of social acceptance can be summed up in the following progression of thought: *If I'm accepted, I'm loved. If I'm loved, I matter. If I matter, I exist.* The need for social acceptance is demonstrated every day by cultural attitudes, moral behavior, the accumulation of material possessions, and religious beliefs. This need is so strong that the more a person longs to feel connected to or accepted by others, the more willing that person will be to give up the powerful capacity of independent will or thought, and submit to group behavior and thought.

All sorts of internal mental conflicts can result when in view of this need a person represses his or her own independent creative thoughts and ideas. Out of the fear of social exclusion for having ideas that run contrary to the group, these strong thoughts and feelings are often suppressed. In many religious organizations this power of independent thinking also will be given up if a person fears the loss of acceptance from some learned idea of the concept of God. This fear often causes people to "sell their soul" in exchange for the perception of acceptance. In this instance the phrase "selling the soul" means giving up the individual creative and intuitive thought that comes from an open and freethinking mind. People often resist their own feelings and thoughts in exchange for the acceptance and approval of others, or to accommodate the learned and believed desires and needs of a supreme being.

The amazing power of individuals to think for themselves is given away in direct speed and proportion to the degree that people believe they need to "fit in" to feel as though they are accepted and matter. This often happens in street gangs or in certain cliques in high school when the desire to be accepted and included is very strong. Other places this can happen are in religious organizations, the workplace, and political groups.

There are many well-known examples of this type of group behavior from history that illustrate the disastrous results that can occur when there is such a strong need to be accepted and matter in some way. Deep fear and survival instincts often combine to completely subvert any hint of rational thought. Some of the more extreme examples from recent history are the Holocaust created by Nazi Germany's Third Reich, the 1978 group suicide in the People's Temple led by the Reverend Jim Jones in Guyana, and the 1994 genocide of ethnic Tutsis by Hutu extremists in Rwanda. In each of these cases, the perceived need for inclusion in a group, combined with the fear of exclusion from the acceptable social norm, was the dominant factor in overriding and stifling creative personal will and truth.

Every life form makes new choices and learns to adapt for the same core purpose, which is to sustain the experience of existing in matter. Everything you can see, smell, hear, taste, and touch has gone through millions of years of action, awareness, and reaction. This has culminated in the form that represents each thing that's in existence today. Specifically, as it relates to us, our mental and physical natures have consistently adapted to the ever-changing conditions of experience in order for us to stay in balance and alive.

In every moment we are changing and evolving in an attempt to remain in balance. The changes we undergo can be moderately lasting ones, such as our skin pigment darkening to protect the body from the sun's ultraviolet rays, or short-term ones, such as perspiring to regulate the body's internal temperature on a hot summer day. Changes can also be social or cultural, such as changing the way we greet and interact with people of different societies, or changing our dress and dialect to become more acceptable to the particular culture in which we are trying to interact.

Just like everyone else, as a sensing being you are continually evolving by perceiving the world around you and choosing new ways to react to the ever-changing circumstances of your reality. All of this is at a core level in the effort to integrate harmoniously with your environment and culture in order to continue to accomplish a particular experience of life.

The path of choices that has brought you to this exact moment is unlike anyone else's in the world. Actually, the pathway of evolution for each object in existence is unique, and it is the reason that no two things in the universe are exactly alike. This powerful creativity is often expressed every time it snows, as no two snowflakes have ever been found to be identical. As these trillions of different, crystallized flakes fall from above, they metaphorically display the magnificence of the universe's infinite ability to create.

As you contemplate the meaning of matter and distinction you may begin to realize and experience the essence of creation.

> **Creation is the ongoing evolvement of distinction in an effort to avoid extinction.**

We live in a world of relativity, meaning that we experience ourselves by distinguishing who we are in relation to every other piece of matter in existence. Our sense of self-definition arises out of endless dichotomies, such as high/low, big/small, hot/cold, wet/dry, up/down, East/West, loud/quiet, hard/soft, alive/dead, and so on. Everything in existence helps us to further differentiate ourselves as individual human beings.

> **Without relativity there is no reality.**

As a human being you define yourself in every moment by how you react in relation to every other "thing" you come in contact with in your life. (This includes people and events.) Each encounter gives you the opportunity to express yourself through your reactions in a variety of ways. The conclusion you will ultimately arrive at if you follow this line of thought is that everything in the universe has purpose. Everything serves to enhance the definition and distinction of everything else by allowing all of life to have an infinite field of context in which to experience itself through self-expression.

- Without the experience of tall there would be no short.
- Without the experience of different cultures there would be no culture.
- Without the experience of sad there would be no happy.

Each piece of matter has a purpose and a reason to exist that serve the whole matrix of experience. Each object gives definition and depth to everything else. This diversity allows life to have an infinite amount of context in which to experience itself through the expression of itself. Likewise, everything in your life has a purpose and a reason to exist that serves you.

Your being as matter is the evidence of your connectivity to all of matter or else you would not be in matter.

Every day and every moment your purpose is being served for everything and everyone whose awareness you enter. All of creation declares it so. You are an integral part of the whole universe that is connected and mutually sustaining. Just your presence is sufficient enough to be serving this purpose. **As a creative human being your journey here is not to decide "if" you are going to matter, but rather "how" you will matter at each step along the way.** This "how" is the essence of the free will that resides in you and every other person.

The less you claim of the power you have to create your life, the more easily you will be manipulated or will submit to the creative power and energy from the people around you. If you are not consciously creating your own path, others—your significant other, boss, kids, strangers, political and religious leaders, or someone or something else—will decide your path for you. The decision available to you in every moment of your life is whether or not you are ready to realize more of the power within you to consciously create and gain full control over your life, or if you will allow your intentions and your creative desires to be secondary to the creative intentions of others.

Life is an endless stream of experience. If you allow yourself the opportunity to open to new creative ideas and experiences, you will simultaneously expand your awareness of the choices you can make for your life. This new awareness about how you can redefine yourself is the essence of your personal evolution. At its core, the idea of evolvement is simply the new choices of self-definition that result from an expanded awareness. It is further revealed:

Evolution is creation expressed.

Evolution and creation are one and the same. Evolution is simply the measure of the expansion of possibilities that have manifested through creative expression. Creation and evolution are both happening in every moment. The main distinction is that creation is the process and evolution is the term given to the measure of the process. The stage to observe this process is where relativity and time come in. Relativity makes the distinction of all things possible and time allows for it to unfold in a way that is observable and experiential.

Since all matter is in a constant state of change, you are in this process of change as well. The distinctive qualities that make up your identity are always shifting and transforming. As soon as a personal characteristic that makes you feel unique changes, you become ripe for a new manner of expressing who you are. The ripeness you feel is due to your need to feel a sense of distinction in the world and to know you are alive through a characteristic that makes you different from anyone else. A sense of satisfaction for the way you are defining yourself to the world is what ultimately brings many the sense of peace.

When a way of expressing the energy of who you are is no longer bringing a sense of personal satisfaction, other means to get back to the feeling of being unique, loved, or appreciated are explored. A sense of personal dress or style with clothes is one of the more obvious examples of the many ways people express their distinction in the world. That's why it is often one of the first things used to achieve a needed change of expression in life. An example in the modern world is the immediate elevation in mood and state of mind through the purchase of a new pair of shoes. The boost to a person's self-worth may be almost immediate. The importance of clothing to identity can be summed up in the example of showing up somewhere wearing a brand-new article of clothing and finding that someone else has shown up wearing the exact same shoes or jacket. Odds are (if you found a sense of your own individuality in this outfit) you won't be pleased.

Popular culture is one of the main ways we are able to see the most current forms of expressive distinction in society. The ever-changing contemporary fashion styles, music, entertainment, technology, architecture, and design of new homes, buildings, and cars are great examples of the constant need for new forms of expression and evolution within a culture. One of the more prevalent acts of self-expression in recent years in the Western world has been the increasing acquisition of tattoos among Generation Xers. This rampant increase is a revelation of the rising desire among younger people to find ways to perceive themselves as unique or distinct. A special marking on their body adds a new sense of individuality that increases the probability of receiving attention and acceptance.

Another very prevalent avenue revealing the strong desire for self-expression and connection is social media. This avenue has exploded in recent years, starting with individual distinctive expressions on MySpace and Facebook, and then even getting down to the moment-by-moment exploitation and tracking of individual expression with the emergence of Twitter. Technology is now an integral part of our personal identity and creative evolutionary journey.

Since the only constant in the universe is change, to remain distinct matter must evolve. All matter has a finite life and a transitory nature. Matter, or form, can only exist for as long as its ultimate nature as pure potential is resisted. The only choice matter has is to evolve and then ultimately dissolve. Even planets and stars must eventually dissolve back into the essence from which they originally emanated. This is the same for you and me. Our transformative return trip will be made as we move from being a collection of individual particles back to being a wave of energy that is only pure potential.

Like the planets and stars, your physical body has a finite lifespan. The degree to which you resist being aware of this truth is the degree to which you will experience pain or suffering as your body begins to submit to this truth. The degree to which you embrace your transitory, finite nature and understand the infinite, transformative nature of your consciousness is the degree to which you will experience peace throughout your creative journey of life.

You are destined to endlessly create and express.

Consciousness "is" and continues to infinitely express its creativity, or else the universe would not exist. As you look around the place where you are right now you can see this creativity in its current perfect form. All of it is the self-evidence of a culmination of billions of years of matter's creative transformations. This continual process reveals that not only are many things possible, but, as we continue to learn throughout our lives, anything is possible.

The expansion of your consciousness (awareness) to a greater understanding of the infinite possibilities that exist for you is the intent behind the force of all of the energy that binds matter. Without an ever-expanding consciousness, nothing would move or evolve. All reality would simply cease to exist. Your life is a journey of the awareness, cultivation, and experience of new possibilities. **Through this unfolding you are led to the realization that it is not death that you are ultimately destined to, but rather the infinite experience of the creative evolution of life.**

Chapter 2

You Create Matter

As you believe it, so shall it be.

One of the most crucial realizations on the path of self-understanding is that you create your own experience of life. Through your five senses you are capable of experiencing infinite combinations and manifestations of matter in the world. Through the senses of sight, taste, touch, sound, and smell, you generate an experience to which you simultaneously apply meaning. The meaning you attach to it based on your perception of the event or experience will reveal how much it "matters" to you. Your perception and interpretation is the great determiner of the quality of your experience.

Only recently has mankind come to understand how matter is created. New advances in the equipment used in modern science have allowed us to examine matter down to its most fundamental level. This advancement has produced an interesting situation. The information that has been discovered by scientists in the field of particle, or quantum, physics during the last century has produced a major paradigm shift in awareness that is only just starting to filter into the consciousness of the general public.

Using high-powered microscopes, science has been able to see deep into the matter that makes up our world. The earliest discoveries were at the chemical–molecular level, where molecules of different elements bind together to form different "things," such as materials and gases. As molecules were then examined at an even deeper level, it was found that they are made up of units called atoms. At the atomic level, scientists were able to see the components that make up an atom: protons, electrons, and neutrons. Atoms were then discovered to be vibrating and oscillating at different rates or frequencies based on how many protons, neutrons, or electrons they contained.

As scientists looked even deeper into the nucleus of the atom, they found it to be made up of particles. Objects studied at this core level of matter obey the principles of quantum mechanics. They exhibit what is called wave-particle duality, meaning that under certain conditions they display particle-like behavior (they appear to be solid matter) and under other conditions they display wave-like behavior (they appear to be pure, formless energy). What this reveals is that at the subatomic level of all things in existence, matter is a potentiality, rather than a certainty. There is only a "tendency" for a particle to exist, and the result of this tendency depends on the manner in which the object is being observed.

The conclusion reached by scientists is that the observer determines the experience of what is observed. Matter is thus created by the intent of the individual observer or by a collective of observers. Observation produces awareness, which is consciousness, which is thought. Thought, attention, and intention create matter.

All that matters is what you make matter. Therefore, you make matter.

When the energy of creative intent is added to the thought of a particular possibility, the result is the miracle of matter made manifest. The wave becomes the particle. The original thought of building the Great Pyramids of Egypt turned into a belief in that possibility, which fostered the intent of the Egyptians, leading to the actions of thousands of builders resulting in the tangible pyramids that we can still visit today. The thought of the electric lightbulb in Thomas Edison's mind led to the process of its invention and ultimate manifestation in reality. The original thought of building the Great Wall of China, combined with centuries of activity to make it real, gave rise to the astounding creation we see today.

Similarly, the notion of designing a flying machine, combined with belief and actions, produced the initial inventions that have evolved into the mass air travel system that we experience today. The thought of organ replacement has become experiential in the modern world through the belief that this type of lifesaving procedure was possible and the intention to achieve it.

Every single thing in creation occurred first and foremost as an awareness of what was possible. An idea that turns into a belief becomes real through the intentional actions and energy that are poured into its creation, thereby making it a reality.

A rock pile ceases to be a rock pile the moment a single man contemplates it, bearing with him the image of a cathedral.

—*Antoine de Saint-Exupéry*

Each thought of what is possible in this world is birthed from all the previous thoughts of what was believed to be possible that have been expressed and exist in some form today. Without all of the previous discoveries in medicine, the thought of organ transplant would not have even been a consideration. Without the thought and creation of the steam engine, the thought of how to create and power an airplane could not have occurred. Without the invention of glass and wire, the design of the light-bulb would not have been imaginable.

With belief and intention anything is possible.

Matter continues to come forth from all that has emerged before it. The direction of this path is not in a straight line nor is it in a circle. Rather, it is in a spiral where each evolution or revolution arises based on what came before it. This is the ever-evolving consciousness of creation.

Take you, for example. You are a result of the merging of a percentage of all the genes of your ancestors. You are the product of two parents, who emerged from four parents, who emerged from eight parents, who emerged from sixteen parents, who emerged from thirty-two parents, and on and on. Retracing your family tree for five hundred years would reveal you to be a product of the DNA of over one hundred thousand people.

Everything goes through this journey of emergence. All is created perfection from the previous expression of perfection. All comes forth from the "ocean" of infinite potential into the finite experience of a reality. You have come forth from the field of infinite possibility for a perfect purpose within the matrix of life. This is a purpose that you are becoming more and more conscious of in each moment. In essence it is the collective awareness of the entire universe that has given birth to you.

As you contemplate yourself as a creator of matter, think about all the things you have chosen to create in your current experience: your friendships and relationships, possessions, job, clothes, hobbies, foods, and forms of desired entertainment. Each of these things remains in your life through the act of putting your focus or intention on it or on something that is related to it. If you do not create the experience of these things, how else do they continue to remain in your reality?

"But I didn't choose this job, I had to take it because there wasn't any other option at the time," you might say. However, you create your continued experience of the job by not choosing to find a way to another possibility. "I didn't pick my neighbors," you could also say. But if you still live next to these people it means you've decided not to move away from them. You keep them alive in your experience of reality by choosing to stay in the same location. The point is not to imply that if you don't like your neighbors you should move, but rather to express how the manner in which you experience the things in your world on a daily basis is based on your choices.

If you grow tired of a piece of clothing you will give it away and it will no longer be a part of your experience. If you then imagine the ideal sweater for you and search stores, you will likely find that item. And if you want it badly enough and can't find that ideal sweater at a store, you could hire someone to knit it for you. You would make it real through the power of creative intention.

This works on a collective as well as an individual basis. If a sufficient number of television viewers aren't watching a certain program, it will be pulled off the air. When the ratings drop it will be replaced. If enough people in a democratic country grow tired of the decisions of the government, the types of officials they elect will change, reflecting this discontent. In a dictatorship, the people may rise up with force against their leader. Your reality at any given moment is always reflecting the current state of the predominant creative will of the individual and collective consciousness.

What matters to you gets its life from your beliefs about who you are.

Who you believe you are gives rise to your intention to experience a certain event, and this immediately shows up in the actions you take to draw the desired experience into your awareness. A good night's sleep, a delicious meal, a fulfilling love relationship, a new car, a different job, a great vacation . . . the list goes on and on. Each desire has a different path and a different set of conditions that need to be met before the experience gets created. The desire to enjoy a good meal, however, may require fewer steps to take and less fortitude than creating a fulfilling love relationship.

Often, by first experiencing the result of what you don't want, your intention brings you the necessary awareness of what you need in order to create what you want. If you intend to have a perfect vacation or perfect relationship, you may experience one or two that are unsatisfying first. The purpose of this is to help you gain the knowledge that you will use later to make much more focused choices. This focus increases the probability of achieving your perfect vacation or relationship. Intent is the key word here. Your intent drives every action that creates what you experience on the way to what you desire.

For an intention to become a reality, you must follow the path of learning to gain the awareness needed to manifest it. This may include accepting both undesired and desired experiences. Unsuccessful marriages, car accidents, financial trouble, family problems, and addictions are just a few of the many tough experiences that life can bring you. Contained within each of these issues is a valuable piece of information that is directly related to an intent you have to experience a certain outcome. On this journey through life you will soon see that every situation you encounter has a purpose and meaning.

What matters and impacts you depends upon how you interpret and perceive events. Even if you were not the direct creator of an event, like the death of a loved one, you do create your *experience* of the event, which is always related to the way you view it. If the deceased relative is a distant aunt aged ninety, with whom you had no relationship, the degree to which her passing would *matter to you* is likely to be less than if the deceased relative is a close sibling under the age of fifty. You do not have conscious control over the experiences of other people. Their journey and choices are their own. But you do have 100 percent control over how you view, interpret, and respond to an event.

Your perception of how much something affects you gives the "matter" at hand its weight, impact, energy, and duration in your life. When you resist the truth that the event has offered you, you are extending the experience of it. Your continued resistance of it keeps it alive as a part of your existence.

Something is matter and impacts you until it doesn't matter to you any longer.

The difference between how much your aunt's passing away matters to you and how much your young sibling passing away matters to you is entirely based on your beliefs about how their passing affects you and affects the world in which you live. All that is created and observed has an original intent for the observer who is experiencing it. Matter cannot exist without intent. To emerge from the field of infinite possibility into finite form there must be an underlying intention. Each observable event has meaning and purpose for those who are interacting with it, or else it would not have emerged from the field of possibility to be experienced by you.

All of creation is designed to give you the awareness of more of the infinite possibilities that exist in each moment.

You have complete control of how you experience reality based on your choices and decisions about what matters to you in life. These choices and decisions originate in your beliefs about yourself. **Who you believe you are gives meaning and life to the matter around you.** You have chosen to experience your life in a certain creative way for a reason—the understanding of which patiently awaits your realization as you continue on the journey of expanding self-awareness.

Chapter 3

You Decide What Matters

Matter and its impact is always up to you.

As you understand and embrace the powerful notion that you are the creator of your reality, an incredible realization occurs. It can be very empowering to finally understand that every moment of your experience is created through your beliefs and your will to confirm those beliefs through your experience of life. It opens up a whole new way to look at your life and the decisions you make as it relates to what matters and affects you along the way.

In each moment, everything in the universe is representing its identity by way of its creative display. For you this identity shows up in your current situation in life and by the way you perceive and react to each situation you encounter. This cycle of perception, reaction, and how much each situation is made to "matter" is what generates your resulting state of mind and the quality of each of your experiences in life.

Who you believe you are and what you believe you need determine what you focus on and what becomes "matter" in your reality. Your intention and attention are what give life to the matter in front of you. What you experience can only have an effect on you in a tangible way if you *make it matter*. If you don't *make it matter*, it will have no effect on you.

Consider a simple example. You and two friends are attending a football game between the New York Giants and the Chicago Bears. One friend is a Giants fan; the other is a Bears fan. You are neither; you don't even care about football. In the last seconds of the game, the Bears throw a touchdown pass to win the game. Your friend the Giants fan immediately descends into a negative state. He is visibly upset. Shoulders slumped, he angrily screams, "Nooo!" Your other friend, the Bears fan, immediately elevates into a positive state. He does a joyful little dance and happily screams, "Yeeesss!" You are completely unaffected by the experience and remain neutral. Although you experienced the same sensory input as your two friends, you display a lack of emotion about the game's ending and sit quietly in your seat finishing your soda and chips.

Three people participate in the same event and have three different experiences. Each has different reactions and memories. Ask the Giants fan how the game was and he'll say, "It was horrible—gut-wrenching and depressing." Ask the Bears fan how the game was and she'll say, "It was thrilling, fulfilling, and fun." If someone asks you, an individual who had no preference about who won the game, the answer will be something like, "It was a football game with an interesting finish." The entire content of this experience was based on three separate individual beliefs. The information was neutral until each person who experienced it benchmarked it against his or her beliefs, which gave each person a context to determine what, if anything, mattered during the event. Because the information was perceived positively or negatively, the experience was perceived positively or negatively.

Your beliefs create the way you experience life and your resulting state of mind.

Now imagine a woman with three children who has been married for over ten years. She and her husband have not been intimate physically or emotionally for the last three years. Ironically, that was exactly when her husband started regularly coming home late from work and making excuses that his absences were business-related. For just about three years he has been taking weekend business trips and making many last-minute calls saying he won't be home for dinner. The wife has chosen to treat the information as if it is nonthreatening to her marriage.

Due to her belief that divorce is shameful and that she will be unwanted and alone if she is a divorcée, she blocks any information she is confronted with that would lead her to the conclusion that her husband is having an affair. She refuses to make any inquiries into the perfume-scented clothes and secret phone calls that her husband is always taking in the other room. "He's tired" is the constant rationalization she develops to make up for her husband's lack of intimate and emotional interest in her. She rationalizes and contextualizes all the information she receives to "fit" it into a story she tells herself that keeps her from any information that would cause her to have to face her fear of divorce.

Through the choice of denying what seems to be an obvious situation, the wife is trying to protect herself from a feeling that she will be alone, doesn't matter, and isn't loved. Although she senses the information, she sees only what she wants to see, and the rest she doesn't allow in or make *matter* in any way that is not aligned with one of her primary intents.

Her friends, on the other hand, can see the truth in her situation. Since they don't need her husband or the marriage to validate them in any way or to protect them from their fears, they see what is happening free of the need to filter out any unwanted and potentially life-changing information. These friends don't have the same beliefs that work to block this information from coming into view, so they allow themselves to see with clarity. They wonder how their friend can be so blind to what her husband is doing. They have no idea of the implications of this information for her life, not to mention the resulting depth of pain she'll feel, if she allows the information into her awareness.

Blocking or avoiding the truth is used anytime we do not want to shatter a belief we are holding that we feel protects us from pain. A common way to avoid truth is to rationalize the actions of spouses, relatives, kids, the government, religious leaders, favorite athletes, and, most important, ourselves. We choose what matters to us and what doesn't based on what we feel we need to do to keep our relationships and the experiences we get from them intact. We do all of this in the effort to feel a sense of balance in order to survive. This is why many are so resistant to changing their beliefs.

The Giants fan whose belief that the Giants are the best team in football naturally assumed his team would win. His desire to feel gratified made the idea of the Giants winning matter a great deal to him. If they had won it would have validated his beliefs and therefore his sense of self. Suffering occurred as the belief in the unbeatable Giants dissolved with the truth of the loss.

The wife who needed to keep her marriage intact for a sense of security and survival purposely kept any information at bay that threatened the status of it. She chose to focus her attention only on what mattered as it related to staying married rather than focus on the information that would cause all sorts of internal conflict. She blinded and diluted herself in an effort to avoid pain. However, in doing so, she actually sentenced herself to a loneliness and pain that would last as long as the current situation in her marriage did—another day, week, year, or a lifetime.

Throughout your life, you have experienced and contextualized your world through the information gained by the use of your five senses combined with what you believe is possible. You have seen the world exactly as you have needed to see it in order to survive. Your attention has always been a result of your intention.

Whether it is a significant other, your job, your appearance, or an activity that gives you pleasure, what validates you is what matters to you and what you focus on. You may be able to relate to a time when you focused your attention on a certain car you were interested in owning. All of a sudden the car appeared in your awareness on a daily basis. Even though you had driven by this exact car regularly in the past, until it mattered to you and you focused your attention on it, your senses didn't allow it into your experience. It simply was not relevant to the way you chose to live and survive. This is a glimpse of how everything comes into being. It is already there. It only takes an intention to experience it to start you on the path to it becoming a reality.

The totality of your accumulated awareness, known as your consciousness, is the sum of all of your beliefs. What you believe to be possible sets the limit on your capacity for experience until that limit is challenged and expanded. Your beliefs determine how you interpret the content of the information you absorb from moment to moment. These beliefs are the gatekeeper of your perception. In other words, if you don't believe it, you won't see it . . . and even if you see it, you still won't believe it. An event can be happening right in front of you, yet, it will not be allowed into your perception to be realized, and understood, until you accept it as a possibility!

An interesting example of this is a story a friend of mine told me about the first time he experienced an earthquake. He was in California working underneath a car that was up in the air on a car lift when an earthquake struck. As he was trying to comprehend the notion of what was going on, his coworkers were desperately yelling at him to get out from under the car. He said he tried to move or run but his legs were completely frozen solid. Finally, after a few more very long moments, his legs reacted and he was able to move out from under the car to a safer area.

Since birth, we are all conditioned to believe that the ground is solid, stable, and unmovable. For my friend, the first time this belief was met with sensory information that was telling him that the ground is shaking and moving, he had no frame of reference or belief for this experience. Because he had not accepted or believed that this was happening or was even a possibility, his brain could not process a response. The lack of a belief that matched what was happening resulted in a state of being frozen like a deer caught in the headlights. This instant can seem like an eternity, until finally the acceptance of what is happening creates a new belief that matches the truth of what is actually going on. Until there is true acceptance with anything in life, the mind can't and hence won't give meaning and proper action to the matter at hand.

Another form of this is what is known as shock. This is when the overwhelming nature of the information is so intolerable that the mind resists the event in an extreme form of denial. As an extreme technique for survival, the mind simply refuses to interpret and react to what's happening. The result is that it freezes into a catatonic state of no reaction. This happens many times to those who have been confronted with the news of the sudden death of a loved one. Disbelief causes the body and mind to go into a complete shutdown.

To a varying degree, you may remember your own shock in the face of the events of September 11, 2001, in Washington, D.C., Pennsylvania, and New York City. Viewing the day's events, you may have felt a certain degree of utter disbelief and shock. How many times did you have to watch the television footage of the planes crashing into the Twin Towers before you finally accepted that it actually had occurred? Just as with an earthquake, your mind may have refused to perceive what your eyes were informing you had happened.

In a last effort of denial, individuals who are having trouble believing what they are seeing often attempt to reconcile the reality of what is taking place by making remarks such as:

- "Did I just see that?"
- "I don't believe it."
- "That just can't be."

At the moment the mind can no longer deny reality, the impact of the event is often also expressed aloud or under our breath. In contrast to the previous notion that what is being seen can't be possible, the final acceptance is often evidenced by remarks such as:

- "Oh my God!"
- "Amazing!"
- "That's incredible!"

These types of statements reveal the process of strong denial followed by the acknowledgment of a new truth. Every moment of every day, information comes into your awareness and is compared with all of what you believe to be true. The information that challenges your long-held beliefs is the most valuable and it is what is at the heart of the evolution of your self-awareness.

How you process what you experience is the key to your state of mind.

The word for the processing of the information that you allow into your awareness is perception. Perception turns the content of your experiences into context, or meaning. The way in which you perceive your world depends upon what you believe to be true, what matters to you, and how you will react.

The way you react to an event is solely based on the level of your resistance or acceptance of it. In the previous example, it was not the outcome of the football game that determined the quality of the reality experienced by the observers. It was their perception of the content of the experience that led to their emotional and physical reactions and resulting state of mind.

What you decide to make matter in your world depends entirely on how it will validate or invalidate who you believe yourself to be.

There are an infinite number of possibilities in the universe that you could experience in this moment. They include: natural di-

sasters, new inventions, birth, championships, illnesses, assassi-
nations, poverty, job hirings, job firings, marriages, divorces, love
affairs, terrorism, heroism, death, graduations, pollution, economic depressions, war, peace, and so forth.

Who you believe that you are will ultimately determine how
you interpret and interact with any of these possibilities. The only
choice you ever have is whether to accept what has happened and
is happening, or to reject these occurrences with the use of physical force or the mental force of rationalizations, judgments, deni-
als, or delusion. How you decide to handle each situation will be
based on what you feel you need to do to survive.

**What matters to you is what reveals who you believe that
you are.**

You will only allow in as much truth as you can handle at any
given moment. What new truths about the world will you be
willing to accept when you are confronted with them? Your
willingness to let go of what you previously thought was true in
order to accept what is currently true is the determining factor in
whether or not something matters and has an effect of any degree
on you and your life. The main question it all boils down to is:

"How does it affect who I AM?"

**You will know peace of mind when what you believe matches
what you experience in the world.** If you agree with what you
see, you are likely to accept it and have a peaceful or positive
feeling. If you disagree with what you are experiencing, you will
likely have some resistance and generate a negative feeling. Your

interpretation of the event is what shifts the polarity of your energy and state of mind. If reality validates your beliefs, you feel peaceful or positive. If reality invalidates or is in conflict with your beliefs, you feel negative.

You then react back to your environment with a certain amount of positive or negative energy based on your perception of an event as either fitting or conflicting with your expectations. You might have expectations about the behavior of your husband, your wife, your children, your parents, neighbors, strangers, community, nature, animals, friends, your nation, and the world. How you react to each situation is how you constantly create each part of your reality. This energy that you send out actually ripples out and has a certain effect on all of mankind. This is why everyone contributes to the effect of what all of us experience. This is the collective energy that shapes the world at any given moment.

The following are examples of how your beliefs lead to the reactions and energy that creates what you experience.

Example: In a store, you see a person stealing (content). You believe this to be wrong (context). You get angry (reaction). As a result of the negative energy of your feeling, you tell the storeowner what's happening and he calls the police. Your reaction was needed to confirm your belief of right and wrong and to attempt to reconcile the negative feeling caused by the theft.

You see a person stealing (content). You believe this is none of your business and that only bad things come from getting involved (context). You do nothing (reaction). No further action is needed to reconcile your feelings since you are acting in harmony with your beliefs.

Here's a second example: The politician you voted for gets elected president (content). You believe this is the right person for the job and so the election validates you (context). You loudly cheer and feel good upon hearing the news (reaction resulting from a validated belief). No conflict exists; therefore there is no further action to take.

The politician you voted for loses the election for president (content). Your belief is therefore invalidated and you feel like everybody got it wrong (context). You are upset and moan about the election results for months to anyone who will listen (reaction resulting from an invalidated belief). You become more active in your political party to prepare for the next election (action needed to reconcile the current invalidated belief).

Here's a third example: Your child comes home with an F on his book report (content). You don't believe that this poor performance is possible from your child (context). You are upset and you tell the teacher that the grade is unfair (reaction of denial needed to avoid the truth and keep the belief alive). You visit with the principal and ask about switching your child to another class (action needed to avoid an undesired reality).

Your child comes home with an F on his book report (content). You knew this was a possibility, but wonder why it has happened (context). You are confused, so you speak with your child to find out what happened (reaction of acceptance needed to avoid this experience in the future). You help your child institute a better nightly study plan, and offer your help and support (action taken to change the accepted but undesired reality).

Life is an endless stream of content that runs through our senses. Our perception interprets and gives meaning to this content as it is compared with our beliefs. The more we can match our perceived reality to our beliefs, the more we feel validated and alive. When we can't validate what we believe to be true, we tend to feel confused, upset, or out of harmony with life.

Anything you make matter in your life is directly related to your need to feel distinct and alive.

The key to the happiness you get from your life is based entirely on the meaning you give to your experiences. What and how something matters to you will always be based on how it fulfills your identity. And it is the fulfillment of your self-identity that puts you in harmony with the universe. You create matter by what you believe you need to survive and by everything you think you need to resist in order to continue to exist. You dissolve matter and the impact it has on you by accepting it and the truth it is offering you on your continual journey.

Disharmony is due to the resistance you feel toward an object or circumstance in your life that is undesired. The irony is that it is the resistance you hold toward any experience that keeps you in the imbalanced state of mind. The moment you accept the event or object for what it is and what it represents in your life is the moment the matter or issue will begin to have less impact on your reality.

As your view of you changes, the matter in your view changes.

You hold the creative power of the universe within you. The path you are on now is one where you are learning that you are far more than who you might have imagined yourself to be up until this point. You are body, mind, and spirit. You are matter, maker of matter, and experiencer of matter. (You are the vehicle, the driver, and the one who determines the quality of the ride.)

You

Who are you?
Have you remembered
Or are you still forgetting—
Forgetting and searching,
Searching to fill the incomplete.
Filling with the outer the false and temporary,
Leaving you feeling emptier than before.
Are you happy with your yesterdays?
Happy enough to choose the same yesterdays tomorrow?
Or are you ready—
Ready to remember,
Remember who you are,
Choosing new tomorrows,
Breaking the string of yesterdays,
Finding fullness,
Fullness with the inner and eternal truth,
The truth that no filling is necessary,
Leaving you more filled than ever,
Lasting forever.
Finally remembering the real.
Reunited unified.
Complete.
You.

PART TWO

How Am I?

Chapter 4

How You View
the Universe

As you define yourself, you define your universe.

You formulate your view of the universe in every moment
of waking consciousness. You are in a constant process of
sensing and interpreting the world around you, as you move
through it. Collectively, everything you see, touch, taste, smell,
and feel is your universe. Sensory data, if it is already known and
stored as memory, is categorized. If unknown, it is analyzed. If
unwanted, it is rationalized. When it is finally understood, it is
realized.

The way you perceive and process your universe is entirely
dependent upon how you define yourself in relation to it. The
relativity of concepts such as big or small, high or low, good or
bad, hot or cold, loud or quiet, east or west all depend upon the
way you interpret such things. The way you perceive the content
that is in front of you is based on thousands of beliefs you have
formulated about your relationship to the world. The total of all
these beliefs at any time is what makes your experience of the
universe unique. Each belief is combined with all the others you

hold to form "your truth." Your idea of "truth" is constantly on display through the actions you take to confirm each truth to be true. This is how the story of your life gets written.

The universe you experience is the current sum total of your beliefs about what is possible.

A single belief or declaration is the nucleus of your entire experience: this thought is the most powerful expression in the universe, as it represents the essence of all creation. This declaration, which is the statement of life itself, is:

"I AM."

How you declare yourself through the beliefs that begin with "I AM" dictates your moment-to-moment reality. Your view of the universe is a combination of all the beliefs you hold about the nature of everything in your life right now and of all the beliefs that you developed as a result of everything you experienced in your past. Whether these beliefs are interpretations of your own experience or you were taught or told to believe them is irrelevant. Your life has been created out of them, is being created out of them, and will be created out of them. The thought I AM is the genesis of you.

Your reality is limited and shaped by your self-definition. The way you perceive things is always determined by the beliefs you hold about who you are. Whatever limits you set for yourself in relationship to the universe are the ones you will experience. If you do not believe you have certain capabilities, you will work to confirm your belief mentally, verbally, and physically. Some examples of limiting statements are:

- "I AM not capable of that job."
- "I AM not worthy of the right woman/man."
- "I AM not capable of experiencing peace."
- "I AM not good enough for love."
- "I AM not fortunate enough to have money."

On the flip side, if you believe you are capable of those particular things, you are much more likely to work to experience them. You will be operating from a state of mind that is open to more personal possibility. This is a state where there will be less mental restrictions that prevent the actions that add up to make the belief a reality. **Having a belief does not automatically create the existence of what is believed, but it does give you the faith needed to take the necessary steps to create it.** As you continually act out of the faith in this belief, you learn more about the conditions that need to be met in order to experience exactly what you want.

All individuals who have lived up to their aspirations and created what they wanted out of life have followed the same path to realize their dreams. They attempted, did not succeed, learned from the attempt, attempted again with new knowledge, did not succeed, learned more from another attempt, attempted again with new knowledge, and so on until their persistence paved the way to the culmination of enough awareness for the conditions that finally gave rise to the success of their vision.

> "If I find ten thousand ways something won't work, I haven't failed. I am not discouraged, because every wrong attempt discarded is another step forward."
>
> —*Thomas Edison*

The mind-set of "can't do" and self-imposed limits is the route of self-protection. It is the way in which the I AM statements that define you are protected from the possibility that they might change into either something "greater than" or something "less than" who you currently are now. The reason change can be slow is that when you contemplate a new self-image (I AM), negative thoughts may come up to thwart any change in the self-definition, such as, "Why risk the possibility of failing and feeling that I AM less?" Or, if you fear the unknown of who you will be by trying and succeeding: "Why bother trying?" You may remember the classic children's book *The Little Engine That Could* by Watty Piper, a story about the power of believing in yourself with intent, desire, and the will never to give up. There is a reason this book has remained a classic.

> **Think you can or think you can't, either way you'll be right.**
>
> —*Anonymous*

Who you believe yourself to be (I AM) is the single biggest factor in how you look at your universe and experience everything within it. Protecting your current identity is what prevents you from receiving the answers to the questions you ask about your life. These are the coveted answers that will change the way you view who you are, providing a state of peace and clarity where you can more efficiently create what you desire most in life. Only a limited notion of who you think you are prevents you from achieving more of the unlimited potential of who you can be. Without demonstrating, by way of your choices and actions, a belief in a particular possibility for you and your life, there is little or no chance of it happening for you.

Some creative statements of being:

- "I AM capable of getting the job."
- "I AM worthy of the right woman/man."
- "I AM capable of experiencing peace."
- "I AM good enough for love."
- "I AM fortunate enough to have money."

The beliefs you hold that form your identity are what you use to measure yourself against in every situation and scenario. **At the core, what you are concerned with most is the successful verification in the world that you exist (I AM).** You are incessantly questioning whether or not you are living up to who you believe that you are. This happens in three ways:

You feel validated. If you feel that what you are experiencing is matching perfectly what you believe is true, you feel validated. This means you feel at peace and in sync or harmony with the rest of the universe. There is no conflict or friction between thoughts and reality.

You feel invalidated. When you feel invalidated by your experiences of life, you feel less energized, less relevant, and less alive. Example: The one you're in love with suddenly ends the relationship. A sense of disharmony arises out of the negatively charged friction created as your beliefs about who you are clash with the limited version you are now experiencing. The inability for the moment to confirm who you believe you are creates the negative energy.

You feel overvalidated. When you experience something that goes beyond the expectations you have of who you are in a positive way, it provides you with the feeling of an abundance of energy and aliveness, a distinct sense of mattering in the world, and a feeling of new possibilities. Example: an unex-

pected raise at work. This experience causes a positive charge
to be generated as the old idea of who you are counteracts
with the reality of a new and much bigger and aggrandized
experience of this idea.

The basic way that everyone feels fulfilled in the world is
through a sense of feeling as though he or she matters in some
way to the world. This is why one of the basic needs in life is
the need to feel loved. If you feel as though you are loved, then
you believe you matter. And if you believe you matter, then you
experience a purpose in existence. Life's first intent is always to
continue to exist. This existence is expressed eternally in the
universe through the constantly evolving manifestations and
experiences of "I AM."

A great irony is that the more ways in which you seek to define
yourself in your universe through the declarations of I AM, the
more you will need the consistent validation from your universe that these definitions exist. All you ever want is to confirm
that who you believe yourself to be is real. Confirmation happens
when the actions you have taken finally produce the experience
of what you desired to be true. Whether you believe you are the
richest person in the world, or the poorest, you will seek to validate this belief throughout your life. Whether you believe yourself to be smart or dumb, good or bad, peaceful or conflicted,
worthy or unworthy, someone who matters or someone who
doesn't matter, someone who is loved or someone who is unloved, you will seek to confirm that it is true at all costs.

**In every case, who you believe yourself to be at your core
is what you will seek to validate from your experiences in
the world.**

Not only do you seek validation but you also focus only on the content in your universe that "fits" the particular self-image. You alter and shape the content of your life until it matches the exact context of this definition. You twist and turn it, rationalize and justify it, judge and accept it, or condemn it until you accomplish this confirmation.

This has been done endlessly with everything in your reality. Self-serving perceptions have been chosen from every experience in your life. You have created reality through what your self-image required in order for it to be experienced. This will continue until the moment arrives when you decide that the I AMs from which you have operated your life no longer serve you. You will experience the same situations and feelings, and get the same results, until you grow tired of this dynamic. This is when you will begin to change your view and create yourself anew through the process of redefinition.

We don't see things as they are; we see them as we are.

—Anaïs Nin

The creation of new I AM statements is the beginning of the creation of a new reality. At the moment you choose a new version of you, your entire experience of life will change. When this will happen is completely up to you and your freedom of choice. One of the most liberating and magical realizations is that in every moment you have an opportunity to re-create yourself. Change your idea of who you are and your perception of the universe immediately changes with it.

Chapter 5

How You Define Yourself

I AM that I AM.

Exodus

The most powerful and creative thought in the universe is "I AM." It is the belief that creates the universe of your individual experience. I AM is the paintbrush of the picture that is your life. How you define and view yourself in and of this universe is the basis for your entire experience in this lifetime. Every thought you have and every self-creative action you take as a result of these thoughts will be based on this view you have of who you are.

Your critical self-defining I AMs are formed in several different ways. Before you were even born many of your physical and mental tendencies and characteristics had been determined through the union of the DNA of your biological parents. This genetic structure has been passed from hundreds of generations before it. Each new generation has come forth as a result of the previous generations and their reactions, expressions, and experience of the content in their reality. Thus you are a result of matter that has gone through billions of years of the evolution of manifested expression and experience.

A mix of genes came together to create the unique and individual you. These genes give you traits and tendencies. All of your physical characteristics, including height, eye color, skin tone, hair color and type, muscle tone, body and facial structure, predisposition to weight, walking and running style, mannerisms of every kind, including emotional style and energy levels, voice tone, metabolism, dominant operating hemisphere influence of your brain (right-brain dominant or left-brain dominant), speed of your neural connections and motor skills, and many other features, have all come from the totality of characteristics inherited from the generations before you. These characteristics are instinctual. Some of these genes are passed from the father's side and some from the mother's side. You are a new creation and generation formed by their union.

What is critical to who you are and who you become is not what you came into this world with, but how you have learned to interpret and accept many of your characteristics. Your level of acceptance or rejection of your genetic characteristics will determine many of your beliefs about your self-image. These beliefs give a context to the content of you, which gives the meaning to the matter of you. This is the second way that your I AMs are formed. This definition and view you have of yourself determines the meaning and type of energy you will give to everything you observe in this world. This view is fully defined and in place at this time in your life. It started to form at the age you became consciously aware of your existence. Many individuals and events have had a hand in your view of you and its formation up until this point in your life.

You are taught and given the initial boundaries of your world first and foremost by your primary caregivers, who are usually your parents. This process of shaping your world of experi-

ence starts with what others pass on to you. Other sources of
input, such as siblings, relatives, teachers, religious leaders, friends,
heroes, famous individuals, and media and advertising messages,
soon contribute to your self-definition. At a young age you are
loving, trusting, and highly influenced by acceptance and nurturing. Because of your inexperience, naiveté, and yearning to
know, you are impressionable and tend to believe everything and
everybody. It is not until you experience pain from naiveté that
you become more guarded and discerning about what you are
told. You quickly learn that what is true for someone else may
not be true for you and your intent to survive and experience
happiness.

How you have experienced your world thus far has had a profound effect on your original nature and on the way you process
and react to information. These adaptations and new learned
behaviors you perceive necessary for survival are what shape your
DNA. It is these new changes that become a part of what gets
passed on to the offspring of the next generation. For example,
many senior citizens are simply not as adept at texting—typing
letters and numbers on a tiny keypad at rapid speed—anywhere
near as much as so many young people. Can you just imagine the
finger speed of the next generation yet to come?

Each inherent genetic tendency that is passed down still needs
to be nurtured in some way to be fully realized. It doesn't matter
if you've been given the best genetically cultivated seeds in the
world to grow a beanstalk. If you don't nurture the nature of
these seeds by providing them with proper soil, water, and sun,
they will not live up to their full potential. The plant's entire
existence from beginning to end will reveal the truth of the
manner in which it was nurtured.

An individual's situation, personality, and disposition at any given moment are a revelation both of their nature and their nurturing. Their nurturing comes both from those who had a major influence on them and from their own personal interpretation of the events they encountered that shaped their sense of identity and value.

How your genetic nature is nurtured throughout this life span determines how much these characteristics are a predominant part of your life. If a child's parents are both accomplished athletes who demonstrated great speed as sprinters and they passed this trait to their child, nurturing will determine if the child expresses this trait. If athletics are never encouraged or allowed, or if the child is not interested in this activity, then this inherent high potential will remain only a potential.

If two people in a relationship have each always used screaming and yelling as a way to deal with stress, there is a high likelihood that this behavioral trait will be passed on if the couple decides to have children. However, if they decide to nurture their children differently, the trait may not surface. If the child is taught to monitor his or her voice level when reacting to stress, and learns other ways of dealing with highly charged emotions, the tendency to scream when under stress has a very good probability of remaining latent. A new and completely different way of dealing with anxiety will emerge.

A child whose parents both have diabetes will have a high potential of experiencing the same issue due to the genetic makeup that was passed on to them. More care will have to be taken in monitoring the intake of certain foods to prevent the actualization of the disease than for someone whose parents do not have the disease.

What is important to acknowledge through these few examples is that your entire personality derives from your hereditary nature and the inherited tendencies of your previous generations, *combined* with the nurturing you have received from others and yourself thus far in your life. Nurturing either activates or alters these tendencies to varying degrees and creates the one-of-a-kind person that you become. This is currently being validated by science through the field of epigenetics. Epigenetics is the study of how genes produce their effect on the makeup of the organism.

The relationship you develop with the world through your nurturing is commonly referred to as your self-esteem. Self-esteem is defined as the level of personal satisfaction and acceptance. Self-esteem is predominantly formulated in the critical developing years of infancy and childhood.

A great portion of the idea of who you are in relation to your universe is formed during childhood through your impression of how you relate to the world. If you have interpreted the manner you were treated as a child in a way that lacks the feeling of unconditional love, you are highly likely to have developed a low sense of self-esteem and a certain negative sense of self-worth as a by-product. This is a critical issue in the building of self-esteem from its core, which says, "I matter." **The lack of this feeling of "mattering" is the basis of all suffering.** Many of the needs and addictions you may feel necessary are rooted in this lack of self-worth or sense of *not* mattering.

The more you feel the need to matter through the experience of acceptance, the more you will feel drawn to certain individuals, groups, organizations, or cultures to feel this way. These needs can include the need to belong to a girlfriend, wife, husband, boyfriend, family, gang, clique, political or religious organization, corporation or company, state, country, and ethnic and cultural background.

The identities that are taken on become a part of who you are and what gives you a sense of purpose and feeling as though you matter, as in I AM a pro-choicer, I AM a pro-lifer, I AM a Christian, I AM a vegetarian, I AM a patriot, I AM a Jew, I AM a Palestinian, I AM a Buddhist, I AM a Muslim, I AM a Republican, I AM a Democrat.

Beyond the general statement that defines you and your values and interests, the need to belong to something larger than yourself or to be accepted within that group, organization, or cause can be very strong. This can lead you to become very influenced by the particular belief system of the group. You will give up your powerful gift of pure, free, independent thought to the degree it is felt necessary to do so to be accepted.

Culture and society can have a huge influence on your fears and may cause you to experience a large amount of pressure regarding what you feel you're supposed to believe in order to feel as though you "fit in" or are accepted. Social influence can end up being a big burden if you can't live up to these beliefs and expectations. It can be an even bigger burden once you find out that lasting contentment and peace of mind cannot be found by conforming out of fear and need. It is only through the faith and love to follow your own true thoughts that true liberation of mind is produced.

Beliefs that you may have blindly accepted due to fear turn into the I AM statements that may have been running your life ever since. These defining statements operate on a subconscious level in every thought and act of your life. You have most likely been completely unaware of this fact. Simply understanding how you have defined yourself to be and how this has created your life thus far will be invaluable to your attainment of peace. **To understand that many of the long-held thoughts that define** how you look at life are instantly changeable may prove to be one of the most powerful and liberating realizations along your evolutionary journey.

Each event and experience in your early years created a defining I AM statement that became one of the building blocks of your later life. Below are some of the commonly taught or interpreted damaging beliefs and their potential I AM definitions. When these expressions from others are believed, they become the resulting force behind the creation of the reality for the individual who takes them on.

COMMENT/PERCEPTION	RESULTING I AM
You are a bad person.	I AM not good.
Money is evil.	I AM afraid of money.
You don't matter.	I AM not loved by anyone.
You failed.	I AM a failure.
You're better than them.	I AM above them.
You're a sinner.	I AM flawed.
That's impossible.	I AM not going to dream it anymore.
Those types of people are bad.	I AM against them.
You're not worthy.	I AM worthless.
You are dumb.	I AM stupid.

None of the above statements on the left are true. These statements only become true for you if you believe them and turn them into the I AM statements on the right.

Another way beliefs and I AMs are formed is through your own experiences and the positive or negative interpretations that you have drawn from them. These beliefs and the energy of the experience that was a part of them are logged into your memory bank to be used for your survival. Generalizations are then formed as a protective measure to avoid what you did not like about a past experience or to keep you engaged in the experience of what was previously enjoyed.

The memory of a hot stove that burned you and the resulting pain that came from it is used to protect the core belief that I AM healthy and alive. Similarly a childhood memory of the first cat you met that scratched you may produce a generalization that cats are dangerous. The issue when it comes to your belief about cats is that each cat has a unique personality. The next cat could be the sweetest cat in the world, but your fear-based survival instinct may prevent you from experiencing this to be true.

The only personality a hot stove has is hot. So generalizing caution around hot stoves makes sense. However, each animal and person has a different energy and intention that they emit through their actions. To be guarded is understandable. To prejudge an individual or domestic animal is to create a future projection that doesn't exist and is only used to confirm your fears. Projections of future outcomes that emanate from a mind-set of fear are what drive prejudice and racism.

If you would eventually like to overcome restrictive and limiting fears, you will need to recognize any false, fear-based generalizations and beliefs and align with new possibilities for the future—possibilities that are open to new experiences, free from the limiting projections derived from past experiences and social pressure.

Each moment, person, and situation in life is unique. Just because the neighbor you had as a child had a tattoo and affected you by being very mean-spirited does not result in the fact that *all* men with tattoos are mean. This generalization has been believed to protect you from interactions with mean-spirited people. The self creates a blanket statement regardless of whether or not it is true in order to avoid the same situation again. The I AM statement developed in childhood is "I AM afraid of men with tattoos." The mind then seeks to fulfill and validate who you are by confirming this belief. You instantly link any man with a tattoo to being a mean, angry person before you even meet him.

At some point in your life you may have said, "I don't like him/her and I don't know why." The "why" is because you have an I AM that says people with the characteristic X are threatening. The X could be height, weight, clothes, skin color, attributes, or mannerisms. It could also be the vibe or sense of reflection an individual gives off. It makes no difference because your mind will link the attribute to anyone with characteristic X to confirm the belief, even if it is not true. This is called prejudgment.

You will experience life based on your beliefs until the beliefs are surrendered to their false nature. This is revealed through a new awareness provided by a contradictory experience. Example: You meet a group of very nice people, all of whom wear tattoos. Aligning a thought with the truth of the moment is what finally changes a belief.

Trying to change self-defining beliefs can prove to be a daunting task since beliefs are anchored deep into the subconscious with I AM statements. At times it can seem that no amount of evidence is enough to change a mind-set that is locked onto these protective thoughts. You have to be at a place in your life where you are ready and willing to experience your world in a different way. As this occurs, the path that is much more quantum, as it relates to change, is the path of changing the I AM statement from "I AM afraid of men with tattoos" to "I AM of the belief that having a tattoo doesn't represent how nice or not nice a person is." The first I AM gives all of the creative power to anyone with a tattoo. The second I AM puts all the creative power where it belongs: with you. Now you could care less if someone has a tattoo or not because you have simply decided that it is no longer connected to a threatening situation. There is no more "payoff" in the belief that all men with tattoos are mean-spirited because tattoos no longer validate the belief. It doesn't "matter" anymore if someone has a tattoo or not. You avoid the exercise of trying to change the belief because it has dissolved on its own by it not "mattering" to you anymore due to your new belief about the world. The old belief then simply no longer influences you.

Another area that will be discussed later in more detail is that your actions will always tell you the I AMs you operate out of in life. You cannot fool yourself into believing that you believe something. Just to say "I AM smart with money" is one thing. To act and "be" smart with money is another. The truth will always be self-evident in your actions in handling money and the results you experience. When you are ready, you always have the opportunity to see how much you are in tune with your reality.

All of your combined I AM statements give you your sense of existence, definition, and worth in the world. That is why the formulation of them is the most critical component to how you are creating yourself and experiencing your life. This also is a major influence on the power you feel you have to change any aspect of your life. Change is directly related to the degree to which you are able to allow answers to your everyday questions to enter your awareness.

One of the most empowering realizations that you can come to as a human being is that you always have the power to change who you have declared yourself to be through your I AMs. Who you were in the past is irrelevant. Your past does not exist anymore. Now is the only moment in which you ever have to decide and declare who you are in relationship to the universe through your powerful statements of I AM. It does not matter how many other people try to label you as your past. **All that ever matters is how you label yourself.**

Chapter 6

How You Experience
Your Self-Definition

Your truth is revealed in the energy of your actions.

Your beliefs about who you are (I AM) form the script for your life. Consciously and unconsciously, they define what you believe you are capable of creating. Your ego, like a dedicated actor, sticks perfectly to this script. Its job is to confirm your script and make it "real" by creating it in the world. Therefore, you could say your beliefs are like the seeds that contain what you intend to "be" each day. Your ego is the mechanism—an automatic process that occurs from within you—that drives the actions you take that attempt to nurture these seeds into full experience and realization.

In order to accomplish the task of verifying your beliefs, your ego will use any way of interpreting the world it finds necessary. Whether or not you are in harmony with the truth of what is actually occurring in life is irrelevant to the ego. All that matters is whether or not your ego has accomplished the job of confirming your self-image through your experience of it. For example, someone can "think" he or she is the greatest wife or husband in the world, but until he or she experiences "being" a great husband or wife it will only remain a theory. The longer it remains a theory, the more an experience of the theory will be needed to feel secure with the thought. Likewise, someone can "think" he or she is a great athlete, but without an opportunity to experience "being" a great athlete the thought becomes susceptible to doubt. They eventually will need to do something that validates the thought, "I AM a great athlete." Incidentally, it is exactly why it is so hard for many of them to officially retire.

People whose self-definitions are in sync with the reality of what is happening at the moment are generally seen to be "grounded" and "down to earth." They usually feel comfortable with themselves, and appear calm about who they are and how they express themselves. In fact, they are unconcerned about how they appear to others. For such people, because their self-identity is in harmony with reality, the ego has little to do.

On the other hand, people whose self-definitions are not in sync with reality are often perceived as "out of touch," "delusional," or as having an "inflated ego." These individuals constantly seem unsettled and tend to act uncomfortable. It can be hard to gain their attention, as they have an inability to relax. Drama seems to surround them on a daily basis. Because their view of who they are is consistently at odds with the evidence in reality, the ego is constantly working to find a way either to distract them from this truth or to reconcile them with the truth.

Your ego will go to any length to accomplish its goal of self-validation and it will fight for any belief you have about yourself. Its job is simply to produce the experience of the self-defining statements (I AMs) you've made that will result in a desired peaceful state of mind. The only time the ego has trou-

ble is when the overwhelming nature of the truth at hand prevents the ego from accomplishing its job. The ego then kicks
into high gear in an all-out effort to repair the conflict. The
ultimate resolution of the disharmony is that you either find a
way to completely avoid what is being presented to you or you
submit to the new truth and change the belief that is in direct
conflict. This process of looking at life and shaping it the way
that best suits you (regardless of the truth) is what millions do
every day.

> **The ego's mission is to take the beliefs of the self and turn
> them into the experience of the self.**

Throughout history there have been many misconceptions
about the ego. Many teachings on the path to peace offer that
you must control or destroy your ego. This is not so. The ego
is neither a good nor a bad aspect of your being. It is simply the
active part that responds to your surroundings to protect the
view *that you have created* of yourself: I AM. **Your ego is not
something you wrestle or fight. It is not something to be
destroyed in order to find contentment and peace. The ego
is simply something to understand.**

> **The ego is not against you, but for you.**

The ego's purpose is to give you a specific experience in the
universe. An issue for millions of people is misunderstanding
that they are controlled by their egos. This is simply not the case.
**What is controlling you is the false belief that you are not
in control**. In fact, this misunderstanding is responsible for the
continual suffering in many people's lives. Your ego is always

under your direction. ("As you declare it, so shall it be.") The ego will attempt to confirm whatever and whoever you declare yourself to be, from "I AM depressed and in debt" to "I AM happy and free."

If your ego has trouble convincing you that you are who you think you are, every possible creative mental illusion and trick will be used by your ego to help you to feel sufficiently validated. For this reason, it is said that people who require frequent confirmation of how wonderful they are always need to have their egos "stroked." Anytime you feel insecure, you are more likely to use an array of different things (people, possessions, events) "outside" yourself to make you temporarily feel secure. Until the false belief that is the source of your insecurity is acknowledged, this continued stream of outside confirmation would be needed to calm your internal conflict.

When the ego finally exhausts every illusion, manipulation, rationalization, and denial, it is forced to make the ultimate submission to the truth that the moment offers. This acceptance immediately ends the conflict and dissolves the pain. A new version of you is born. The work your ego needs to do diminishes when your I AMs finally harmonize with your current experience of reality. Your ego only takes action when you need to confirm a certain belief about yourself or the world that is not currently happening or is being challenged in some manner.

Your ego generates both the content of your experience and the interpretation you give it. The interpretation determines your emotional response to any situation. The ego decides whether information (content) is good or bad, fun or boring, dangerous or safe, evil or godly, exciting or mundane by comparing the information to your beliefs about yourself and the universe to see how well it matches up. For example, let's say you have declared:

"I AM a fashionable dresser." In order to have the experience of being fashionable, complete with all the pictures, sensations, sounds, and feelings, your ego will urge you to:

1. Drive to a store to buy the clothes you deem fashionable, and then to put them on. (content)
2. Give yourself mental approval of your look as fashionable. (context)

These steps would represent your ego acting upon your instructions. If the ability to construct the content and context occur as anticipated, you will feel validated and be at peace. If not, you will feel uneasy about this particular aspect of your self-image until you either change your belief ("I AM not interested in being fashionable") or it is validated through something that occurs in your life. If your own approval is not sufficient to validate that you are a fashionable dresser, then you'll probably seek the approval of others for further confirmation of a new, subtly altered definition: "I AM a fashionable dresser *to others*."

When you give away the power of self-validation to others, your ego runs an even greater risk of not being fulfilled in a way that would help you to remain peaceful. If others confirm your idea of being fashionably dressed, your ego's job is accomplished. The self remains at peace. But if others tell you they don't like what you're wearing, your ego will kick into alert mode. A conflict has surfaced between who you think you are and who the world is telling you that you are. In this case, the self would be temporarily invalidated and your damaged ego is sent back to work.

In order to reconcile the difference between an I AM statement and the current information that is the cause of your temporary suffering, your ego has different strategies it can implement. Your ego can react by:

Option 1: Completely dismissing whatever an individual says to you and moving on, ignoring the person and his or her words.

Option 2: Destroying the credibility of the person with the damaging information by believing and offering to others that the person is crazy or has no idea what he or she is talking about.

Option 3: Getting angry with the person in an effort to manipulate him or her to change the opinion so that it conforms to your belief.

Option 4: Ask several other people to confirm your belief to minimize the impact of the first one's opinion, hence making the first person's opinion "matter" and impact you less.

When your identity is challenged, it's as if an I AM statement has been put on trial and the ego is its defense attorney. In this case, "I AM a fashionable dresser" has been accused of being a false statement. It is the ego's job to defend this belief to the bitter end to prove the idea so that it will remain true for you. The ego uses any means necessary in order to keep this personal truth real for the self. The ego will rationalize, deny, dismiss, manipulate, coerce, and judge anything or any person that delivers contrary information. This is all done in an effort not to have to accept and change into what you don't believe you are. In this case: an "unfashionable dresser."

Ironically, your acknowledgment and acceptance of what you are *not* to others would enable you to receive the information you need to fulfill the experience you desire: being a fashionable dresser. Let's call this *Option 5:* Accepting an opinion from another person as their truth.

Every experience you have is filtered through your ego, which frames it within a context that's based on how you believe the experience best validates your identity. The ego is the guardian of your identity, and this identity is always evolving and transforming. What the ego is always working against is any perceived reduction or change to what is known and believed. This is essentially the essence of a change in you! It means the end of a known way of existing and viewing the world that now leaves space for a new self-image to emerge.

A change in You is possible anytime a belief about the world is challenged with sensory information that points to the contrary. Most often this information is perceived as a threat by the ego, therefore the ego responds to the potential change with resistance of every imaginable shape and form. The ego is a master at deception and illusion. It will go to any length to protect you from information that produces an unsolicited change. It will do this until it perceives no other choice but acceptance and change.

Consider the example of a man who resists asking for directions when driving in the car with his wife or love interest. Through aeons of evolution males have defined themselves as hunters, gatherers, and protectors in relationship to females. Due to this genetic and social coding, being in control and knowing how to get somewhere safely is a big factor in many men's self-worth, sense of mattering and being needed, and path to being loved in the world. Many men who define themselves this way would rather risk running out of gas by driving thirty miles in the wrong direction than break down and have to admit that they are lost by asking for directions. They will usually hold out to the last possible moment in the hopes that they will find the correct route and protect their identity as the capable protector who is in control.

Examined objectively, we can see that the man's determined nature (or what some might call stubbornness) is based on the fear of being a poor protector and looking foolish and incapable by asking for help. Yet by being stubborn (and then getting even more lost), his worst fear is fulfilled. After a period of wasted time and frustration, he finally asks for help and is immediately shown the way. The thing to do, if he actually wanted to exhibit the qualities of protection and wisdom rather than merely imagine that he has them, is to face the truth that he is lost and ask for directions sooner. By acknowledging and accepting his own limitations, and the truth of the situation, earlier, he would ironically reveal this sought-after display of intelligence and control. Interestingly, people usually find this type of personal humility attractive and comforting because it implies that if they are willing to accept their own learning experiences, they may be much more likely to do the same for others.

It is irrelevant whether you define yourself in your relationship to the world as a successful businessperson with an abundance of money or as someone who constantly struggles in life and always feels poor. Your ego will protect your self-definition by working with you to shape both the content and the context of your experiences to make this idea real. **In fact, your self-definition is the core of your experience of life.** Every time you believe the thought, "I AM X or Y or Z," your ego immediately responds by seeking to validate X, Y, or Z through your experiences in the world.

It is not what you say to yourself and to others about who you are; it is what you *believe about yourself* (I AM) that is demonstrated through your actions.

Your identity is a composite of your interpretations of every experience you have had since childhood, up to this moment. The actions your ego takes are directly related to this composite identity. Right now, in reading this book, you are learning more of what is possible for you beyond your previous view. By doing so, you are simultaneously sending your ego new instructions, which it will draw upon to create new choices and actions. In each moment, you are in a constant process of evolution and re-creation.

While at first it may be tough to accept that your idea of who you are creates your experience of life, especially if you have been unhappy with what has been created, it may bring you a great sense of relief to know that because of this control you are just as capable of creating the experiences that will make you consistently happy.

Just as you created the quality of the experience of your past based on what you believed, you hold the same power to create your experience of the future.

Many times during life we desire to be, do, and have more. We feel there is no reason why we shouldn't be able to experience what we want, and yet we cannot find a way to take the steps that are necessary to create it. This is a result of the ego refusing to take action. The inability to take action is a revelation that your self-definition does not yet include what you desire to be. Rather than being filled with the faith that creates immediate action, the self is dominated by fear and inaction.

When you're afraid you'll fail in your quest to be "more," it is a result of the fear that by failing you'll become "less" after the attempt. The ego's resulting nonaction is based on the declaration: "I AM afraid to be less than I currently AM" or "I AM not capable or worthy of *this* particular experience." These beliefs are evident in the lack of attempting to be "more." You want all the things you desire, but you aren't yet willing to face the truth of the dedication it takes to create the necessary conditions to experience these desires. There is too much feared vulnerability that will be encountered on the road to the desired experience.

Failure has taken on a negative and shameful connotation in today's culture. Many who experience failure end up defining themselves in an unfavorable way by it. What failure really offers, as many who have experienced their dreams have found out, is information. Failure is nothing more than an opportunity to gain feedback about what conditions have not been met yet in order to accomplish your intent. This is the necessary path of awareness on the way to your desires. When failure is looked at from this perspective it can remove many misinterpretations about events from your past, thereby freeing you to take new steps in life. Seeing failure this way leads to the new belief that you cannot be "less" in this world, only "more," through the awareness that comes from any experience of failure.

There can be no real freedom without the freedom to fail.

—Erich Fromm

True creative power in life is gained by realizing the nature of the real you beyond all of your self-imposed limitations. This is the key to achieving the experience of what you desire most in this lifetime. Undesired states of mind result from trying to hold on to limiting false ideas about who you are and the world you live in. Until now you may have been unaware that who you *think* you are is creating the limits on the possibilities you experience. You will experience more of these possibilities the more you *know* who you are.

You may have heard a story about someone who wins a lot of money in the lottery only to find himself a year later broke or in a worse financial situation than before he won. When looked at from a new perspective, this seemingly unbelievable scenario begins to make sense. If the individual's identity as it relates to money doesn't change after he wins, he will find a way to keep this identity intact. If the identity did not include the belief in achieving this state of wealth and financial freedom, he will find a quick way to rid himself of it. This is a great example of how the ego works as the guardian of self-definition. The truth of a lottery winner's current self-definition becomes evident in the ego's actions and treatment of the new money in how it is carelessly spent.

The specific thoughts and actions taken by the winner to spend the money are irrelevant. The bottom line is that the universe mirrors back to the lottery winner the exact experience of who he believes himself to be. This could include one or all of the following definitions: "I AM unfortunate," "I AM not worthy of money," and "I AM foolish with money."

The game of golf is another great example of the ego in action. Almost all golfers have an idea of how skilled they are at the game. The score at the end of a round, however, demonstrates how aligned (or misaligned) this conception is with the truth. In golf, the ball doesn't move before you hit it off the tee, and you have no teammates to blame for a poor outing. Therefore it isn't as easy to rationalize your results on the golf course as it is in other circumstances in life. This leaves little wiggle room for the ego to fool you when the score doesn't match your thought of who you are (I AM).

The ego's first attempt to protect a golfer's identity will be to grab on to any explanation it can use to keep the golfer from facing the truth: "It was too windy," "My clubs are horrible," "I'm tired," "My shoulder hurts," "This course stinks," or "The people in front are playing too slow." All of these ego-generated rationalizations are designed to help the golfer deny the reality of their score as it collides with who they believe they are. For in golf, as in life, there is only room for one perceived truth at a time. Relief occurs when these rationalizations and excuses finally wear out and the golfer allows the real truth in. Because the golfer is finally in tune with the truth, the golfer now knows immediately what he or she needs to work on in order to improve at the game. All the pressure the golfer has previously put on himself or herself to be somebody he or she is not dissolves as well.

How hard your ego is working in any moment to keep your identity "together" is revealed by how you feel at any moment. These feelings represent your state of mind.

For example, the more you need to believe you are loved and needed in your current romantic relationship, the more you will need your ego to confirm this to you. This arises at the extreme end of the spectrum when you constantly require your significant other's attention, demand a certain tone in the "I love you" or in the hellos and good-byes, and become paranoid or jealous on a regular basis. The more uncertain you are about yourself, the more you will direct the ego to help you feel secure. Insecurity leads to doubt, doubt leads to fear, and fear leads to the

actions that will actually attempt to confirm the original insecure belief.

At extreme levels of need almost everything becomes threatening. If you tell yourself that your relationship is your "whole
world" or something that "completes you," you will be susceptible to your whole world crashing down or feeling incomplete
if your significant other decides to end the relationship. The
same thing occurs with anything you attach to as your self-
definition: your job, your family, your physical appearance, a
sports team, money, inclusion in a social group, material possessions, or anything else.

When the ego becomes overextended and has trouble confirming any of your beliefs, its inability to do so shows up in a
very negative state of mind. The outbursts from this state come
out in expressions like: "I can't take this anymore," "I just want
to scream," and "I need to run and hide." These are alarm sig-
nals that a truth can no longer be held at bay. The only way out
of the suffering at this point is to accept the truth about yourself
that the situation is offering. With the acceptance of this truth,
you can then ask the right questions that lead you to the necessary understandings for real change.

Imagine that as you leave your job at five P.M. you say, "I AM
going to be home in twenty minutes." Since you can never
know this for certain, you are setting yourself up for a potential
conflict. If there is a traffic delay of any kind your ego is going
to have a hard time manipulating the three thousand other driv-
ers on the road with one beeping horn. Nonetheless, you may
start honking your horn in the futile effort to keep your self-
definition intact.

The most fluid path out of this type of conflict and the suffering that accompanies it is always submission to the truth.

Once you modify your self-defining thought to "I AM going to be home after traffic clears," you instantly take all the pressure off your ego, and it no longer needs to attempt to manipulate the situation to fit your view. You will no longer feel conflict, frustration, or suffering from being stuck in traffic on the way home. The work the ego needs to do to express your identity is reduced as you have decided to harmonize your beliefs with the reality of the environmental conditions of the moment. As soon as they match, you are back in sync, harmony, and contentment.

Each of a person's I AM statements is linked to a bigger and deeper I AM. In the example above, if your significant other has repeatedly stated that he or she would like you to be home by five-twenty P.M. and you fail to do so, the I AM that defines you as in a happy and healthy relationship may still be in conflict with your new belief, "I AM going to be home after traffic clears." Even deeper than that, the declaration, "I AM in a happy, healthy relationship," may exist to keep a bigger, more important one alive: "I AM not divorced." Then, if we take a further look at this belief, it leads us to one of the most common of human fears—disconnection, solitude, isolation—which you may protect yourself against with the declaration, "I AM not alone."

Now you can see why someone *really* feels the need to be home in twenty minutes! We put so much pressure on ourselves with conditioned fears that it is no wonder so many of us become affected by the seemingly smallest things. These aren't really small when you understand they are connected and holding together much bigger self-defining statements. This is why we tirelessly attempt to keep them intact.

As you peel back the layers of the onion of your actions to see the sponsoring thoughts you are really operating from, you will discover more truths about how you have defined yourself.

Within these truths you will discover the false notions you have about yourself that you are using your ego to protect.

Here are a couple of other ways the ego commonly acts and reacts to validate and protect a self-definition. These are times when the self-belief is in conflict and being challenged as false and when a self-belief is being validated as true.

EXAMPLE 1:

Self-Belief	"I AM an irreplaceable worker."
Ego action	Lackadaisical attitude about job performance.
Result	You get fired for being irresponsible. (Conflict)
Ego reactions	Label the boss as an idiot. Justify that the job didn't pay well. File a lawsuit.
Payoff	Protection of the belief that you are irreplaceable through judgment and deflection of the truth.

EXAMPLE 2:

Self-Belief	"I AM not worthy of love."
Ego action	Uncaring, antagonistic attitude toward those who offer love, creating unpleasantness and making them feel uncomfortable.
Result	Most people who initially offered you their love choose to avoid social contact with you. (No conflict)
Ego reactions	None.
Payoff	Validation of the belief through the creation of the experience of it.

The universe is consistent in always presenting you with the truth when you ask for it. However, when you are not ready to face the answers you ask for, you put your ego to work to make sure this information is avoided. The ego does its best to deflect or rationalize these answers so that any particular belief in who you are (I AM) that you are not ready to let go of can stay intact.

It takes a certain amount of force to resist the truth. It can be very energy-draining to go through the day trying to protect certain illusions you have about yourself, such as that you are a great golfer, an irreplaceable worker, or not worthy of love. It's no wonder so many people are exhausted by day's end, requiring plenty of sleep to rejuvenate their bodies and renew their minds. Only when what you believe is in tune with your reality does the workload on the ego diminish. This is the highly sought-after state of peace.

The more you can learn to find acceptance and love for yourself as you are in this moment, the less impact these external events will have on your state of mind. Whether you believe it or not, you are in control of how you interpret the experience of life. The work your ego does through the way you act and react to the events of your life will always reveal the degree of this acceptance and love.

It is important to know that you are never without an ego. As your awareness expands and you learn more about who you are (I AM), your ego may not seem to be used as much or find itself in as much conflict with the events of the world. However, it is still always operating in a way that allows you to validate who you are.

Some of the most peaceful souls on the planet still have an ego, but it does not require much in the way of activity. These individuals are not under any false illusions regarding who they are. Their egos are operating on a much more powerful level of self-acceptance and self-love. All of their energy is focused on validating this identity by offering acceptance and love to others. Rather than drain energy from them, this state of being is actually the source that supplies them with an endless amount of energy.

Your ego's actions are always aligned with who you truly believe you are. You never have to fight your ego, because you can always take more conscious control of what it is seeking to validate. If you are willing to look at the truth about yourself, and embrace and declare this truth, your experience of life can change instantly. As with every other act in life, self-examination is a choice. It is likely that you will only choose this path when you have exhausted all other perceived ways of attempting to experience fulfillment and contentment. By reading this material, you could be choosing it right now.

Chapter 7

How You Create,
Your State of Mind

Your state of mind is the essence of your life.

Your state of mind at every moment is the only thing relevant to your experience of life, for it provides the quality
of your life. All human beings on the planet frame their perception of the world in a way that attempts to achieve a contented
and balanced state of mind. This is the moment-by-moment
intention of our consciousness.

When a moment brings us the feelings of contentment and
peace, we feel as if everything in the world is as it should be,
that all is perfect, and that all is right with the universe. There
is a serenity and sense of comfort that can sometimes be difficult
to express. Throughout history, the world's many religions and
cultures have given different names to this state of mind, especially when it lasts for a certain length of time. Enlightenment,
samadhi, bliss, nirvana, the kingdom of heaven, and being at
one with God are terms that have been used. Each term is de-
scribing nearly the same state of being, which is often offered as
the ultimate state of mind to attain.

Historically, individuals described as having this experience bask in a glow that seems to shine forth from their faces in a tangible radiance. They emit a healing and peaceful energy that can be felt by others in their space. Their presence is calming, accepting, and loving, due to the simple fact that there is no conflict or disharmony in their mind. This place of balance allows them to offer deep wisdom and insight to any others who seek it.

This same state of being is available to you at any time you choose. There may have been times in your life when you have experienced it for a moment or maybe even an extended period of time. It is never far from you, nor do you lack the ability to enter into it at will because it is the core of who you are. The journey you are on in life is consistently moving you toward this realization. It is your destiny.

No matter how many individuals throughout history have attempted to explain this state of being and offer the world their understanding of how to attain it, this peaceful state of mind continues to be elusive for most people. Many find themselves constantly fluctuating between the polarities of feeling good and feeling anxious, first feeling positive about life and then feeling negative and hopeless about it. They are rarely able to achieve a true lasting state of balance. Shifting back and forth leaves people constantly questioning how to achieve a consistent state of contentment and happiness.

If you are intent upon having more moments in your life filled with this peaceful experience, one of the first things you will be offered to contemplate is the truth that there is no place to "get to" at "some time." The irony is that the state of mind you seek is HERE and NOW. It only requires your awareness and acceptance of "what is" in this moment—the phrase "what is" meaning *what is known as the truth*. This is the understanding that everything that exists in this moment is perfect, including you. Embracing this truth is the only thing required to set you free to experience this beautiful state.

While the state of peace and serenity is a deep-rooted desire of mankind, there is much misunderstanding and confusion about the path to attain it. The current state of affairs in so many areas of the world is evidence of these misunderstandings. Throughout the globe and predominantly in Western cultures, people are fed abundant information through the media about what will provide us with happiness. The information usually involves a certain way to look, a certain amount of money we should have, and a specific collection of material possessions to own. It is interesting to note that the United States, while being one of the wealthiest countries in the world, is also one whose inhabitants are reaching to ever greater extremes in an effort to experience peace and happiness.

Culturally programmed images centering on money, power, looks, love, sex, and possessions are usually presented to the public both to fill a need and by those looking to profit from the message being conveyed. Many people measure themselves against the benchmark of these images of what is required to be loved, liked, and to matter in the world. This creates feelings of inadequacy and insufficiency that are a breeding ground for discontentment and unhappiness. Constant discontent is the catalyst for the depression and feeling of loneliness that so many people throughout the world experience.

The number and variety of methods people are currently using to shift to a more pleasurable state of mind are evidence of the degree of discontentment that now exists. Illegal drugs, prescription drugs, alcohol, sex, pornography, Internet chat rooms, video games, material possessions, drastic weight loss, and plastic surgery are some of the more prevalent compulsions or addictions that have surfaced in a pronounced way in the past several decades. All result from the collective desire to experience a state of mind free of negativity and suffering. The cultural portrayal and programming of what is acceptable, admirable, and desirable has reached a level that is highly improbable for the majority of individuals to attain. As a result, millions of people influenced by this programming are plagued by feelings of unworthiness.

Fortunately, negative states of mind born by misunderstanding the nature of peace and contentment are entirely changeable. Through the simple intention and desire to experience a peaceful and balanced state of mind, every human being is offered the path to achieve it. Not a single person is denied it. A state of grace and peace is available to everyone who truly and intensely desires the experience.

To achieve the state of mind you desire, you must first realize some key insights about its creation. One of the first and most important things to realize is that you have always been the creator of your state of mind. You may have been unaware of this, but that doesn't make it any less true.

Your vision of who you are (I AM) in relationship to your ability to experience this declared vision (the confirmation or denial of the ego) creates your state of mind from moment to moment.

In each moment you are in one of three possible states of mind. You are in:

1. **A negative state of mind** of a greater or lesser degree that has arisen from the fact that who you believe yourself to be

(I AM) has been met with sensory or experiential information that is not allowing you to confirm this self-definition.

2. A **balanced state of mind** due to the fact that who you believe yourself to be (I AM) has been met through your sensory perception with its exact experience in reality.

3. A **positive state of mind** of a greater or lesser degree that
has arisen from the fact that who you believe yourself to be
(I AM) is not only being affirmed by your experiences and
perceptions, but has expanded into an even grander self-
definition than you had formerly believed possible.

Here's a simple example. You are sitting down to pay your bills
and you have a certain amount of money in your checking account to cover them. You pay the last one and realize:

1. You are significantly short of money in your account. You
expected to be able to pay all of your bills and have a certain
amount left over. Instead you can't pay them all and will be
behind next month because of it. This does not "sit well" and
sends you into a negative state of mind due to the conflict
between what you believed about you and your ability to
budget your money and the reality in front of you. The ego
attempts to do its job to protect the belief of being well able
to budget money, but the truth of the reality of the balance
in your account won't allow for any rationalizations to work
in this moment. Your negative state of mind could presently
be characterized as sad, angry, depressed, shocked, horrified,
or confused. Statements that arise in this state of mind are
ones such as: "I don't believe it!" "I'm really upset." "I AM
so pissed!"

2. You are perfectly on plan with your bills being paid and the perfect expected amount left over for saving and spending. Your definition of exactly who you are is being validated in the moment with regard to this issue, putting you in complete peace and contentment. Your balanced state of mind could be characterized as fulfilled, peaceful, at ease, or content. Statements that arise in this state of mind would include: "That felt good." "All seems right with the world" and "Perfect." Sometimes there is even a big sigh of relief, "Ahhh," as you realize you are in harmony and peace. The ego has done its job perfectly to satisfy the self-definition. No different action needs to be taken by the ego at this time.

3. You are significantly under budget and have excess funds in your account. This amount is above and beyond what you expected to retain after all your bills were paid and money saved. This "sits very well" with you and sends you into a positive state of mind due to the conflict between what you expected of yourself as a good budgeter of money and the reality in front of you. The ego not only did its job to protect the self-defining belief, it enhanced your self-image so it has become even greater than it was before. Your state of mind could be characterized as happy, joyful, ecstatic, euphoric, shocked, confused, pleased, or bewildered. Expressions arising in this state of mind are ones such as: "This is great!" "I can't believe it!" "What luck!"

Each life experience offers you a choice to accept or deny "what is." It is created by the meeting of who you define yourself to be and your actual experience in reality. If your self-definition (I AM) is affirmed, you feel in harmony with the universe. If it is not affirmed, you feel less alive and end up in a negative and disharmonious state. If your self-definition is not only affirmed but increases in distinction, you go into a joyful, positive state, as you feel more alive than ever before.

Your desire to experience a more tolerable state of mind, combined with your beliefs about how to achieve that state of mind, will always be the driver of your choices. That is why many people choose to pursue addictions to elevate their state of mind. If you're depressed or anxious, take a pill. If you're lonely, have a drink. If you're unhappy with your looks or body, pay to change them. If you're not feeling loved, buy something. These quick-fix shortcuts to an elevated state of mind are temporary (creating the addiction) and carry the potential for a damaging downside effect. At the end of the day, the root cause of the perception of the unfulfilling existence has not been addressed. The cycle simply repeats until the desire for a more peaceful state of mind starts you on an inner path of insights that allows you to begin to discover who you truly are.

Many do not understand that they have the power to change their experience through their self-defining statements of I AM. Because of this misunderstanding, they tend to believe their past experience is a reflection of *who* they are now and that they are tied to this identity. For example: I AM a bad student (rather than "I failed a lot of tests and was a bad student, but now I AM a good student"), I AM not responsible with money (rather than "I had no discipline with money and was a bad budgeter, but now I AM responsible with my money"), I AM a drug addict (rather than "I previously used drugs a lot and was addicted, but now I AM no longer addicted"), or I AM a mess when it comes to my relationships (rather than "I used to make rash choices about who I got romantically involved with, but now I AM smart about my choices in relationships").

Even in one of the most well-known examples, "I AM an alcoholic," at some point with a strong enough will and faith this notion can be transcended. The shift to a believed new self-declaration immediately begins to create a new experience while leaving the unwanted identity and the energy that created it in the past.

> Who you were in the past is not who you are now.
> You decide who you are in each and every moment.

Your former self-definition will be as much of your present and future experience as you allow. This fact is critical on the path to understanding more of your true essence. Your state of mind is everything. As you come to understand more of how this state of mind is created, you begin to understand how to take conscious control to create it just as you desire it to be.

A peaceful place of contentment and serenity comes from being in a powerful state of awareness where you see that all things are possible. In this state of balance that is void of any emotion, time stops and you are in pure harmony with the moment. You merge into the moment when you come to total acceptance of where you are in life in relation to everything else in existence. To be in this state of mind is to be filled with a complete understanding and love for the self, knowing and understanding that for this moment you are perfect and all else is perfect around you.

In order to come to this liberating state of mind, you have to take a look at the dominant thoughts you hold about yourself that keep you from seeing more of your beauty and perfection.

These are the thoughts that say you should be more, and they are what cause your energy and state of mind to be out of balance and in disharmony. It is not until you recognize the cause of the "disconnect" and embrace the truth and perfection that the moment is offering you that peace can be realized.

The chart below displays the different levels of conflict that can occur when your beliefs of I AM are confronted by the truth of "what is." Each level represents the words used to contextualize the state of mind that has resulted from the friction created by the conflict of thought. Each of these "states" is accompanied by the resulting feelings and emotions.

In any given moment, your state of mind can fall anywhere on this spectrum. The amount of time you focus on a thought

---

CHART OF POSITIVE AND NEGATIVE STATES OF MIND

+

Level 5	**Madness, Hysteria, Insanity, Shock**
Level 4	Nirvana, Ecstasy, Bliss, Euphoria
Level 3	Exhilaration, Elation, Intoxication, Dreamland
Level 2	Jovial, Happy, Joyful, High-spirited
Level 1	Buoyant, Glad, Pleased, Lively

↑ **Positive States**

O Balanced, Content, Harmony, Peace, Clarity, Calm, Neutral, Tranquillity, Well-being, Unity, Fulfilled, Egoless, Placid

↓ **Negative States**

Level 1	Unease, Displeased, Annoyed, Discontent
Level 2	Pressured, Anxious, Sad, Upset
Level 3	Disgruntled, Frustrated, Angry, Inflamed
Level 4	Exasperated, Infuriated, Depressed, Enraged
Level 5	**Madness, Hysteria, Insanity, Shock**

that you resist is directly related to the amount of time you'll spend in an unbalanced state of mind. If your attention is focused on a sick family member who you believe shouldn't be sick, your resistance to the thought of your relative's condition puts you at some level on the negative side of the spectrum. If your attention then shifts to the fun of your budding love relationship, this thought will shift you to some level on the positive side of the spectrum. Shift your attention to your poor financial condition, especially if needing money is not in harmony with who you believe you are, and you're going to find yourself back on the negative side. Think of the playful puppy you've got waiting for you at home and you're back to the positive side.

Whatever you put your attention on is always being measured against your beliefs about who you are. Thus the interpretation of the moment-by-moment information you encounter is what is always responsible for your state of mind. The key to consistent peace of mind is one of attention and perception. If the perception you have of who you are (I AM) is in line with the truth of "what is" (reality), you will be in a state of balance. Staying in balance means constantly accepting a purpose for what is happening around you. The more you can do this, the more tranquillity you will experience throughout your life.

It is important to note that the word "happiness" is commonly used when people are talking about the ultimate state of mind they want to achieve. We often hear people say things such as, "I just want to be happy," or "I want to find happiness." It is critical to distinguish between the definition of happiness as being joy and elation, and the definition of happiness as being contentment and well-being.

Joy and elation are states on the positive side of the state-of-mind spectrum, meaning that conditions must be met in the experiential world in order to produce them. Whereas the happiness that is defined as contentment and well-being is characteristic of perfect balance and harmony, a neutral state of mind. No conditions outside of you need to be met to experience this sought-after state of being. There is only a simple sense of peace. This form of "happiness" is a state of pure, unconditional acceptance, love, and understanding. As you progress on your unique journey of conscious evolvement, this will be an important differentiation for you to make.

Each of the levels in the Chart of Positive and Negative States of Mind on page 104 represents a different degree of friction or conflict between a person's self-definition and the truth of the moment. This works on both sides of the spectrum. When you believe you are loved and your significant other breaks the relationship off or files for divorce, this produces a conflict between your truth and the truth of "what is." On the flip side, if you believe yourself to be average in luck and you win a raffle for a trip around the world, this will also produce friction between your self-definition and reality. In each case a shift in your energy and state of mind will take place.

If your spouse files for divorce unexpectedly, how much this threatens your self-image temporarily determines the *degree* of the shift of your state of mind. How long you take to accept the new identity of being divorced is how long your negative state of mind will last. If you have based your entire sense of self-worth on having the love and acceptance of that particular person, you are most likely going to wind up depressed or enraged at level 4, or shocked and hysterical at level 5. You'll remain in suffering as long as you see your survival as dependent on the other person.

The degree to which you defined yourself by the relationship is directly related to the size of the "hole" left in your heart that is the source of your breakup pain. How long it takes to "fill" this "hole" with something or someone else dictates the duration of the state of mind. This is why many people have "rebound" relationships. It is an easy way to fill the "hole" and temporarily numb the pain.

On the other hand, if your sense of self is mainly based on your own sense of love and acceptance, then when the relationship ends, you are more likely to feel sadness and discontent at level 1 or feel frustrated and upset at level 2. Because the part of your identity that was defined by your relationship was much smaller than in the previous example, your negative unbalanced state of mind will have a shorter duration.

Let's go back to the example of the positive state of winning the raffle and exceeding your personal expectations. How much this experience improves your sense of self-worth determines the emotion. If you entirely redefine who you are to include the concept of yourself as "very fortunate" and "extremely lucky," most likely you'll have a temporary experience of level 4, bliss and euphoria. If you interpret winning to be interesting and fun, but feel you are not much better off for it, most likely your state of mind will move to just being jovial or high-spirited at level 2. It all depends on how you view who you are because of the event.

Your state of mind is always based on your last thought.

Following are examples of how your believed identity when met with a particular experience determines your state of mind.

I AM	Experience	State	Level	Emotion
Responsible	Lost wallet	Negative	2	Annoyance
Average-looking	Told gorgeous	Positive	3	Elation
A provider	Fired	Negative	4	Depression
Childless	Have a baby	Positive	4	Blissful
A son	Parent dies	Negative	5	Shocked
Thankful for life	Alive	Balanced	0	None— Peaceful
Understanding	Yelled at	Balanced	0	None— Peaceful
Compassionate	Mugged	Balanced	0	None— Peaceful
Faithful	Anything	Balanced	0	Infinitely Peaceful

The key to the way you go through life ultimately resides in how you define yourself. When you think less of yourself, you often need more from the world in the form of such things as money, power, vanity, possessions, and attention to neutralize the feeling. This mind-set can put you in a very protective and fearful state as these "outer" things tend to change. As you become more self-aware, you see that your survival is less dependent on anything outside yourself. This allows you to more easily integrate with the constant state of change. Less can be taken away from you when you are not attaching the ultimate idea of who you are to these material or physical things and when need is not generating big expectations from the people and the world around you. This reduction in fear is what will keep you closer to a state of balance and peace as you go through your daily life.

A key to a life filled with peace and happiness is to avoid becoming attached to your current identity, while simultaneously enjoying the experience of it.

An example of this is working hard at your job every day without expecting anything special for it. One day in your workplace, you alone get a nice raise and a compliment for doing great work. This sends you into a temporary positive state of mind. If you then expand your self-definition to include the idea that you're an especially great worker who deserves a big raise every year, you are setting yourself up for a "less than" feeling if it doesn't happen.

If you remain a humble and hard worker who perceives himself or herself as no better than anyone else, you've not only eliminated the possibility for future disappointment, but you are also positioning yourself to be surprised and elated if you get a raise and praise the following year. This doesn't mean you don't try to better your situation every year, but doing so in a humble and grateful way always puts you in a winning position. The I AM that is egotistically expecting to be treated a certain way always sets you up for a high potential of a disappointing experience and a negative state of mind.

While we constantly fluctuate between positive and negative states of mind, the place that has been the most elusive to mankind is the one at perfect balance, the state of tranquillity and peace. This is the state that has been spoken about through the ages. It has been conveyed from almost every religion, spiritual practice, and sacred philosophy as the ideal state of mind to achieve.

As mentioned earlier, every human being is mentally working

toward this exact "holy" or "whole" state of being. Whether you buy a new pair of well-fitting jeans, ride a roller coaster, make love, tell a joke, start a business, have children, or hug a loved one, each and every act ultimately represents an effort to be at peace with the universe. We all desire the answers to our deepest and most sacred questions. The centered and balanced state of being is where all the answers are—every single one of them.

> **The way to experience a clear and peaceful state of mind is to realize when you are not in it and why you are not in it.**

Experiencing this "holy" state of mind requires an expanded level of self-awareness. You must be able to recognize when you are in a state of nonacceptance or resistance to the truth of the moment in order to begin to change it. Fortunately, the journey of life itself offers this opportunity to you endlessly.

Polarity

Experience comes in through our minds like the wind.
We take it and twist it, and give it a spin,
To provide for the show that all of us are in,
One we don't lose nor any of us win.

The vision gets charged from our thoughts deep inside.
And sometimes it seems that there's no place to hide
From the conflict we feel that constrains us like vines,
All of this fiction created to keep our eyes blind.

We cry out for reason to try to keep ourselves sane
Any thought will do, no care, no shame,
As long as it keeps us from illusions of pain
And holds us together with a conscious that's lame.

The pain goes away for a short length of time
As the charge takes a shift to the pleasuring kind,
Until truth creeps back through the cracks in our mind
And we're confronted at last with the things that we find.

We learn that no thought can cause to erase
The soul's deep desire for peace in this place.
And nothing we do will make it leave without trace,
Only fear is left, will we finally face?

So listen to your gut, your heart and your feelings.
Have faith in its desire to bring you to healing.
For vibrations contain answers if you open to meaning,
And you'll find that what's there is beautifully revealing.

There's no charge in the world that can give you pure love,
Full peace and freedom, symbolized by the dove,
Because if you want the experience of all you're made of,
It's eternal balance you'll seek to be anointed from above.

PART THREE

Why Am I?

Chapter 8

Why You Have Emotions

*Your emotions are the clues that lead
to the treasure of everlasting peace.*

If your state of mind is the essence of your experience of life, then your feelings and emotions are the essence of your state of mind. Your emotions display the feelings or mood you are in at any particular moment. Happy, sad, tense, lighthearted, depressed, elated, anxious, repulsed or invigorated, are just some of the many words used to describe the character of your state of mind.

Since we know that all matter, including you, is composed of energy, the way that the behavior of your energy is revealed is through your emotions. Your emotions expose the degree to which your energy is out of balance. The more out of balance you are energetically, the more pronounced and intense your resulting emotions and aura will be. Your emotions are designed to help you rebalance and achieve a more tolerable state of mind.

As you become more aware of what is causing your emotions, you start to see more of the answers that they are offering you about your life. You begin to see exactly what these emotions are trying to reflect to you regarding where they stem from.

Ultimately they will be realized as signposts pointing you toward the path of lasting peace.

The word "emotion" originates from the Latin word *emovere*, to "move out," and can also be looked at as E-Motion, or "energy in motion." When you exhibit an emotion, a buildup and imbalance of energy from within you is moving and being released. This is the mind's way of equalizing your energy in the attempt to find a tolerable state of existence. This same process of energy release, while it is not called emotion, occurs with everything else in the universe. This type of a release is observable in some things in the world and goes virtually unnoticed in others.

The "emotion" of the sun could be called radiance. With the exception of the occasional "flare-up" (pun intended), the sun radiates virtually the same energy to the solar system each and every day. The sun's emission of energy will change and diminish over time as it runs the course of its five-billion-year life cycle. However, you and I are not likely to see any change in its luminosity in our lifetimes.

You are just like the sun in that you emit energy out to your universe every day, and, just like the sun, this energy has an effect on everything it comes in contact with.

One of the differences between how the sun emits energy and how you do is that the intensity and style of your output of energy changes depending upon the polarity of your energy. If you get a job promotion, fall in love, have a baby, triumph at sports, or win money, generally you will shift to an imbalance on the positive side of the energy spectrum, and positive emotions are likely to result. If you experience the passing of a loved one, lose a job, undergo a financial crisis, get hurt, see others hurt, or experience the undesired end of a relationship, you will likely shift to an imbalance on the negative side of the energy spectrum, and negative emotions conceivably will follow.

Anytime your state of energy shifts to a point that is deemed *intolerable* by you, a release of some of this energy will need take place. The avenue for this release is the purpose of your emotions.

While emotion is the way this release happens for human beings, the word for the degree of buildup and release in all other things is "entropy." Entropy is scientifically defined as the degree of disorder or uncertainty in a system, while other definitions describe it as the universe's constant (and unstoppable) movement toward balance.

For each of us, emotions are a sign of the disorder of our perceived system, which is caused by our uncertainty. The degree of our uncertainty depends upon our perception of the reality that we are experiencing. When we are conflicted and uncertain, it produces a shift in our mental balance. As we move further in degree into an intolerable state of mind, we release the extra negative or positive energy that is creating the imbalance. A release of either positive or negative emotion occurs through the behavior we display, like jumping up and down for joy when receiving good news or crying when we hear about the passing of a loved one or friend.

The reason for the release of positive or negative energy is always to attempt to return a system (or a human being, in our case) back to a state of balance. At balance, there is clarity and peace.

There is order in chaos.

All chaos manifests for the same underlying purpose: to restore balance. Whether we are discussing an individual, a small
group of people, a culture, or an entire nation, the process of
releasing charged energy (chaos) is a natural effort to escape
disharmony and return to a more tolerable existence. This is also
known as a *catharsis*.

The type of energy you generate that seeks release through
your emotions depends upon the way you perceive what you are
experiencing. The core factor that determines whether what you
are perceiving will generate negative or positive energy is always
based on what validates or invalidates who you believe that you
are. It originates either from your resistance to an experience that
does not align with your self-definition (I AM) or from your
acceptance of an experience that reinforces your desired image.

SELF experiencing a desired increase in definition
   (Overvalidation of existence) = Increase in positively charged
   energy

SELF experiencing an undesired decrease in definition
   (Invalidation of existence) = Increase in negatively charged
   energy

You resist any experience that invalidates your self-image, because this causes you to feel "less than" or threatened in some
way. The feeling of being "less than" shifts your energy to the
negative side of the Chart of Positive and Negative States of
Mind (see chapter 7). For example, you might resist the ending
of a relationship with the person you are in love with, you might
resist someone with a different point of view than yours, or you
might resist the physical reality of aging.

Alternatively, any type of experience that causes you to see yourself in a pleasant or fulfilling way is considered desirable and increases your sense of personal validation. A good example is receiving a genuine and unexpected compliment. This feeling of being "more than" shifts your energy to the positive side of the Chart of Positive and Negative States of Mind. This produces a release of positive emotions.

Interestingly, the reason a negative experience may seem to hang on longer than a positive one is that you are more likely to quickly accept an experience that gives you a positive sense of validation. In contrast, the truth that generates the negative experience is often resisted for a much longer period of time, producing the friction that keeps the negative energy alive.

Everything you experience throughout your day that is not perceived to affect who you are in any way generates no friction and is observed neutrally.

How you interpret yourself in relationship to your moment-to-moment reality is the key to your state of balance.

When there's a difference between your self-image (I AM) and your perception of reality ("No, you are not"), the difference causes friction that generates the shift in energy that results in certain feelings and emotions. The more you are content with who you are, the less likely you are to be thrown off balance by what the world confronts you with on a daily basis. The less you are thrown off balance, the more centered you will be and the more you will experience peace.

The following flow chart reflects the different phases in the Experience-Reaction process. First, matter is detected by your five senses, giving you an experience. Next, in a nanosecond, these sensations are checked against your memory bank of beliefs about yourself and the world (I AM). Third, this action of checking against your beliefs determines your perception of the experience as good, bad, or indifferent. Fourth, your perception generates a positive, negative, or neutral energetic response. Finally, there is an emotional release of some type and degree in the attempt to rebalance. Anytime you meet information that is outside the realm of your expectations or conflicts with your beliefs, the resulting friction sparks a feeling or emotion.

Let's look at how this could work in a real-life situation. Imagine you leave work one evening and find that your car has been stolen. Your perception of the experience will determine your state of mind and your resulting emotional response. If you love your car, have personal things inside it, and don't have it insured, having it stolen may prompt a high degree of disbelief and resistance to what has occurred. The result will be the feeling that a part of you has been lost with the car, and that you are now "less than" you were. The energy derived from these thoughts will put you out of balance on the negative side. A release of negative emotions must then follow. You could feel a range of emotions, such as grief, confusion, rage, and sadness. An overload of negative energy can make you feel heavy, low, or downtrodden.

But if you hate your car, don't care about what's inside it, and also have it fully insured, instead you may indulge in thoughts of driving a brand-new car that your insurance company will cover financially. Since you did not expect to experience a sudden change in self-definition ("I AM the proud owner of a new car") and can easily accept the idea of owning a new car, you generate positive energy. A release of positive energy must follow this shift. Emotions that would accompany the release may

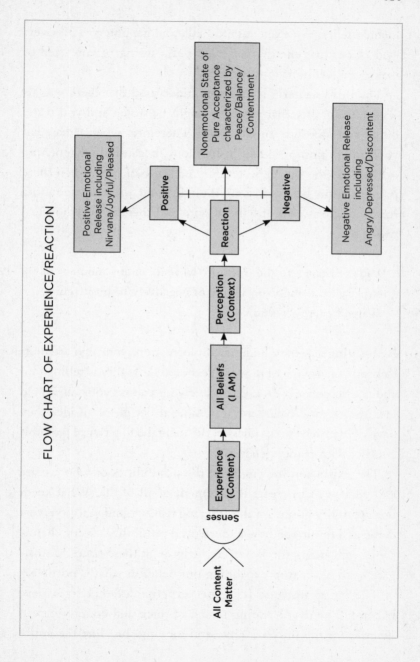

FLOW CHART OF EXPERIENCE/REACTION

include relief, joy, excitement, thrill, and happiness. This over-load of positive energy may even put a spring in your step or make you feel light on your feet.

The third scenario is that you understood that there was always a possibility that your car might be stolen and you really didn't care one way or the other. Therefore, when it happens you remain unmoved and in harmony, because the happening is in line with your expectations and sense of self. When there is no friction between your thoughts and the corresponding reality, there is no unbalanced state and there is no emotional response.

Your resistance to the truth of "what is" in any moment of experience is the main source of negatively or positively charged energy within you.

By resisting any new undesired information, your ego attempts to keep you as you were regardless of what reality is telling you about who you are. To take on a new idea about yourself, an old idea must "die." Many are unwilling to let go of an idea they have of themselves regardless of the mental and physical pain this conflict with reality generates.

The expansion into more of the possibilities of who we are and what we can create is the intent of all of life. What keeps our creativity going are the amazing feelings and emotions that come as a result of a new experienced possibility. Every chemical of well-being is released in the brain at these times to instigate us to never stop expanding our belief in what is possible.

The entire universe is in the perpetual attempt to achieve balance. The never-ending match of force and counterforce is what keeps the universe alive and moving. Just like the entire universe, you and everyone you know are constantly ebbing and flowing and doing whatever is deemed necessary to stay in harmony with the ever-changing universe.

Remember the troubled kid in your grammar school or high school? That child was doing his or her best to find a balanced state of mind and sense of peace. Trying to gain attention by goofing off was the effort to gain acceptance or compensate for a lack of positive identity reinforcement at home. Acting out was most likely the child's only perceived way to attract the attention that compensated for a low self-image. It was one of the child's only known ways to feel alive and to *matter*.

Our minds and bodies are perfectly designed to work together by using our actions and emotions to regulate our state of mind. Creativity cannot flow from a chaotic and disharmonious state. That is why it is so important to learn to let your emotions out when you feel them. The emotions, when not restrained, provide a cleansing and rebalancing that allow us to be in the best possible frame of mind to accomplish what we desire. They also are a critical component that offers each of us a litmus test of how tuned into and accepting we are of what we experience in our world. Constant movement toward balance is the intention of every action and emotion of life.

The mind-set of clarity, contentment, and peace is a sign of a balanced state of energy.

When people go through life interpreting events in such a way that their energy gets polarized to the negative side of the spectrum, a buildup of pressure occurs. When this pressure continues without release, the imbalance moves to a level that becomes highly unstable. The large buildup of extra energy then becomes ripe for a release. Just like a dam that is under too much pressure, one small crack and the emotional floodgates are sure to burst open.

Perhaps you know someone who is always on the verge of a breakdown such as this? If so, you may often feel like you have to "walk on eggshells" around this very fragile individual. For many different reasons the person's perceptions of the world and his or her place in it have generated an abundance of negative energy that has not found an avenue for release. This overload can only last for so long until, like an active volcano, they are ready to blow. The energy of this individual is highly charged and can be tangibly felt by those in the person's presence.

When you are in a room with someone who is depressed or angry, you can often feel the heaviness of the person's negative energy, which can affect you to the point where it "brings you down" or "wears you out." When you are around an individual who is volatile and has an unstable energy about them, the unpredictability of the person's behavior can have an "unsettling" and "unnerving" effect.

Being around someone in a state of extreme joy or excitement can have an equal effect on us on the positive side of the emotional spectrum. Experiencing their happiness or ecstasy has the literal effect of lifting us up, as we "feel their joy." Their highly charged energy is infectious and stimulating, and we often feel "energized" and "inspired" after being around them.

Individuals whose energy is constantly fluctuating typically create scenarios that can give their energy an outlet. "Drama" is one of the words we use to describe someone who has a need for frequent outlets. "She is such a drama queen." "He is highly affected." "That guy seems completely bipolar." All such comments are used to describe people who demonstrate a wide range of pendulous emotions. They undergo quick shifts in energy, as they are continuously affected by the truth of the moment. Continual conflict is produced by their self-defining I AM statements that have a hard time being realized in reality.

Every one of your own I AM statements has the potential to be challenged by a world of infinite possibility. The more rigidly you adhere to specific ideas and beliefs about the world, and what you expect from it, the more you enter a state that is ripe to be thrown off balance. It can feel like the world is constantly assaulting you.

Negative Imbalances: Each of us may easily remember an experience that created negative energy in our minds and bodies. Anger, shock, disbelief, sadness, repulsion, rage, and hysteria are states of mind manifested from these experiences, as your belief system leads you to resist the truth of the moment.

When you read the following list of some of these well-known events, you may recall the exact place, time, and feeling you had at the moment the event entered your awareness.

- News about the unexpected death of a loved one.
- News you received about a personal illness or disease.
- A time the person you were in love with told you that he or she no longer was in love with you.
- A past experience of a sudden and material loss of money or financial security.
- The death and destruction from the earthquake in Haiti in January 2010.

- People flooded out and stranded without food and water in New Orleans, Louisiana, after Hurricane Katrina struck in August 2005.
- The deadly tsunami that struck Indonesia on December 24, 2004.
- The terrorist attacks on September 11, 2001.
- Princess Diana's sudden death in a car wreck in Paris on August 31, 1997.
- The U.S. Space Shuttle *Challenger* explosion on January 28, 1986.
- The murder of John Lennon on December 8, 1980.
- The sudden death of Elvis Presley on August 16, 1977.
- The assassination of Martin Luther King Jr. on April 4, 1968.
- The assassination of U.S. President John F. Kennedy on November 22, 1963.

The intensity of your emotions upon learning of undesirable news was always related to how much you did not want to acknowledge what was occurring or didn't want to believe it was occurring. A piece of who you were that was defined through your beliefs was being dismantled by the truth, and you fought it for a certain length of time.

Since the core intent of matter is to achieve balance, when our energy is overloaded, the brain, which is the body's key organ in charge of balance, starts the process of entropy: crying, screaming, clenching and waving fists in the air, pounding the ground, and spitting. The metaphor to "spew venom" is appropriate for this action because negative energy truly has a poisonous effect on our minds and bodies. In extreme cases, like the untimely death of a loved one, vomiting, fainting, and even catatonia occurs. At this extreme level of resistance, negative energy is being generated faster than the brain and body can release it. A complete mental shutdown takes place in order to avoid the truth.

Back in March 1991, Rodney King, an African-American taxi-cab driver in Los Angeles, was brutally beaten as he was being arrested by a group of policemen after leading them on a high-speed chase. The district attorney of Los Angeles charged the officers with the use of excessive force. However, at their trial the policemen were acquitted. We only have to remember the destruction, riots, and looting that followed the verdict to see ways in which negative mental imbalances work themselves off. From the perspective of many African-Americans living in South Central LA, the verdict handed down by the justice system was an unacceptable statement. It became a symbol of how poorly African-Americans had been regarded by the law in relation to other races. Years of social injustice and repression—being profiled, judged, and unfairly treated by the justice system—boiled over and resulted in an emotional explosion that was tripped by the King verdict. The ensuing destruction from fires and rioting was a massive collective display of entropy and release.

The fact that African-American businesses in the community were looted and burned in the process of expressing rage against the system is the irrepressible truth of the degree of intent of the brain to immediately release any negative energy causing an imbalance. A highly charged, chaotic state of mind is far from rational and objective, as evidenced by the pure intent to release energy on anyone anywhere. This destructive energy will even be self-directed if the negative imbalance is large enough.

There is no greater fear to a human being than the interpretation of events to mean, "You are nothing." The ego will go to any measure to get the self to be seen and heard when the self feels it is not heard. The April 1992 riots that followed the Rodney King assault trial were the response of the collective consciousness of a specific community saying, "I AM," and "If you won't acknowledge that I AM, I will create a release that will cause you to notice that I AM."

There have been many other examples of such releases throughout history. Most of these incidents were many times larger in magnitude. Thousands of years of revolts, genocides, and wars have been the result of a shift to a negatively charged state of mind and the perceived need for a certain way to exist. In many cases, it is only in the aftermath that the initiators are able to reflect on what has occurred. This type of reflection is usually marked with disbelief, shock, and horror at the behavior that was used.

The description of violent behavior by its perpetrators may include statements such as, "It was like I was possessed" or, "I felt out of my mind." Of course, "possession" is really nothing more than the energy system within an individual or group purging the energy imbalance (entropy) through heightened emotion, chaos, and the *seeming* loss of control. The mechanism setting off the imbalance is always the protection of a certain piece of one's perceived identity (I AM) and the resistance to the current truth being experienced that threatens it.

In a highly volatile or imbalanced state, the possibilities one believes they are faced with have been reduced to only the ones that generate the greatest amount of fear. In this very irrational and nonobjective state of mind the most primal survival instincts emerge in the fight to remain alive.

The way out of the chaos and confusion is by ending the source of the friction that is causing the negative energy. This is done by the will and control to take pause and open to a new perspective of the situation at hand, or by safely releasing as much excess negative energy as possible through the emotional system. The intent is to get back to a sense of inner peace and balance with the situation at hand. This state of balance (also called the state of grace) is where clarity can be found. In balance, we realize more of the possibilities that exist, as opposed to perceiving only the most feared and limited possibilities that we have previously focused on and reacted to.

At one time or another in the course of your life you may have "flown off the handle" or had an outburst of emotion that you reflected on later as unbecoming of you. What simply happened was the event you experienced was way out of line with your belief system. At that point, you determined that you couldn't and wouldn't take it anymore, so, to end the mental conflict, you attempted to manipulate the situation back to your definition of normal through an energy outburst.

When someone says, "You've hurt my feelings," that person is really saying, "You told me something that was in direct opposition to what I believe about myself." The person's "hurt" comes from the invalidation they feel through the message that is being conveyed. "Thin-skinned" people, as well as those who typically seek other people's approval to compensate for the lack of their own approval, are the most susceptible to getting "hurt." It is never the person who says something that causes hurt, or even what the person has said, but always the listener's interpretation of it.

For the majority of people in a negative state of mind and body, a big outburst usually exhausts them and brings them to the point where they can regain some sense of balance. After a "good cry," they tend to feel drained, but also more accepting and open-minded to the potential changes they are faced with in their lives. Before crying, screaming, or yelling, focusing on the image of the worst and most feared future scenario is what generated their negative energy and state of mind. The more these projections are focused on, the more intense these physical releases can become, as in, "She cried so hard I thought she was going to pass out."

Below are some common expressions we hear in everyday life to describe people who have been affected by unexpected and undesired events and are still having trouble dealing with the new reality. These comments reflect the fact that they have yet to accept "what is" and are still in a state of imbalance.

- "She seems lost."
- "I don't know who I AM anymore."
- "I still can't believe this happened."
- "He hasn't been himself since."

Each of these descriptions reflects the negative polarity of the individual's energy as they try to protect an I AM statement, such as, "I AM a mother," "I AM a husband," "I AM living in a safe country," "I AM healthy," "I AM loved," that has radically and abruptly changed. Many people fear letting go of any piece of identity no matter how much pain it has caused. However, the more we can embrace the truth of each moment, no matter what it represents to our ever-changing identity, the easier it is to release the destructive negative energy within us. Allowing this energy to flow out and be purged by way of our emotions is what allows for healing to begin.

We call this the "grieving process." The loss of a major piece of one's identity is "grieved" as one moves to accept the new and present self. There is no set timetable on the grieving process. It can take years or days. It is completely up to the individual who has experienced loss and that person's will and desire to return to a life of peace and balance.

When energy and the way it moves through the mind and body is looked at from this perspective, it can easily be seen how all sorts of varying emotions occur.

Procreation has a powerful way of defining us as human beings and thus sex and conception can often be surrounded by strong emotions. And when things don't go as expected or according to plan in this area of our lives, these emotions can become negatively charged.

While many men experience a deep sense of connection with their partner through sex, it can also be very self-defining for men. On some profound level, their identities as procreators provide a substantial sense of fulfillment. Thus, a feeling that there is a lack of frequency or any issues surrounding an ability to perform the act of intercourse can generate negative energy and lead to an array of different emotional responses. The incredible amount of money spent each year on erectile dysfunction drugs such as Viagra further highlights the priority that is placed on this self-defining act.

For many women, sex is often more deeply related to the emotional connection that goes with it—the feelings of being loved and appreciated. Negative emotions can arise when a woman feels that this loving, sincere connection is lacking. Another issue that holds the potential for the creation of negative energy surrounds pregnancy and birth. Since one of the more powerful acts of self-creation is the act of procreating, a lot of pressure and expectation can be put on both men and women to conceive successfully.

When this process does not go as planned, it can be a source of much internal conflict and emotional unrest.

Another example of the challenge to validate and maintain a certain core identity is found with those in the entertainment business. Many famous actors, actresses, musicians, and sports stars find themselves constantly working to keep up a certain image and public identity. Those who have trouble accepting the height of their fame, or those who have trouble dealing with the loss of any of it, tend to end up battling a very negative state of mind as a result. This often leads to problems with addiction to drugs and alcohol, which has plagued many notable stars throughout recent history.

Many famous people who started their careers as children and never had a chance to develop their own personal identity outside of sports, music, theater, television, or film come to mind. If they get injured or go on the "out" with pop culture and can't get work, they are often left with a deep struggle and conflict adjusting to a new, unknown identity. Anger, depression, and frustration are common among such individuals as they try to cope. Drugs often are used to counterbalance the pain of the new, undesired reality. The consequences from this can be devastating, as the drugs only compound the problem and move them away from the real cause of the suffering.

Aging and the sudden changes it brings is another area that has the potential to create resistance and mental suffering. As people age and their physical attributes or abilities diminish, many struggle to accept the new limitations and changes. Examples are general aches and pains; the loss of body shape, strength, and hair; wrinkles; thinning of the skin; and problems with memory. When an individual constantly resists the reality of who he or she currently is, it can be emotionally draining and physically damaging.

The more insecure a person is about who they are, the more their ego is on display as it works to reconcile the fear-filled thoughts. Manic swings in mood and volatility in general are a constant by-product of this thought pattern. Also, the more distinct and powerful an individual thinks they are in relation to others, the more concerned and paranoid they become about losing this definition. When something or someone threatening enters the space of a highly defined "egomaniac," no time is spared in removing it.

Behavioral examples from history of massive narcissism from dictators like Saddam Hussein, Adolf Hitler, and Joseph Stalin reveal the extreme nature the ego will go to in order to protect any delusional idea they have of themselves and the way they believe the world should be around them. These individuals murdered and killed not only many perceived enemies and in- nocent men, women, and children, but also members of their own political parties.

This reveals not only the lengths that the mind will go to in order to accomplish its objective of feeling alive and distinct, but also the extreme emotions and behaviors that manifest when one is operating from a very negative state of mind. In the case of extreme insecurity, the ego must work very hard to both purge negative energy and get what they feel they need from the outside world to confirm who they believe they are on the inside. The bigger the disparity, the more likely a person is to lose a sense of objectivity and become delusional in the attempt to reconcile the gap. Extreme and volatile emotional reactions will then be the result.

The more "distinct" and "finite" you feel yourself to be in
your world, the more "fragile" and "volatile" you become.

The vital significance of the emotional system can be seen in
individuals who have a very difficult time with emotional release. When negative energy imbalances build to a high intensity
and there is no perceived method of release, the pressure and pain
of living can seem overwhelming. Extended periods of "depression" are often the result of this inability to emote. The negative
imbalance, rather than being purged, remains within the individual, where it creates the feelings of gloom and despair.

When an individual perceives no acceptable outlet for an
overload of negative energy, he or she is left in a constant state
of either fear or apathy. Without help, the affected individual's
feeling of not being able to experience himself or herself as valued and alive inflicts more suffering on the person than the
imagined act of physical death. This can be when and why suicide is considered or chosen.

When an individual is unable to emote, it usually stems from
childhood programming. The use of emotion was either taught
as a sign of weakness (usually in males) or as the precursor to
the pain of corporal punishment ("If you don't stop crying, I'll
give you something to cry about"). To be able to emote and
release is critical because it is the outlet that moves people from
a perception of what is not possible for them in the world, to a
more objective state, providing an outlook of what IS possible.

The ability to emote is a critical factor in the process of living
a more contented life. The process allows for a place of clarity
and balance where self-acceptance might occur. It is what can
bring us back to see the infinite possibilities for our lives that
allow us to experience healing and peace.

. . .

Positive Imbalances: On the other end of the spectrum, when your beliefs about your identity expand, you experience an imbalance of your energy on the positively charged side, resulting in positive emotions. Any new or desired experience has this effect. Exploring a new part of the world, opening a present, or falling in love will increase the charge to the positive side. What is happening is that the experience makes you feel more distinct, separate, and defined. As a new I AM is born, the self is aggrandized by the experience and positive energy flows.

Under these conditions, the brain sets off the release of chemicals such as dopamine and serotonin that produce the feelings of happiness and well-being. By keeping us addicted to certain experiences of life, nature reveals an intricate part of its perfect process.

Because all things in the universe are finite and have a beginning and an end, the only way to keep creation going is through the constant process of creating, dividing, and multiplying. The infinite force that is life persists in its never-ending intent to divide creatively. It is why Mother Nature unleashes an extra helping of oxytocin during the reproductive activity of sex, just to ensure we keep coming back for more.

A great example of positive emotional release is when children are in the act of opening gifts. The excitement and anticipation of opening a present is a reflection of the positive creative experience in front of them. The unknown is about to be known. The result of the experience will be a new self-definition. At times, if they are opening multiple gifts, children may seem more interested in the act of opening the gift than in the gift itself. This reflects the mind's addiction to the creative experience.

Positive imbalances cause an inordinate amount of positive energy to be generated as the mind realizes that what has just occurred is outside the boundary of its previous beliefs. The resulting emotions include joy, exhilaration, stunned silence, and ecstasy.

Below are some examples of public and private experiences that may have sent you into a positive emotional state. Depending on their impact, you may remember the exact time, place, and emotional response you had when you learned about these events.

- The first time you fell in love.
- The experience of the birth of a child.
- The experience of your team winning a championship.
- Watching the first man walk on the moon on July 21, 1969.
- The U.S. ice hockey victory over the Soviet Union in the 1980 Olympics.
- Watching the fall of the Berlin wall in November 1989.
- A desired sexual experience.
- Listening to a beautiful and moving piece of music.
- Enjoying the victory of your particular political party or politician.
- A time you got an unexpected promotion.
- The experience of winning money gambling.
- When you asked your significant other to marry you and he or she said yes.

The ways the brain seeks to correct the positive imbalance created by the information are screaming, jumping, laughing, crying, running, and in extreme cases (such as being sung to by a favorite rock star at a concert) fainting or otherwise having a complete physical shutdown. **These are the exact same behaviors that occur upon release on the negative side of the emotional spectrum.** The only difference is that positive energy gives you a release of pressure that makes you feel lighter and more energized than normal, a feeling of being uplifted, grander, and free. Negative energy adds pressure to your system and is draining on the body, making you feel heavier, downtrodden, and smaller in significance.

You only have to look at the bedlam and destruction that typically occur when a city's home team wins a major sports championship to find one of the ways that positive mental imbalances (entropy) are worked off through the process of an emotional release. Anyone who has attached his or her personal identity to a sports team instantly feels a larger sense of self after the win. The personal identity (I AM) has jumped to a level of a champion, which makes one feel like they are "on top of the world." When this surge in positive energy occurs, the brain immediately seeks to restore balance. Leaning on the horn in front of the stadium, yelling while jumping up and down, turning cars over, throwing objects, breaking windows, setting fires—all of it is done in the desperate and seemingly uncontrollable attempt to rebalance energy and get back to a tolerable and clearer state of mind.

The comments heard from those who have had emotional outbursts and from others who describe them are statements such as:

- "I just lost it."
- "He was in la-la land."
- "They went crazy."
- "I'm on cloud nine!"

All positive imbalances depend upon the conflict between who you believe yourself to be (I AM) and what your experience indicates that you are. For example, if someone with minimal income buys a scratch-off card at the local gas station and wins $500, the person is likely to be sent into a higher positive state, with much more pronounced emotion, than if Donald Trump won the same amount. The resulting imbalance is always related to the subjective nature of the experience. As we experience a grander version of ourselves, positive energy is released. This is the essence of creation. Something new, an evolvement of the previous creation, has taken place—an expansion of awareness of the possibilities for self-definition has occurred. **This is the process that provides for an infinite universe.**

A moment of desired creation generates a significant amount of positive energy, which is why it is no wonder that at the pinnacle of orgasm there are moans and screams of ecstasy.

One of the results of being tilted to one end of the emotional spectrum or the other is the effect it has on your objectivity and rationality. At both ends of the spectrum we tend to focus on only the possibilities that we perceive will validate the corresponding emotional state. Just as negative emotional imbalances lead us toward doom-and-gloom scenarios, positive imbalances tend to cause us to believe in and see only the best possible outcomes. We tend to take on an extreme Pollyanna-ish or rose-colored outlook. The mind and the way it uses memory for survival link our experiences to the future so that we *expect* and *believe* we will experience the same types of outcomes every time. That's why someone who experiences a lot of losses or failure often feels stuck in a reality where he or she will lose every time, thus adding to the creation of this outcome. The one who tends to win or succeed more often does the exact same thing on the opposite end of the spectrum, but believes in victory.

The skewed view that many take on when they are having an emotional surge to the positive end of the spectrum can make them feel invincible. This often happens to gamblers who are on a hot streak and to powerful sports teams when they are playing a severe underdog. When a highly favored sports team goes into an event with a high expectation of victory, it only takes the slightest puncture in those expectations to throw the whole team off balance. If the underdog takes the lead in the event, this could shake the favored team up just enough to allow the less-skilled team with no pressure or expectations on them the window of opportunity to go on to achieve victory.

Many investors experienced something like this during both the stock market bubble of 1999–2000, and the real estate bubble of 2006–2007. The euphoria of a continual period of rising prices led to such a positive emotional state that it caused them to drastically underestimate or even completely ignore risk. Many only looked at what they wanted to see to keep the positive energy and good feelings rolling. All that was perceived was profit; the idea of declining prices or losses was not given much consideration in the decisions that were made.

As these expectations were confronted with the early stages of the market's downturn, many investors froze like a deer caught in the headlights, as their minds tried to conceive of the seeming impossibility of declining prices. In the stock market, when the reality of what was happening was finally acknowledged, the previous euphoria shifted to panic and fear, and there was a stampede as many investors all tried to sell at the same time. Many of the investors caught in this situation ended up selling their investments at drastically lower levels. This was the price to pay, literally, for resisting the possibility that prices could go down.

The teenage years are certainly filled with plenty of experiences of what is possible and what is not possible. Teens often test and seek the limits of their physical boundaries. Because they do not have enough experience with cause and effect, many young people share a feeling of invincibility. New creative experiences of driving fast or climbing high give them a rush of excitement. When they are in this larger-than-life state they tend to lose their objectivity. They do not see the true level of risk in their behavior. Just like in the investing example above, the individual becomes primed for the surprise of an undesired and unforeseen result. When risky behavior is displayed, parents often try to snap their kids back into reality with comments like, "Just who do you think you are?"

The graph on page 141 illustrates the poles of the emotional spectrum and the perceived possibilities in different emotional states. Limiting the possibilities increases the odds of experiencing a possibility that was not accounted for, which will always create an energy imbalance. In contrast, the balanced and peaceful state of mind is the one in which the mind is completely aware and ready for all possibilities.

As your emotions constrict your vision, and also destroy your sense of objectivity and truth, they simultaneously are telling you that the beliefs you hold are false. The more you can become aware of the beliefs you hold that are false, as they relate to your intent in life, the more you are led to the truth that gets you to what you desire to experience. Being in an emotional state is the evidence that you are out of balance. Being out of

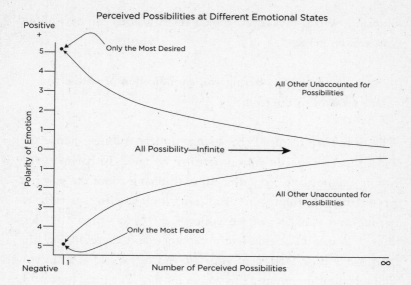

Perceived Possibilities at Different Emotional States

balance means you are denying some part of the truth of what is currently happening in your life.

Emotions are a great signal of where you are in terms of ignorance and lack of awareness. They offer you the choice to acknowledge and accept "what is" and experience the relief and grace that comes with it, or to deny "what is" and go through another emotional buildup. The truth will NOT go away. You cannot move to a negative emotional state unless you are resisting some part of what is occurring in your life. You cannot move to a positive emotional state unless what you are experiencing is desired and at some level not fully accepted as real yet.

If you want to be free of a constant negative feeling or emotion, you will have to look at the reason you refuse to accept what is happening. This will always lead you to an idea you have of yourself (I AM) that you cannot currently experience. Your emotions will always reveal the current illusions you have about you and your life.

Your emotions are offering you an indication of where you are resistant to the truth.

The only state of mind that brings understanding—hence the most peaceful and fulfilling state—is balance. In balance, you are in the moment. You are neither thinking about the past nor projecting into the future. You don't look at things as right or wrong and you do not see yourself as "better than" or "less than." You are in complete acceptance and therefore see the purpose and perfection of yourself and the world around you and what it is representing to you every day. The most powerful, creative, and harmonious actions take place from this state of pure clarity. This is where your dreams are conceived, believed, and created.

In mankind's attempt to achieve a more peaceful and liberating state of mind, many seeming shortcuts have been developed. Rather than look at the source of the painful thoughts that keep us in a state of emotional disharmony, other means of relief are used to manipulate our state of mind. Enter the use and eventual addiction to drugs, alcohol, gambling, codependence, money, sex, food, and vanity.

Chapter 9

Why You Have
Need and Addiction

The thought of imperfection is the root of all addiction.

The desire to be alive and experience life automatically places each of us in a constant state of need. A need is defined as a perceived requirement to achieve a particular experience.

Essentially, as human beings, our ultimate intent is to continue the experience of living. Therefore, we often have cravings for food, water, sunlight, shelter, love, and many other things that we feel are necessary to continue to survive. Cravings also occur for thousands of nonessentials to staying alive, and these fixations arise each time we desire a new life experience. The moment we decide upon a certain way we want to live life, a set of needs is born alongside that decision. In order for the desire to materialize, these needs must be met.

For example, if you decide to experience a different part of the country, you *need* to know where you are going, and you *need* to know how to get there. You then *need* a means of transportation to achieve your intent. If you decide to experience a fulfilling love relationship, you *need* to know how exactly this relationship will have to look, feel, and be for you to be fulfilled by it. Once you have this idea in your mind, you then *need* to put yourself in a position that increases the probability that you will meet the person who will complete the original intent.

The core intent behind all of the "needs" that result from your desires is to help you realize a certain state of mind.

Anytime you engage in an experience that confirms your self-image, you immediately feel a sense of satisfaction and peace. "I AM a traveler to new places," or "I AM in a loving relationship." Each of these is a declaration of creative distinction that gives you a sense of who you are. As your needs are met and you successfully have the experience you desired, the result is a sense of contentment and harmony with the universe.

In essence, we are all addicted to constant self-creation, which enables us to know that we are alive and matter in the world.

This knowing can only come from the experience of actually being whoever we declare ourselves to be.

The word "addiction" generally has a negative connotation in our language and culture. Addiction is thought of only as something harmful or damaging. However, to the addicted, "good," "bad," "harmful," and "damaging" are irrelevant concepts. The only thing that is truly relevant is whether or not the addiction helps them achieve a more acceptable state of mind. This is the deciding factor for the user when the impulse leads them to participate in the addictive behavior.

Since we all have a need to live life, we all have a massive need for food and water. This creates the cravings necessary to search out and find food and water. We only have to see news reports of what happens in countries where food and water are scarce in relation to the size of the population to see the acts of desperation that people will commit in order to meet this need. Under these circumstances, the object or experience that people crave can easily be seen as the addiction that it truly is. This is the same with every other perceived need as it relates to survival in life.

Every person who has an addiction is doing what he or she perceives is necessary in order to survive.

If an individual feels as though a certain altered state or experience will bring them to a more tolerable state of mind, they will seek this avenue at all costs. Many times these costs are heavy in terms of the resulting suffering that is created. When an addicted individual is in an intolerable state of mind, they only focus on the short-term benefit of achieving a temporary state of gratification and the relief that comes from the means they use to get there. Costs and consequences basically become irrelevant. The damage, downside, and repercussions to their bodies, finances, relationships, and quality of life in general all become of secondary concern. Here are some examples.

- The money-addicted workaholic who sacrifices his or her marriage, relationship with children, and physical health.
- The codependent-addicted individual who refuses to face the reality of a relationship with a controlling, abusive, and insecure individual.
- The addicted gambler who doesn't consider the financial damage and effects on personal relationships and family.

For an addicted person, all that *matters* at the moment is achieving a shift in their state of mind through the act of the addiction, thus temporarily releasing them from a discontented state of mind and the suffering that entails.

Addictions are not to any particular "thing" but to the state of mind that the experience of the "thing" provides.

The quest for the state of mind of peace and tranquillity has a powerful universal appeal. What humanity is in the process of learning through addictive behavior is what is true and what is false as it relates to achieving the experience of lasting peace. Remember, all things in matter (formations of energy) either are in a sense of balance or are seeking balance through a process of trial and error. Addictions are part of the process that is error because it is falsely believed that the addiction will help with finding lasting balance. What ends up being discovered through a sometimes long and painful road is that it serves only to send the addict further out of balance.

It will eventually be discovered that a sense of balance is achieved faster and lasts longer through the expansion of awareness that reveals more of who you really are. It is this understanding that ends the old idea of who you thought you were that was driving the suffering. As you continue to expand the awareness of who you are, the result is a permanent change in experience, rather than the temporary and unfulfilling path of outside attachments and addiction that puts you in a repeating cycle.

Addiction is like trying to fill up a bucket that has a hole in the bottom. The water may fill the bucket temporarily, but the bucket will always end up empty again due to the leak, causing the addict to be in a constant search for more "water." When finally the root of the issue is found and the hole is fixed, the bucket stays filled, and the need or craving constantly to fill it vanishes.

When dealing with someone who has an addiction, the use of resistance, anger, force, disdain, or manipulation generally only serves to compound the problem (evidence of the universal principle of force/counterforce). The state of mind that originally triggered the perceived need came on some level from a place of self-rejection and repudiation as a worthy or valued person. As the individual incurs a further lack of acceptance and approval through another's disapproval of what they are currently doing, it actually exacerbates their negative state of mind. This new additional validation of the person's poor self-identity causes these individuals to slip even further into an addictive state.

The most effective means by which one can help in the healing of another human being is to start from a place of understanding, compassion, acceptance, and unconditional love. If you aren't at this level of understanding, simply know that your resistance to an afflicted individual's behavior is part of the energy that helps the addicted person to confirm his or her lack of self-worth. It is this exact state of mind that searches for the damaging method of relief in the first place.

Some of the most prevalent addictions in today's society are addictions to money, power, drugs and alcohol, codependence, gambling, vanity, food, perfection, material possessions, and compulsive behavior. Each of these avenues is simply a different method of rapidly elevating the state of mind.

Three major issues stem from using outside methods to shift to a positive state of mind. One issue is the temporary nature of the gratification. As much as this state feels good, it will not last unless the act of addiction is repeated. As people start to "come down," they are faced again with the negative state of mind and sense of suffering that was avoided in the first place. The intolerability of a negative state of mind causes addicted people to crave the method used to get back to a better-feeling state of mind. They become obsessed with finding any avenue to experience it again.

The second issue is that the mind and body are designed to constantly adjust to keep all systems working and in balance. This adjustment happens both chemically and psychologically. Because of this, over time it takes more of the particular addiction to reach the same positive feeling or "high."

The third major issue is the nonobjective, irrational mind-set that results from being in an emotionally charged positive state of mind. At this extreme, the effect and consequences of individual behaviors are not clear. As mentioned in chapter 8, unbalanced states of mind limit objectivity and possibility, increasing the potential for behavior that has a damaging result.

With addictions all the focus is on the new state of mind. So the drug addict keeps on using to stay high regardless of how much they are out of control; the gambler keeps on gambling no matter how much they are losing; and the shopper keeps shopping regardless of their poor financial condition. Thoughts of consequences produce a "buzz kill," so they are not entertained. This denial has meticulously been constructed by the ego, which is trying to avoid the feared state of suffering that will replace the euphoria once it wears off.

The path to a sound "cure" or "healing" to this repetitive cycle is in understanding the true underlying cause of the constant shift to a negative state of mind. This requires the path of self-inquiry. Individuals must be at a significant point on their journey where they are finally ready to ask questions and embrace the answers that will set them free from the counterproductive and damaging personal story and thoughts. A free and clear mind is where new choices can be made from. In this state of being, addictions aren't necessary for there are no misunderstandings and no sense of self-devaluation to result in suffering. This leaves no need for a method of release because there isn't a negative energy imbalance. Let's take a look at some ways that addictions show up.

Addiction to money: Money has been said to be "the root of all evil" because many people will seem to do almost anything for it. The attraction factor to money is that it allows us the means to create new experiences in ways that are unregulated and at times out of control. A misinterpretation that many have, and a reason why they can fall into the act of worshipping or being addicted to money, is the illusion that having a lot of it buys happiness. However, money can actually do the opposite. By providing its possessors with the distraction of a constant stream of new activities, money makes it easier for them to believe they are happy because of what they have or what they are doing. It allows them to avoid the true root cause of mental unease and suffering.

When you are feeling unfulfilled, money can temporarily buy you a boost with flashy clothes, a big house, or an expensive car. What happens eventually, through the principle of diminishing returns, is that the thrill fades and cravings for more money and bigger experiences assert themselves. When you believe it takes more material things to be happy, constantly achieving "happiness" in this way becomes increasingly harder and more taxing to maintain.

Ours is a culture in which many look at success in terms of net worth. Many idolize and are captivated by those who have achieved financial levels far beyond the norm of the rest of society. Extravagance and luxury seem like the answer to the problems many are going through. "If I only had x amount of money, all my problems would be gone." This is a lie the ego tells the self to avoid the real true core of the problems and undesired state of mind.

A lot of experiences and self-delusions can be bought temporarily with money, including power, sex, material objects, prestige, and cosmetic changes. Of course anyone can choose how he or she experiences the use of money. There is no "right" or "wrong" in how much they have, in how much they spend, or in what they spend it on. It is their life and these are their decisions.

Almost everybody in the world has a certain need for money. It is only when money becomes an obsession beyond the basic necessities that a problem can surface. This is when we may find ourselves in a situation where we can't find balance unless we have a certain amount of it to spend. Rather than realize that we have the power to create our own peace of mind, we often give that power away to money and how it creates us.

As many people chase the positive acceptance, respect, love, and approval of others, money tends to be the appealing way to achieve it. A decade or so ago the goal of having money was to "keep up with the Joneses." Recently, however, many people have found themselves in an all-out sprint. Ultimately this has the effect of wearing a person down. They adopt tireless work habits and take on increased financial risk and debt to compensate for their addiction to spending. Due to the recent global

economic slowdown, many have been forced to face the consequences of this manic behavior.

Using money to manage constant comparisons to others is a
draining and never-ending task. It leads many to ask, "Where
does it all end?" To begin to find the answer that would end
this obsession, reflect upon what you are trying to "get" from
the outside world with money. The feeling of being loved, respected, and powerful may be achieved for a moment through
the use of money, but the idea that respect is real when cultivated this way or that you will experience this feeling continually is a mirage that will not last.

It is interesting how many people are trapped in an addictive
cycle with money, craving it to such a degree that they cannot
experience peace, no matter how much money they make.
There are endless stories of extremely wealthy people who live
lives of complete misery. This is clear evidence that peace and
serenity come not from money and what it brings on the outside, but from a sense of inner self-acceptance and self-love.
Money is a useless currency for the achievement of a loving state
of being. What cannot be bought, no matter how much money
a person attains, are true love, true peace, wisdom, and eternal
happiness. These intangibles are priceless, leaving money pow-
erless as a means to create them.

The true path to a lasting experience of a peaceful and fulfilled
state of mind is the path of self-awareness that empowers you to
re-create yourself (I AM) in a way that emanates a self-love and
self-respect from within. To embody this self-love means you are
constantly in a state of acting out of it to everyone and everything
in your reality. **What really impacts the people in your world
most is not what you have or what you do, but rather who
you are.** Offer kindness and love to others, if for no reason other

than the relativity and reflection they offer you in your world, and you will be loved for it. Respect others by seeking to understand who they truly are and the feeling of true respect will be yours. When you can demonstrate this you will never again need to use money as a means to "get" these things because you will already have them through who you have created yourself to "be."

Addiction to codependence: Codependence is defined as being psychologically dependent on a relationship with another person for your balance, happiness, and sense of peace. Codependence can occur in romantic relationships, parent-child relationships, and friendships. In many cases those who are emotionally codependent connect themselves to individuals who have issues related to control and manipulation. In the universe's continual display of perfection, each individual in such a codependent relationship gets exactly what he or she needs from it. One gets to control and the other gets to be controlled. Both fulfill their I AMs through the other. One says, "I AM fearful of not being loved, or not being able to survive," and not coincidently the other one says, "I AM fearful of not being loved or not being able to survive."

Since severely codependent people are in fear of not being able to survive without the other, either they make no effort to take more control of their lives, fearing this would cause them to lose the connection with the person or people controlling them, or they try to take complete control of somebody else's life. The fear of loneliness and isolation is so pervasive that many codependent people easily submit to the demands of the other and allow themselves to be constantly manipulated. Manipulation occurs in every way imaginable, and in many cases it includes physical abuse.

Codependent individuals who subject themselves to this type of abuse do so because they see limited opportunities for themselves outside of the current relationship and would rather not face the alternative fear of being alone.

Manipulators use "love" as the hook. "I'm sorry, you know I love you," is often heard when someone who has been controlled shows signs that they are tiring of the experience. Addicted codependents may also have learned the notion of love to be only conditional, which can make the manipulation seem normal. Being controlled and manipulated is often rationalized as a trade-off for experiencing their idea of what love is. They simply do not know love to be any different, or may be too afraid to consider that a higher form of love exists because it would be evidence that they are in a relationship that might need to be changed or even ended.

The manipulator in a codependent relationship feels as though the only thing keeping the other person involved with them is their control over them. They fear that by letting up on manipulation and control, the other individual will find their sense of strength and identity, and then muster the power to leave them. Pressure is constantly applied through the use of negative personal attacks, physical domination, and the fear of retribution. Verbal abuse often tends to be used to keep oppressed partners in a low state of self-esteem. This helps quell their continual fears and elevate the sense of control that a manipulator feels they must have.

The addiction to codependence originates from a negative sense of self-worth. Due to a deep negative sense of self that most likely developed in childhood, many of these individuals often feel as if they are unlovable or incapable of surviving on their own. When someone comes along who offers them the experience of being loved, they are instantly sent into an incredibly unbalanced positive state of mind. They often feel a sense of bliss and personal validation that they never felt before. The thought of losing this person and the new love the person brings can become terrifying. Rather than connect the experience to the new understanding that being loved by another human being to this degree is possible, they believe this particular person is the only one on the planet who can offer them this feeling. Now they are "under the spell" of another and will do anything to keep this individual in their life out of the fear of going back to being unloved and living in a negative state of mind.

From an onlooker's perspective of the codependent relationship, we often hear comments such as: "What in the world is he doing with her?" or "Why would such a nice girl be with someone who treats her so poorly?" It can oftentimes seem hard to fathom why people do what they do unless we have walked through every experience of their lives with them.

From the perspective of the person creating it, every act is perceived as an act of survival.

Depending on how much fear there is in not being loved and in being alone, codependent relationships can go on for months, decades, years, and even for the remainder of the participant's lifetime. A change can happen only when one or both individuals are ready to change. This happens in two ways, which are demonstrated in the following Desired Experience Comparison Chart.

In the chart, two possible experiences that an individual can have are compared to illustrate why the individual chooses one experience over the other. At time interval A, the individual is starting a relationship because the desire to be in one is greater

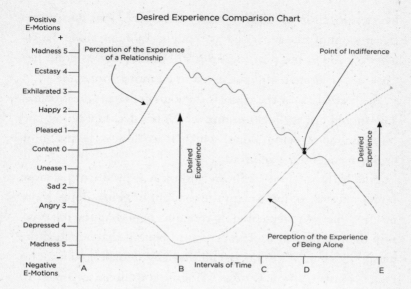

Desired Experience Comparison Chart

than the desire to be alone. The top line shows how the person thinks and feels about the idea of being in a relationship. The bottom shows how the individual thinks and feels about being alone. At point A, being alone causes a certain degree of sadness, whereas the idea of being in a relationship brings a sense of contentment.

The relationship builds into full-blown love, and at interval B the individual is in a state of ecstasy that borders on madness ("He is madly in love"). At the same time, the thought of being alone has now dropped to a new, feared low of hysteria and depression ("I can't live without him").

As time goes on, the relationship starts to lose its luster. At interval C, as the feeling that occurred from that initial experience of love from the relationship slowly erodes, conforming to being controlled and manipulated is less appealing to the individual. Here the individual is also growing and maturing, and has developed more self-love and self-respect. This diminishes the amount of fear generated by thoughts of being alone. However, staying in the relationship is still desired at this point because being alone is still perceived to be more intolerable.

At interval D on the chart is the experience of indifference. The thought of the relationship, which has declined in joy, and the thought of being alone, which is no longer feared, now produce equal states of mind.

Finally, at interval E, the relationship is producing a more undesired state of mind than the thought of being alone. More positive energy is generated by thoughts of ending the relationship than staying in it. The perceived benefit that attached the person to the relationship and all they endured along with it no longer exists. Action is now seriously considered or taken to create a new reality of freedom from the relationship in order to alleviate the negative imbalance and its resulting negative state of mind.

When well-meaning and concerned friends and family members express anger, resistance, and disapproval to someone in a codependent relationship, it can have the opposite effect of causing those addicted in this manner to feel like they need the relationship even more. What the codependent individual really needs in the way of support is more evidence of others' understanding, compassion, and unconditional love. Understanding and love demonstrate to the individual that they are accepted just as they are, which helps to add to their own acceptance. By loving themselves more, they honor themselves more and begin to realize that they do not need to put themselves into these types of self-destructive relationships to fulfill the experience of being loved.

. . .

Addiction to gambling: Compulsive gambling can be defined as the addiction to random reward. What people seek from the act of gambling is the positively generated state of mind that occurs simply from the possibility that they might be rewarded. In this case "rewarded" means the experience of being "right," which is validated through the experience of winning money on a particular bet. The feeling of being "right" that comes from a win results in a positive imbalance of energy and its accompanying sense of well-being. The self-identity is lifted and aggrandized in that brief moment of "win" to the feeling of a new I AM. This could be one of hundreds of I AMs, including "I AM a winner," "I AM smart," "I AM worthy," and "I AM rich." Whichever I AM is being sought after is one that was not previously included in the gambler's identity.

The catalyst for an addiction to gambling is the negative state of mind brought on by a potential self-image of being "less than" that creates suffering, such as "I AM not a winner," "I AM not smart," "I AM not worthy," and "I AM poor." For addicts, gambling is perceived as the avenue that can alleviate these undesired identities and negative states of mind. They crave the feeling of the opposite, which they believe will result from winning a bet and being "rewarded."

What actually happens is that the ego ends up ultimately fulfilling the true thoughts of "less than" by creating the experience of manic gambling and losing money. When instances or periods of winning prevail, addicts are lifted into emotional states of everything from joy on up to euphoria. People who have linked their good feelings to winning at gambling perceive this as the preferred path out of any negative state of mind they may have. They seek self-validation and love through their attempts at being randomly rewarded.

The reason consistent profit is so elusive for addicted gamblers is that the intent of these individuals is not for *consistent* profitability. The ego may use the idea of consistent profit as one of its rationalizing tricks to keep them engaged in the act of gambling, but this is not their true motivation. The intent of gambling addicts is elevation in their state of mind through the *anticipation* of winning, which expands who they believe themselves to be. The key word here is "anticipation." Who they briefly might be able to experience themselves being drives them ("I AM a winner"). For this reason, the joy derived from winning is a fleeting feeling.

This is true for every kind of gambling there is, including sports betting, card games, lotteries, horse racing, slot machines, and even the stock market. The type of game a gambler chooses is dependent on which one the person's ego feels will get the job done with the most impact. For some this means keno, the lottery, or roulette; for others it is slot machines. For those who use gambling as a means to experience a positive validation of their analytical intelligence, there is poker, horse racing, and sports betting. The more sophisticated the game, the larger the ego and work needed to be done by it to achieve the shift to a positive state of mind. A win on a slot machine does not generally elevate the state of mind of the hard-core poker player or horseplayer. This type of gambler needs to believe that their intelligence has something to do with winning. Part of what makes them feel so good about winning is the feeling that they have outsmarted everybody else.

As we've seen, the mind is wired to link our experiences for survival. When something specific happens to us we tend to believe—and then we begin to expect—that we will experience the exact same outcome under similar conditions. But since one of the unavoidable truths of the universe is that every moment is distinct and unique, this presents a huge issue for the gambler trying to repeat a past "win." You may know somebody who has hit it big at one time or another while gambling, only later to fall under the false belief that this was the new way he or she was going to make a living. Only after losing many multiples of what was originally won do such people face the truth of the self-deception they used in order to justify going after that feeling again through more gambling.

As an example, let's look at the rationalizations of an addicted slot machine player. Once the individual experiences the shift to euphoria after hitting a jackpot on the slot machine, the individual is now "hooked" on the experience. The word "hooked" is very appropriate because the mind now links pushing a slot machine button to a high degree of probability that they will experience the machine's bells and whistles going off and the immediate pleasure of the big win. As bells and whistles go off, the brain releases pleasure-enhancing chemicals. The ego did its job. The individual's self-image (I AM) is instantly aggrandized by the windfall of money, causing them to momentarily feel distinct and valuable. What happens from this moment on is exactly like what happened in the famous experiment of Pavlov's dog.

In a historical experiment, Ivan Pavlov noticed that every time a dog was about to be fed, it salivated to aid in the digestion of its food. He then decided that immediately before he was to feed the dogs he would ring a bell. What he realized through this process was that the dogs started instantly to salivate upon the ringing of the bell, regardless of whether they were fed or not. The conclusion was that the dogs' brains had linked the previous experience of hearing the bell with being fed and now expected this same outcome of receiving food every time they heard a bell.

Like the brains of Pavlov's dogs, the brain of the slot machine player starts immediately to release pleasure-enhancing chemicals in anticipation of random reward. The belief is attached to that one time, 942 button pushes ago, when the gambler hit the jackpot and won a hundred dollars. Now every button push is believed to be the next jackpot. Just like the dog that drooled in anticipation when the bell sounded, so, too, does the mind of the slot player ooze with anticipation upon the next push of the button and potential jackpot. The addicted slot player temporarily experiences a positive state of mind just by virtue of having projected thoughts of winning.

As the gambler gambles in a more addictive manner, the belief in winning starts getting assaulted with the undeniable truth that more money is being lost gambling than is being won. (You would think the evidence of the continued building of those enormous hotels in Las Vegas would be an indication of this truth.) The ego now has to get very creative to protect the I AMs that allow the underlying addictive behavior to continue. The ego's next step is to fool addicts into believing that the reason they are losing is because they haven't yet learned all the angles of slot play: which are the best times, which machines pay the most, which are the best locations, how hard they should press down on the button, and the correct way to rub a rabbit's foot for good luck. Basically, the ego can use anything to rationalize the false notion that addicts can beat the game. Its goal is to help them keep getting the "fix" of the brain chemical that is released upon the action of playing slots.

As the gambling becomes more sophisticated, so, too, do the rationalizations about what needs to be learned to keep the gambler believing that now they've got the answer to consistent success. This helps them avoid the real reason they are addicted to gambling. There is no "right" or "wrong" with gambling in and of itself as an experience in the world. There are many who use games of chance strictly for the purpose of recreation or entertainment, while a minute percentage of people have made it their intention to play at a professional level. "Right" or "wrong" is relevant only when individuals involved in gambling cannot cope in life when they are prevented from gambling, and would like to be able to find true peace without the addiction. Gambling would be perceived as "wrong" when an individual realizes that the suffering resulting from financial loss, relationship loss, or physical and mental health related to gambling is not worth the temporary elevated state that the act of gambling produces. It is then that the need and desire for the addiction wanes. At this point the addiction can be looked at from its deeper level of origin.

The double-edged sword of addiction to gambling, as with all addictions, is that the backside of using it to elevate a state of mind is an even lower negative state of mind than the one a person originally was attempting to escape. The irony is an individual who gambles to try to feel better only makes matters worse by losing. Not only do they fail to attain a positive validation, but they also further validate an already low sense of self-worth. This drives them even deeper into the addictive cycle because the addictive action is the only perceived path out of the suffering! Many gamblers keep gambling and "pressing" when they have already lost a significant amount of money. "Just one more roll, one more hand, one more stock trade, one more spin, one more game, or one more race" is what they convince themselves is all they need.

What may be even more interesting to realize is that this inability to stop gambling happens on the upside, as well. When an addicted gambler has a big winning streak, if the self-identity and corresponding I AMs are not changed to believe themselves worthy of the possibility they are now experiencing, the ego, as the loyal protector and servant of the self-definition, will see to it that the money is lost back. Rather than quitting and changing the view of the self to "I AM a winner," the money will be gambled again and lost in order to put their true identity back in sync with reality. There is nothing but perfection in the universe. We are all a perfect representation of who we believe ourselves to be in every moment of our existence.

Addiction to sex: Since the way in which a shift to an abundance of positively charged energy occurs is through the experience of creating yourself anew, it is no surprise that one of the biggest and most powerful shifts to positive energy occurs through the natural ecstasy of orgasm. The universe's intent is obvious here in making this one of the most powerful feeling experiences known to human beings. Without the desire to reproduce there would be no human experience. This desire has been biologically wired into our brain and body. As this is understood, it should also be of no surprise that this particular path to the temporary feeling of an increased state of mind is one of the most addictive on the planet.

Addiction to sex stems from the same desire of experience as any other addiction: an elevated state of mind. Sex simply has become the chosen path to achieve it. If we look a little deeper into this, we see that it is not "sex" that drives the addiction, but what the sex represents. For many, sex has become the only idea or way of experiencing love. For the person with a limited understanding or experience thus far in life of what true love is, sex is often substituted for a higher understanding. For some, it is the direct means to achieve the euphoria of orgasm.

Of course, sexual release is not limited to intercourse, but can also be achieved through masturbation, which is the reason that the pornography industry is a multibillion-dollar-a-year business. A multitude of avenues have been created to get "turned on" on the way to the ultimate experience of sexual pleasure, including everything from magazines, videos, and strip bars, to prostitution. In today's world, the evolution of the Internet has made it easier than ever to view material designed for the purpose of sexual pleasure. Many people have since become addicted to this form of getting a quick fix of positive energy.

When an individual is addicted to sex in a relationship with another who is not addicted, this can present all sorts of challenges. If the other individual is not as in "need" or as eager as the addicted person, the couple will not be in harmony and conflict will occur. Addicts may try to manipulate their partners into the act. This will cause resistance from the one being manipulated, mainly due to the resentment of being used by the addicted individual. The fact that the one addicted to sex is using their partner as an object to make them feel better, regardless of their partner's feelings or concerns, will cause karmic consequences that will surface at some point later in the relationship.

For those addicted to other avenues of sexual release, such as pornography, strip bars, or prostitution, the "problem" occurs when the resulting time, money, or relationship damage has reached a point where more negative energy is generated as a result of the addiction than the positive energy gained from the experience.

In any case, the intent on the part of the afflicted individual is to have an experience that lifts the state of mind to believe that either "I matter" or "I AM loved." "I matter" is achieved through the act of procreation or the experience of orgasm. This is why addicts continually repeat this experience. They have a strong need to feel as though they exist, and the euphoria associated with orgasm momentarily accomplishes this intention. The "afterglow" of orgasm is a state of serenity. This peaceful, balanced state is a result of the harmony that is felt by experiencing who you believe yourself to be. In this case, the experience of being procreative puts you perfectly in tune with the universe, which collectively always is the exact same thing.

For those looking for the feeling of being loved to achieve balance, another person is needed. This could include the person they are in a relationship with, a person they just met, or even a prostitute. Many people who have one-night stands do so to attain the fleeting feeling of being loved. Women predominantly fall into this category to the degree that they are looking to feel love. Out of their need, they will use sex as a means to achieve an experience of love. Many men are just the opposite. They offer love as a means to achieve the experience of sex.

As a result, neither person will have a high probability of experiencing lasting peace. For this addiction, the sex will never be enough for the man, and for the woman the love is just an illusion that will ultimately be unveiled. The consequence of this type of sexual union is a feeling of emptiness and a negative state of mind that are experienced until one or both of the participants realize they are in the repetitive cycle of need.

The recent notoriety and certain acceptability of strip bars in

pop culture make for an interesting case study on human motivation. The curious thing to look at here is the fact that at a strip
bar there is no orgasm or sex. It is simply a woman or man danc-
ing provocatively on the lap of an individual who pays for it. For
the duration of that three- or four-minute dance, as far as the
recipient is concerned, he or she matters to someone. The fact
that the dancer is staring at the addict and for that few minutes
"loving them" through the erotic nature of the act is all they
need in order to enjoy the illusion. This mental stimulation along
with the physical is what instigates a surge in positive energy and
release of good-feeling brain chemicals that provides the "in-
toxication" that lifts the addict to an elevated state of mind.

People addicted to sexual acts are using the medium of expression to fulfill who they believe themselves to be. People who use
one-night stands to find love, and inevitably never find it, are
fulfilling an I AM that says, "I AM not worthy of true love."
Their lack of self-respect becomes evident in their lack of respect
for their body by the use of it. For those who are engaged in a
deeper connection or what is called true love, sex cannot merely
be called "sex," but is a higher state of "making love." In this
state, two people are joined not only by body, but by mind and
spirit, as well. This actualized expression of oneness only occurs
between two individuals whose energetic wavelengths, thoughts,
and intents are in perfect harmony. To achieve this experience
with another human being, you must first believe you are worthy
and capable of both giving and receiving the higher experience.

Sex addicts are on their way to understanding and becoming
aware that the feeling of love and mattering in the world cannot
be experienced consistently through acts of addiction. When
this realization is achieved, the true path to the feeling they seek
will be revealed as being an inner one that stems from the truth

that they are their own source of love and mattering. Until they realize this inner love and give it to themselves, they will be unable to receive love consistently from the outside world through the experiences that revolve around the addiction to sexual pleasure.

Addiction to alcohol and drugs: Alcohol and drugs represent the perceived "magic pill" or "serum" to help us escape a negative state of mind. Negative energy imbalances produce negative feelings and emotions that include fear, anxiety, and stress. Mental pain ultimately localizes itself in the body as physical pain. The combination of these "pains" can be temporarily relieved with both prescription and illegal drugs and alcohol. People use these substances to help "take the edge off" or "cope" with their undesired circumstances of life. The feeling of "pressure" is what addicts seek to release or dissolve temporarily with the use of drugs or alcohol. When individuals are said to be "feeling no pain," it is because the suffering generated by their perception of themselves or their circumstances has temporarily ceased to exist—or, at the very least, it has been altered to *matter* less than it did before. The instantaneous shift in reality and temporary freedom from the painful state of mind is the addictive feature of this particular method of relief.

The addiction to alcohol not only is an avenue for the release of pressure, it also has an important social element. There are a multitude of bars and taverns in the world that serve the needs of those looking for relief while also adding the human connection factor. People want to know that they are not alone in the troubles of their lives. They gravitate to others with similar issues to make themselves feel better, not only about their issues, but also about the fact that they drink to feel better about them as well. There is an undisclosed bond that forms with other drinkers and it is why they are happy to see friends and acquaintances when they enter the bar.

As a person becomes addicted to alcohol and the relief that it provides, many of the dangerous consequences become secondary. These consequences include personal safety, health, the safety of others, damage to relationships, and poor job performance. The deep cause of the individuals' suffering is consistently avoided through the use of alcohol and its pain-numbing effects. The feeling of mattering to other drinkers as a "drinking buddy" becomes an important self-identity, especially to those who have been led to their drinking by the feeling of not being loved or mattering in the world. Drinking relationships become coveted and help to counter the previous painful reality of the lack of social interactions and the desolate feeling of being an island unto themselves with their perceived problems.

There are also many who drink alone. For them, drinking is used purely for its numbing effects on the pain they feel, and the social element is not an issue. Individuals who drink alone reveal that they are avoiding many more aspects of reality.

What alcoholics are faced with when they attempt to break free from the addiction has four major elements. One is the fear of having no perceived way of mitigating the mental and physical pain they feel by their sober self-image. This negative emotional state and intolerable reality is avoided at all costs.

A second major issue is breaking loose from an entire social scene composed of people who have helped to validate and define who they believed themselves to be. When they are down at the bar drinking, they matter to those people. Everybody knows them and accepts them, as is. Bar friends are like a beloved family from which you have to divorce yourself. Alcohol also has an accepted social club built around it. You rarely see public establishments where heroin is used, or a bar and grill where all Prozac users go to commiserate while popping anti-depressants.

A third issue is the issue of constant temptation. Drugstores, grocery stores, nightclubs, restaurants and bars, inviting commercials, and almost every social scene make for an endless stream of opportunity to continue the addictive behavior.

A fourth issue is the pain of the withdrawal process. When a drinker initially starts drinking, the drinker's body automatically adjusts and compensates. Since the brain is designed always to strive for a state of balance, the body reacts to the consistent influx of alcohol by making all sorts of chemical adjustments over the time frame of consistent drinking. A biological tolerance is built up, as much as the body can build it, to adjust and survive. Many marvel at the amount of alcohol an alcoholic can consume and wonder how the drinker remains alive. This is the magnificence of the body and it illustrates how it will do just about anything to adapt and evolve to continue to exist. When the individual can't get alcohol or attempts to go "cold turkey," the body is thrown completely off balance. This is the withdrawal process, and it is usually marked by a violent balance adjustment in the form of shakes, sweating, vomiting, convulsions, and hallucinations. Combined, these issues are what make the battle with alcoholism such a major issue.

The addiction to illegal drugs is similar to addiction to alcohol in many ways and different in others. However, the core reason for the need is the same: escape from the current perceived reality that produces an experience of suffering. The desperation level that a drug addict reaches at times often moves them to extreme behavior to get drugs or to achieve the means to accumulate them. It is said that there is nothing a drug addict won't do for a "fix," including theft, prostitution, and even murder. The mind-set of how needed the drug is for survival leads to a breeding ground of crime, sickness, and economic despair. This is common in many poorer segments of the population that are known for having a low sense of self-worth and heavy drug addiction. The cycle becomes a constant one in these areas, because children are often neglected and subjugated to the effects of the environment that create a bleak outlook on life and low self-esteem. This causes them to seek the same methods of release. Threat of incarceration is useless to those in this state of existence for nothing could be worse to a person in this state than the inability to be in a drug-induced state of mind. This truth is demonstrated by the rap sheets of users who have been in and out of prison numerous times. If the time in prison is not combined with education about a new way to look at who they are, they will see no new choices for themselves when they get out but rather only the same ones that put them in there.

Society keeps assuming that drug users *should* know "better," but the truth of continued addictions and addicts' corresponding levels of desperation show that they do *not* know any better than their actions currently exhibit. A society that continues to live under the illusion that "they should know better" is avoiding or is in denial of the real truth of the issue and will be destined to continue to experience the same undesired reality.

For people addicted to illegal drugs who live in middle-class and affluent neighborhoods, the core negative sense of self-worth is the same but the catalyst may be different. Rather than being brought on mainly by economic disparity, addictions in many wealthier neighborhoods can also come from the pressure of "measuring up" and the parental use of conditional love. These addicts are children of parents who are driven and have been successful in their business and financial lives. The success in large part for these Type A parents is due to their ability to control and manipulate a great deal of their environment to meet their goals and expectations. Their expectations can extend to their children, causing a heavy amount of pressure to be put on them to conform.

As the children in these situations grow up, they become fearful of not measuring up and of losing their parents' acceptance and love. This feared disappointment and lack of acceptance and love transform inside them into self-disappointment, loathing, and lack of self-love. Their unbalanced, unsettled state opens them up to the lure of drugs and other addictions through which they seek to find balance and compensate for their constant negative state of mind. The access to money for many in this economic status is not an issue. Drug addiction tends to be a lifelong battle if the core root of the suffering is not uncovered for its false nature.

Prescription drug addiction has taken on a whole new look in recent years. A steady increase in the general anxiety level of the overall population, combined with a change in the marketing strategy of drug companies, has created a boom in legal drug addictions. In the last ten years, there has been a major increase in the amount of prescription drugs available for people with varying degrees of anxiety and depression. Drug companies have come out with an endless array of medications and advertising offering people help from negative states of mind. So-called "antidepressants" and "anti-anxiety" drugs have surfaced, such as Prozac, Valium, Paxil, Xanax, and Zoloft, to name a few. Millions of people have become dependent on these prescriptions just to get through the day.

The reasons for the rise in prescription drug abuse include both the number of new prescription drugs being produced and advertised by drug companies and the number of doctors in the medical community who are very quick to prescribe them. For the individuals using these drugs, their desire for a new state of mind also puts tremendous pressure on the medical community to solve their problems.

The feeling of "pressure" in everyday life seems to have been on a significant rise in the Western world over the last decade. One cause of this "pressure" is when an individual's view of himself or herself is not being realized in reality. Many are looking for relief from the feeling that life is not going the way they want. This could translate into feelings of being stuck financially, emotionally, creatively, or physically.

Another reason for the increasing anxiety in today's society is that many people are finding out that the contentment and state of peace they thought they would achieve from attaining certain material possessions hasn't happened. This realization can be very destabilizing in a society that promotes financial success as the secret to being happy.

And then there is the prevalent, excessive, fear-based media programming, which many inundate themselves with on a nightly basis through television. Our culture has become accustomed to having the television on at all times while we are at home, during which time ratings-driven news programs constantly report and sensationalize the worst of humanity's acts. It is no wonder so many look for something quick and easy to combat the resulting anxiety.

The number of prescriptions filled today supports the idea that drugs are used as a "quick fix" to solve negative mental imbalances that cause anxiety and depression. As with every other addiction, taking drugs has the effect of diverting attention and prolonging the time it takes for people to get to the real issues that need to be addressed if they are looking to be free of the need for an addictive substance. The constant use of an artificial mechanism to find balance produces temporary relief, causing patients to "need" the drug every single day. This is like treating skin cancer with a Band-Aid. Every day a new Band-Aid needs to be applied, as the sores it covers never go away. Eventually it will take more "Band-Aids" to keep patients feeling like they are treating the issue. Until the core issue of the suffering is addressed, prescriptions will be a lifetime affair.

For each different manifestation of the addiction to drugs, whether it is to alcohol, illegal drugs, or prescription drugs, the intent is the same. All are perceived methods of survival for individuals who know of no other way. They have found a path that is available to them and works to ease their suffering. While they may achieve relief for the short term, they also have become slaves to the addiction and the karmic repercussions that are instantaneously created by the diversion from the truth of who they are.

You can close the door, but truth will keep knocking.

Running from truth is tiring and energy-draining. The monster people run from in life when they are addicted to drugs is the same self-created monster that they feared lived in the closet or under the bed as a child. In one moment of a faith-filled look the fear is unmasked for the illusion that it is. All that is found to exist is an empty closet. True desire and courage do have their rewards. It may take many unpleasant consequences for the addict to summon the will necessary to search for another answer to the mental pain. But with a strong enough will for change they will find an answer that is more satisfying and eternal than the temporary and damaging nature of relief from drug abuse and alcoholism.

There is no "right" or "wrong" with the use of drugs or alcohol. This is simply another one of an infinite number of choices that exist within the experience of life. "Right" or "wrong" only becomes relevant when the intent of using these means is not being realized. For example, for the person whose intent is to conform to the laws set down by society, using illegal drugs may be "wrong." For the individual who is intent on experiencing the effect of an illegal drug, it may be "right." The same is true of alcohol. Daily use may be "right" for some and "wrong" for others. The use of legal anti-anxiety drugs is helpful to many and hence "right," but unhelpful and worse for others, making it "wrong" if their intent is to find a lasting, peaceful state of mind.

All of us must decide what we are willing to do to seek balance and survive in this world. This is just as true for individuals as it is for cultures, societies, and countries. That is why each country has its own set of laws. In free societies, laws represent collective majority decisions of what codes of conduct are acceptable for people to live in balance. Of course, laws are always susceptible to causing resentment due to the fact that there are millions of angles of perceptions on what is acceptable. Uprisings and revolts that occur around the world illustrate this point. As a culture evolves, the rules of acceptability also change and evolve.

For this moment, "what is" is, and it is up to each individual to make his or her own decisions about the truth and bear the consequences within the culture or society in which he or she has chosen to live.

With drug addiction, as with any addiction, it is vital to understand the essence of its creation and the driver for its continued use. Resentment and contempt directed at an addicted individual are acts of resistance that only affirm their negative personal story and need for drug use. Addicts are desperately running from a constant place of self-rejection. Compassion, understanding, and love from those they are closest to gives them one less thing to run from. Offering love and compassion is not condoning the behavior but is simply offering the understanding that you cannot ever fully know the depth of the pain and the suffering of mind they are experiencing. The reality is that the afflicted is doing his or her best to cope, just like every other human being in every moment of existence.

Addiction to vanity: Receiving the attention of others is one of the strongest ways of confirming we are alive. It starts in infancy, as we cry for our mother's attention. As we grow older we learn new and creative ways to get attention when we need it. In today's world, outer appearance has become a predominant method. People feel highly rewarded by the positive attention they receive for the way they look. Positive attention not only confirms that we exist, it also confirms that our existence has meaning—that we are significant to someone other than ourselves.

Although what's considered attractive varies from culture to culture, our brains are hardwired for mating and procreation by positively responding to certain shapes and looks. When we receive attention for our looks we instantly feel more "loved" by others. Just the anticipation of such attention can produce a rush of positive energy. That is why buying a new piece of clothing or a new pair of shoes is often sufficient to generate a "feel good" state of mind. Those who feel a great degree of personal insecurity often place great importance on outer attention to feel loved, validated, and at peace. Some of the ways to attract favorable attention are through jewelry, clothes, physical conditioning, and plastic surgery.

For an extremely vain person or a person addicted to outward appearances, self-defining statements might include: "I AM unattractive," "I AM unloved," and "I AM unimportant." The ego makes efforts to validate these I AMs by constantly doing things to improve a person's self-image. (If the I AM were, "I AM attractive just as I AM," the ego would have no need to respond in an effort to constantly modify a person's appearance.) Steps to enhance appearance can become addictive, and can include addiction to clothes and shoes, addiction to jewelry, obsession over hairstyles and makeup, addiction to working out and weight loss, and addiction to plastic surgery.

No matter what is done, unless the core defining self-image is changed, the individual who is using these methods to alter his or her looks will maintain a negative frame of mind when it comes to personal appearance. Rather than taking an inward journey to develop the self-acceptance that could change them forever, such individuals develop a constant hunger for more clothing, harder workouts, starvation tactics, or more plastic surgery.

Cultural programming relating to appearance starts at a young age with messages received from parents, friends, and the media.

These messages teach children a mind-set that a certain type of appearance is what is needed to survive and be loved. For girls, programming might begin during playtime, by comparing themselves with the physiologically impossible dimensions of a toy Barbie. For boys, programming might begin by attempting to live up to the image of an anatomically "perfect" and strong superhero. Enormous pressure is placed on children these days to seek acceptance from the outer world. Few are instructed that the way our bodies look is largely due to our genetic heredity, which predisposes us to different bone structures, weights, and features. This makes it nearly impossible to fit into an idealized picture of what is attractive and lovable.

As people get into their teens and early twenties, depending on their childhood ideals, a mind-set that places a high value on appearance can become even more demanding and illusionary. Obsessions with outer appearance and unrealistic physical expectations can lead to preoccupations with bulimia, anorexia, excessive body piercing and tattoos, steroid use, plastic surgery, and unchecked spending on clothes and accessories. There are also many other noncosmetic ways people compensate for the pain of not feeling noticed, including sexual promiscuity and drug and alcohol abuse. Financial problems soon arise as a secondary issue.

In the early teen years, a stage of life when physical changes are rapidly occurring and the mind is trying to keep up, there is a hypersensitivity to the idea of fitting in and gaining social acceptance. The pressure to fit in leads to extremely volatile emotional states that occur as this pressure is released. Parents become prime targets of emotional expression, as their children know the family is a safe place for release. If, as a child grows into adulthood, issues of vanity are not reconciled and balanced by increased self-acceptance, cosmetic addictions will ensue.

True outer beauty emanates from an inner spirit of self-acceptance and self-love.

The need to gain attention to feel loved and accepted, to matter to someone else, is perceived as vital for many people. Making changes in personal appearance is seen as an immediate solution to satisfy the need. If a big part of an individual's self-image is built upon the foundational idea that they are loved due to their looks, an even bigger challenge will lie ahead as they get older. As we age, we have to face the finite nature of the body and the skin covering it. The fear of losing these physical qualities in the eyes of others causes many people to use every possible technique to avoid the aging process. The mirror becomes a despised object.

Ironically, resistance to aging and lack of self-acceptance add to the aging process. The negative energy of worry and the draining effects of self-criticism flowing through people's cells take a physical toll that becomes visible to others. Many people become so worried that others won't accept or love them for what they look like that they actually create it by the negative energy they emit through their outer appearance. The belief produces the reality.

There is nothing "right" or "wrong" with nice clothes, jewelry, makeup, creative hairstyles, working out, losing weight, or any type of plastic surgery. "Right" or "wrong" is only relative to the person inside the experience. If a peaceful, balanced state of mind cannot be reached in life without constant need or obsession for the preceding list of items, the addiction will need further evaluation to get at its true roots.

If you want to free yourself from a compulsion with your appearance, the true result you are trying to "get" from the outside world through the use of cosmetic means needs to be seen and understood for its true intent. You cannot "get" anything from the outside world with any permanence without first believing yourself capable of experiencing it. What you feel you lack on the inside will be sought from the people and things outside your own approval until the day arrives when you realize you no longer need it. All human beings are as beautiful and as loved as they believe themselves to be. When this is realized, your deep need for constant attention through what you do with your appearance will cease to exist and the addiction will vanish with it.

Addiction to food: Food has become a major source of addiction for millions of people on the planet. In this case, the preferred method of feeling better or elevating from a lower to a higher state of mind is eating. Everyone has his or her "vice" of choice. Food provides millions with a path to a more pleasurable state of mind. People become addicted to food due to the pleasure they feel when eating that compensates for other areas of sensation that have not been utilized to allow this feeling to exist.

There are many different benefits to those who find themselves addicted to food. Eating can be a comfort and something to do when sitting still doesn't seem like an option. Eating a bag of chips while watching TV has a meditative property associated with it due to repetitive action. You don't even have to be hungry because the pleasure that results is not about eliminating hunger. Activation of the taste buds can offset personal thoughts that navigate toward suffering and negativity. The repetitive action of chewing can be a way to burn off the nervous (negative) energy coming from these thoughts.

Eating can also be a source of comfort that was learned during stressful times of childhood. Food, preparing and then eating it, may have been a sanctuary of sorts from surrounding circumstances that were unpleasant.

Many people also use food addiction to create and fulfill self-identities that relate to excessive weight. Weight becomes an excuse to rationalize why a particular thing hasn't yet been experienced in life and a means to avoid things that are feared. Examples range from getting the right job to meeting the right person to marry. Weight becomes a perfectly placed element in the story that people can blame for feelings of deprivation rather than take responsibility themselves. Weight can be a form of self-protection.

There is a saying: "Habits are hard to break." In fact, survival instincts that get wired into our brains to seek pleasure do not go away simply by "trying" to do better or trying to change behavior. "Hard" is a relative term and can turn into "easy" based solely on the will of the addict for change. The way this happens is by identifying and then changing the sponsoring thought that keeps them using food to feel better. If the sponsoring false thought about themselves ("I AM . . .") that is the source of the negative state of mind can be identified and its false nature exposed, it can be changed. Once truly changed, the "need" will no longer exist to use food in the same way to reach a higher state of mind.

There is nothing "right" or "wrong" about the nature of how much someone chooses to eat. It is the sole choice of the individual to decide and judge. "Wrong" is only evident if, for the person addicted, due to chronic health issues or weight gain food becomes more of a negative experience for them than a positive one. Beauty is in the eye of the beholder. As long as people who enjoy eating a lot of food are happy with the experience they get from it, and are content with who they are, who is anyone else to judge?

Other addictions: Many other activities and methods are used in addictive ways to raise one's state of mind. It is always worth reflecting on compulsive behavior to better understand how the brain is in the constant search for self-validation and balance. Other prominently felt "needs" and addictions include the addiction to lying and cheating, smoking, tattooing, people pleasing, sleeping, personal drama, meditation, perfectionism, gossiping, surfing the Internet, watching TV, computer games, and any other activity deemed necessary by an individual to feel alive or to find balance.

Regardless, all the experiences we define as needs are related to our personal views about the best way available to survive our reality. Nobody likes to feel negative or depressed or to suffer. Addictions simply are the best ways many can come up with to find a new creative state that is closer to peace and balance.

If you are seeking a permanent end to a "need" or an addiction, your view of the world will need to be examined. Personal inquiry will be your path. Ultimately this process will lead you to the core self-identifying I AMs that are driving the current truth of your life. Answers are always available to those who earnestly ask for them. Your eagerness to open to and accept the answers you receive during your reflections will reveal the true state of your will to experience a new reality.

Many times the level of pain an addict must go through gets excruciating before they are ready to face the real truth about their life. Near-death experiences are common life-changing moments for addicted people, while for others the release of their resistance finally comes down to the simple realization that they've had enough. Hitting "rock bottom" is a term often used to describe the moment when the realization finally occurs that the addiction or behavior is not the answer and is actually destroying their lives. The continuation of the addictive act is then seriously questioned and may finally no longer be desired.

Seek first to understand, then to be understood.

—*Stephen Covey*

From the addicts' perspective, not being understood is the same as if your need for food and water was not understood. You have a need to live, and food and water are what allow you to accomplish this intent. Addicted individuals are exactly the same, as they perceive their only means of survival is by way of the addiction. Force, manipulation, and resistance to what is occurring will mainly solidify the issue rather than dissolve it.

There are certainly many biological and developmental issues with the brain that can play a major role in the nature of behavior as it relates to addiction. All of these issues should be taken into consideration when dealing with anyone who has a serious addiction problem. However, nothing can replace the nature of a loving and accepting mind-set as it relates to healing for all parties involved. This acceptance is not for any of the behavior itself but rather for the individual and the validity of their experience and personal need for survival, however different from yours it may seem. There is a distinct purpose for each person and each situation that gets presented in your life. A true gift from the experience waits to be realized.

The main challenge for loved ones is to release the addicted to their own destinies while unconditionally loving and accepting them regardless of the choices they make and the consequences they face. At the same time it is important to always be ready for the moment they ask for help.

In cases where the addiction has become life-threatening and intervention is felt to be the only route left to take, it is vitally important to do it from the most loving and accepting state of mind possible. The energy of compassion and understanding is an energy that greatly aids in eliminating the reason for the resistance and addiction. At the root, negative energy is a result of self-invalidation. Unconditional love and acceptance offers an addicted individual a completely different way of looking at who they are and helps to move them to a higher state of mind where they learn to become more accepting and loving of themselves.

Raise yourself to a higher level of thought and you will raise others with you.

There is a reason for everything that happens in your life and resisting "what is" brings you no closer to understanding that purpose. Your life and your experience of it are in your hands. If you are intent upon understanding how to be an active and conscious creator of your life rather than an unconscious reactor and resistor to your life's events, you must uncover the reasons that lie behind your resistance to change. You will need to realize how and why "what is" in your life continues to "be" in your life and how, in an instant, it can all change.

Chapter 10

Why You Have Yet to Experience the Reality You Desire

It is the limits of your beliefs (I AMs)
that set the limits on your experience.

Each of us has certain desires and ideas of what we want to experience in our lives. We each also have different views of the world and what is possible to achieve within it. Because of this, every human being has different results when moving toward a specific goal or dream. Some people achieve feats that can only be described as amazing, while others have trouble merely surviving. Some people get the results they imagine for themselves, while others never achieve their goals or even give them a chance to materialize. Ultimately, the major driving factors of these results are one's true belief in personal possibility and one's will to see these possibilities become real.

What separates those who experience the fulfillment of their desires from those who stay in "want" are their beliefs about who they are.

Luck is a concept that the mind uses to help compensate for the discrepancies in human experience. We sometimes use the word "luck" to rationalize what we experience or fail to experience and to alleviate or avoid having a certain feeling of insignificance in comparison to others. Such feelings arise when we perceive others as having better fortune or success than we do. For example, we may decide it is lucky when a coworker gets a promotion, a best friend finds true love, or an acquaintance wins a lot of money. There is always a specific reason why others are having an experience of good fortune. But if we do not want to see, or cannot perceive, the real reasons, we call it luck. This is an easy way to mitigate feelings of low self-worth we may feel as observers of other people's life circumstances, especially when we wish the same type of experience were ours.

Nothing happens by chance in the universe. No matter what the situation seems to be, calling it pure luck is a misunderstanding. Each of the individuals in the examples above had to create in some way the conditions for those events to occur. The coworker had to show up and do a good job at work; the best friend had to take the opportunity to talk to the individual he or she fell in love with; the acquaintance had to risk some money. Each one of these individuals had to make certain choices when the conditions and the opportune moment arose.

The point is that at any given moment, no matter what the probabilities are, whatever happens to each person is the result of many causes and conditions that developed beforehand. Inherent in this continual process is perfection and purpose for everyone involved in the situation, including you, the observer of the event.

Every choice and resulting action that has been taken prior is why this moment is occurring exactly as it is for you, exactly at

this time, and exactly at this place. If your previous actions had
been different you would be experiencing a different reality
entirely. That is why each and every moment for each person is
completely distinct and unique. To say that luck is involved is
to deny on some level the perfection of each person's path, including your own.

> When you look at your reality and ask, "Why has it yet to
> change?" it is important to realize that all desired changes
> in your outer reality begin with a change in your inner
> reality.

Your inner reality is the sum of your I AM statements. These
are your beliefs in what is possible for you. Each of them works
like a code that sets you on a course to experience them. If you
do not believe it possible, you won't take the necessary action
to create it. You cannot consciously experience what you *do not*
believe is possible. You can only experience what you *do* believe
is possible.

If you have been trying to make a change in life and nothing
in your outer reality has changed yet, it most likely has to do
with your actions or lack of them. The reason that certain elements of your life remain the same over time is that you are
interpreting the situation the same way and essentially making
the same choices over and over. Under these conditions, it will
be nearly impossible to get a different result.

**In order to change your choices, you have to change the
beliefs you hold about who you are.** Your actions are what
express and declare to the universe who you truly believe yourself to be. Your actions and the energy of intention behind them
are the only things that the universe can respond to in your

reality. The power to change your experience of life comes by changing the way you interpret yourself and your relationship to the universe. As this relationship changes, the energy you emit to your universe changes. A change in the polarity of the energy you send out (positive or negative) will alter the way you create the events in your life and hence the energy of the experience you encounter coming in. **The universe is a perfect mirror that works with complete symmetry—thus the true magic and power behind the creative declaration I AM.**

If your actions have changed and you are still not experiencing a desired result, then the self-evident truth of the issue is that those particular actions are not what are keeping your desired reality from you. Rather, you have not yet faced the truth of the real actions and issues that need to be addressed to change your reality. You are distracting yourself with "other" changes in your actions that are not related to experiencing what you truly desire.

The ego is a powerful illusionist. Denial is one of its favorite tools of protection. In an effort to protect your truths, the ego often uses anything that will help to distract you from facing the real issue that would produce a change in your life. Denial can take many forms, such as the *denial of responsibility* for a situation ("It's all his/her fault"), *denial of your true feelings* to yourself and everyone else ("I'm totally fine"), and *denial of the truth of the situation* ("I have it all under control"). This is meticulously done by the ego to prevent you from having to face the roots of your issue and keep you from change.

As a result of denial, changes may be made, yet these changes have nothing to do with the core beliefs preventing you from making a shift. Vital energy is drained during the charade, as the time it takes to experience what you really desire is pushed

further out into the concept of the "future." You are left feeling
frustrated, confused, and angry, especially if you feel you should
already have your desired experience. Thoughts can quickly
turn to rationalizations such as "The world is out to get me" or
"I'm just unlucky" or "Life isn't fair." These rationalizations are
just another form of denial that stretches time. The frustration
is nothing more than the fear and refusal to accept where you
are in relation to what you desire.

Here's an example. Let's say John is desperately trying to get
a promotion at work but can't seem to make it happen. He starts
working longer hours, believing that this is the key to getting
promoted. After weeks of taking this action, John still does not
get the promotion. In this case the truth is that it is John's negative attitude that is the impediment rather than his work habits.
John's boss may have communicated this reality many times and
in different ways over the course of his employment, only to
have the information ignored. In not wanting to see the truth,
John has distracted himself by deciding that the real thing the
boss wants is for him to work longer hours. The core belief
being challenged is "I AM someone with a good attitude."
John's personal truth is in conflict with the reality of those in
charge, who don't quite see it the same way.

If John really wanted to know why he hasn't been promoted yet, he would ask what is preventing him from getting a
promotion. The truth would then be made clear and John could
begin to take the "right" action. However, rather than face the
truth that his attitude is poor, John's ego, as directed by his I
AMs, deflects the thoughts and feelings that come from having
his belief challenged, so his experience of reality can remain the
same. John is under the illusion that he is someone who he is

not to his boss. Who he is in the eyes of his boss is what has cost him the promotion.

At the very heart of the denial in this case is a core belief that says, "I AM not worthy of getting a new position or promotion." The truth that this self-defining statement exists is John's refusal to acknowledge his poor attitude. If John believed himself to be worthy, he would not have been in fear and denial about his poor attitude. He would be willing to face any feedback about himself in order to achieve the desired experience. If he faced the poor attitude, he would at least be able to make the choice to change it. This would allow John to align with the "right" beliefs and identity necessary to allow the experience of a job promotion to occur. The output of John's fear of finding out who he might actually be by blocking the information is coming back in the input of the experience that was feared.

The preceding example can be used to reveal how every moment and situation in reality has certain purpose and meaning for everyone concerned. John's frustration indicates an energy imbalance that was created by the conflict between thinking himself worthy of a promotion and the reality of not getting one. Truth was trying to get through to John through an emotional experience: a job promotion *not occurring*. It will try again to reveal itself through the frustration he will feel from putting in even more hours and still not advancing in the workplace. Once John has exhausted all other rationalizations for why he may not be getting promoted, he may finally face the truth. In this instance, it is the truth of having a poor attitude in the workplace.

When our inside reality is in harmony with our outside reality, we are aligned with the truth. In this place clear choices of action can be made that lead to real change.

It is always up to you, through the act of free will, to accept or reject the truth that each moment holds for you.

Your work life functions no differently from any other area of your life. Whether you are confronting undesirable realities relating to your children, your marriage and love life, your finances, your health, or your job, your reality won't change until you accept the truth that the experience is offering you. Experience is directly related to your desires, and to the questions you ask about how to create and experience these desires. The answers always exist but only become apparent when you are ready to receive them.

As we contemplate what we desire to experience or change about our lives, we also contemplate and evaluate how painful it might be to face what we need to accept in order to create desired changes. We often avoid acknowledging the "reality" of who we have been in our relationship to the outer world due to the degree of pain in the feelings of guilt, shame, and regret that we have been taught to carry. The more pain we feel as we look at and evaluate ourselves, the more we use rationalizations and denial to buffer ourselves from these painful concepts. A rationalization is any self-satisfying, but incorrect, reason we come up with for our behavior. Of course, avoidance only further delays the achievement of our true desires.

Many of us resist the opportunity to understand and learn more about ourselves when we fear that the truth will unveil that we are not who we thought we were. Ironically, this resistance only makes it worse because it reveals a lack of faith in who we really are. On some level there is a certain amount of guilt, shame, or regret that is being avoided. Avoiding these feelings only serves to perpetuate them, which means they will have to show up again in another experience. Reality will remain the same because the idea of the self remains the same due to the inability to let new life-changing information into our consciousness.

When a core self-defining belief is "I AM unworthy," the thought process is as follows. First, the ego seeks to confirm this self-concept through an experience of it. This happens by a person making the exact choices that produce actions that are looked upon with guilt, shame, and regret. Thus the feeling of being unworthy arises and is confirmed. The ego's mission is accomplished. This creative behavior will occur repeatedly until the I AM statement is changed. Reality is always a mirror of the self-image. This leads to another undeniable truth:

All human beings are perfect representations of who they truly believe themselves to be.

The truth is always the reality being experienced by you at any moment. Although truth is self-evident and undeniable, many people are reluctant to embrace it. Your reality cannot change until you accept what the moment has to offer you about your personal beliefs and how they may or may not be in harmony with your current reality. An example would be trying to get to Los Angeles, and believing you are in Chicago, when in fact you are really farther away in New York. Because you have refused the truth of where you are, you read the map and make choices as if you started from Chicago. These choices bring you no closer to an intended destination or experience and can ultimately lead you further away. When you finally acknowledge and get in harmony with the truth that you are in New York, you will be able to make the correct choices to get you to your ultimate destination: Los Angeles.

By refusing to look at what reality offers you, you destine yourself to repeat the same experiences. "Reality loops" are designed to wear you down to a level deemed intolerable, which is when new actions will be taken to change it. "Why does this keep happening to me?" or "Is my life ever going to change?" are common questions that will find answers only in the current self-definition of the afflicted. It is your current view of yourself that is not allowing change to take place.

Many who pursue this line of questioning are filled with a sense of fear-induced stubbornness that ultimately leads them to go through many years of pain. Human beings often define themselves by the "dramas" going on in their lives. This is all a perfectly choreographed piece of the story of their life. When the story no longer is tolerable, they will change it by choosing to experience life differently.

Resistance to the truth and the repercussions from this resistance bring to mind a conversation I had a few years ago on a golf course. On the first tee my friend and I were put together with an individual who was playing alone. Halfway through the round he started talking about his journey through Alcoholics Anonymous. He told me how the program had turned his life around, and he made a comment I'll never forget. Breaking the drama of his tough story with a dose of humor and a great sense of humility, he said, "So here I was, fifty years old, divorced, broke, jobless, and living on my friend's couch, all because I was still trying to do it my way." Revealed in this statement was the profound implication of how the ego, ignorance, and resistance to truth create so much of what we perceive as chaos in our lives. Acceptance that "my way" wasn't working was the turning point in this man's life. His submission to the truth of his life at the time allowed him the clarity to make the correct new choices related to a new, desired way to live life.

Individuals with a high degree of resistance to the truth often suffer greatly for their resistance. Protecting I AMs and personal truths can be very painful to people who are not grounded in the reality of the universe. Many times the limits of their ability to create and achieve desired outcomes are shown to them in an abrupt and unexpected fashion.

Ignorance's destiny is awareness. The ignorance of this truth is what causes it to occur in a painful fashion.

The universe doesn't beat around the bush. If you don't know your limitations or you are under a false notion of your limitations, they most certainly will be shown to you, oftentimes in an experience that includes physical or mental suffering.

Take the example of the skier determined to ski a downhill run designated as difficult and reserved only for the most advanced skiers. Ski runs are designated with colors: green for beginners, blue for intermediates, and black for experts. This particular skier has not had much experience on the slopes, but wants to feel cool at the lodge later when telling his friends that he skied down a black run. The skier starts by going down an easy run. Although it's not a perfectly balanced run, he makes it down without incident. As soon as it is completed, he says he's ready to do an intermediate run, labeled with the color blue.

His next run takes much longer to complete. There are many uncontrollable moments when he nearly finds himself in a severe wipeout and only narrowly avoids injuring other skiers.

This blue downhill run is barely completed when, so strong is his need to feel defined by having skied an expert run, he decides to ignore all of the warning signs that come from his inability to ski a blue run under control. The skier heads down the next steep black run he sees, avoiding the truth of his ability, and disaster occurs. He has a major wipeout and he breaks both of his legs. Ignorance has met awareness as karma, a self-created moment of fate.

> Karma is the experience that arises out of the conditions that have been created from previous self-defining choices and actions.

In this example, a degree of force meets the same degree of counterforce. The skier's ignorance about his limitations meets the experience of broken legs. But while this painful incident offers awareness, it is still up to the skier to accept it. He could deny the awareness by saying, "I had bad luck," or he could acknowledge the truth and say, "Wow, I was really trying to ski beyond my skill level."

The amazing thing about the perfect symmetry of the universe is that it offers the gift of awareness to us through our experiences, and we always have the free will to accept or deny that awareness. If the skier chooses, he could wait until his legs are healed, go back to the mountain, and repeat the same reality loop. Of course it would be complete denial (perhaps close to the definition of insanity) to do so, however, under less dangerous conditions people go through repeating reality loops all the time and continue to ask, "Why is this happening to me?" It may remind you of what many parents say to their kids who repeat the same misunderstood choices: "When are you ever going to learn?"

Overestimation of ability and underestimation of limitations can occur in any situation you find yourself in: driving a car, managing finances, consuming alcohol, using drugs, personal relationships, business, sports, and many other activities. Each of these situations puts you in a high degree of propensity for karmic repercussions to the exact degree of the illusion and denial that you make choices out of. Each of these situations offers you a chance to gain the valuable awareness that comes out of the experience.

> Your reality always offers you the answers. Their value in relation to your intended reality will always be based on your willingness to accept them.

When you ignore or reject the new information and awareness that each of your experiences offers, your beliefs won't change. If your beliefs don't change, your choices won't change. If your choices don't change, the actions you take won't change either. One follows from the other. Each instant of your life offers you the opportunity to recognize and receive the answers you are seeking to every question you have ever asked. Everything you perceive with your five senses is based on what you asked for through your deepest desires, including the current state of your life, your circumstances, your conflicts, your relationships, the movies you watch, the music you listen to, your religion, this moment, and this book right now. All of these avenues provide nothing more than the opportunity to experience, choose, and react. Through your actions and reactions to the circumstances of your life, you get to know more about who you are. More important, you get to experience how much this conflicts or harmonizes with who you intend to be.

Reality is constantly giving you valuable feedback in the form of your mental and emotional responses. Each response serves a great purpose by showing you whether or not you are in tune with the truth of the moment. If you are resisting anything in your life, in essence you are resisting an answer to one of your questions. You are thus preventing your awareness from expanding and your life from changing. You are ensuring for this moment that a lesson is not learned and that a certain reality will remain the same. However, the beauty of the universe is that each and every moment offers you another great opportunity for acceptance and transformation.

The life you know is the result of living and experiencing the sum total of what you have believed. Whether you are Bill Gates or a man or woman on a street corner begging for money, your life is the product of the personal beliefs and truth you have put into action. If you want to begin the process of transforming your life, the key element going forward is how you decide to interpret and react to the stream of experience that shows up every day. What is its purpose for you and your life? Why have you drawn this information into your field of consciousness? How will you respond to it? Will you see it the same way today as you did yesterday? How you react will expose your true identity, which is exactly what you need to see in order to uncover the I AMs that are currently holding your life in place.

Remember, you must change your thoughts in order for your life to change. "Right" or "wrong" is only relative to what you desire to experience. If you have a belief that holds you back from a desired experience, then it is necessary to identify the belief as "false" in relationship to what you want to achieve.

An example of a necessary change would be a woman who believes she isn't "good enough" to attract a certain type of man as her lover or life partner. If she is content without a relationship, then her belief aligns with her life circumstance. However, when she tires of being alone or desires a relationship with this particular type of man, her belief that she is not "good enough" will be counterproductive to the life she desires to make for herself. If she really wants to attract this type of man as her lover or mate, she has to believe herself worthy of it. She must change her self-definition to "I AM worthy of a relationship with the type of man I prefer." As her I AM changes, the ego immediately responds and begins to prepare the conditions necessary to actualize the experience.

Whenever you change an I AM, your energy shifts. Everything from having a higher level of confidence to the actions you take transforms to match and attract what you believe you are worthy and capable of experiencing. When there is sufficient faith in the new belief, it will overcome any fear that was connected to the old belief. The ego will then change its actions to support the newly declared identity. You will finally say "yes" to experiences and actions that you previously said "no" to. You will respond in a different way and "be" a different way and thus your experience will change.

Examples of new actions the aforementioned woman might take after having the thought "yes" would be calling the man who interests her and asking him out, or approaching him at a party, conference, or chance encounter and introducing herself. The new choice of I AM ends up giving rise to the conditions that lead to the reality of I AM. As the idea of the self expands, thoughts change and a new reality is born.

Until we change the intent of what we want to experience or we accept a needed lesson, the conditions of our lives remain the same. No matter how you choose to react to events, know that they are simply opportunities for you to experience and understand who you are. Once you begin to see this, the only thing left for you to decide is whether or not you want to continue to be the person you are currently creating and experiencing.

> Your universe is a mirror of self-reflection whose purpose is to give you the experience not only of who you believe yourself to be, but also ultimately the essence of who and what you truly are.

Even the things you go through that you consider to be the most challenging or unpleasant have immeasurable purpose for your journey. The greater your resistance to understanding the personal significance of an experience, the more time you will destine yourself to live with a painful or confused state of mind. An unwanted situation can eventually have an extremely positive impact on your life if you are willing to embrace the meaning of it in your life. Each challenging event holds a great message for the person going through it. The manner in which you react to these events will determine where you are in relation to the message of it in your life. The degree of your resistance, as evidenced by your mental, physical, and emotional reactions to the circumstance, is indicative of what you have yet to understand and embrace about the current truth of life as it relates to you. A big part of the path to living a more peace-filled life is understanding exactly what is causing you to become unbalanced and why.

If you are protecting yourself from the truth on any issue in your life, in essence you are choosing to stay in disharmony with reality. This is exactly what keeps your desired reality out of the present moment and in the concept of time called "the future." Time becomes a factor in relation to creating your dreams based on how much you deny or stay ignorant of what conditions need to be in place and exactly where you are in relation to the creation of those conditions. Time begins to dissolve the more you ask the right questions, allow the answers in, and then take the action that aligns with the answers. And lastly, this all needs to be done without the expectation of a certain outcome. There is nothing "wrong" with intending an outcome but the most powerful creators know better than to expect certainty in a universe where anything is possible. The rest they leave to the great power of faith.

Resistance and the world of relativity that this force produces give birth to the concept of time. Einstein once described his theory of relativity and time this way: "Put your hand on a burning stove for a minute and it feels like an hour. Sit next to a beautiful girl for an hour and it feels like a minute. That's relativity." In one example there is resistance, in the other there is none.

Each of us has experienced the feeling of time dragging or time flying. Maybe you can relate to the time you were sitting in school on the first warm, sunny day of spring, watching the big clock on the wall as the hands barely moved and the minutes seemed to pass so slowly. In contrast, being at the end of an exciting vacation always brings the proverbial "I can't believe how fast this week went!" Time is only relative to our desire for the experiences we are having and our intent to be in the midst of them.

The memory of falling in love, especially for the first time, has been known to throw off a person's sense of time more than any other experience in life. Being with the one you are falling for generally puts you right into the essence of the moment. Perhaps you can relate to the memory of when you were younger, spending time with your boyfriend or girlfriend talking or being intimate when one or the other looked at the time and said, "Oh no, I can't believe it got this late so fast. My parents are going to be really mad if I don't get home right away!"

Time is relative to the exact degree you lack the realization that you are the creator of the experience of time.

A desired experience always puts us into the present moment, the place where our attention is focused on neither a past memory nor a projected future outcome. In the present moment we are not concerned with how slow or fast time is going because we are simply immersed in reality. "There is no time to think" is a perfect statement. Since time does not exist, we are simply "being," engrossed only in the truth that is the experience.

Some people believe that time is defined by rotations of the earth, or night and day. However, measurement of the earth's movements is only one way to measure time. For each of us, our personal experience is up to us. What can feel like an hour to one person can feel like a minute to another, offering that time is relative to the angle of perception of the observer.

For example, time slows down when you are experiencing something that does not gratify you, such as being at an undesired job, waiting in line, sitting in traffic, or spending an afternoon with someone whose company you don't enjoy. Anytime you're in a situation that you have no interest in being in, there's a feeling of being stuck in eternity.

Conversely, time speeds up when you are experiencing something you like, such as an enjoyable vacation, a good movie or concert, or spending an evening with someone you love. Time seems to "fly" so much in these experiences that you feel as if there is never enough of it. The feeling of time running out is due to the way in which your identity becomes tied to the outer experience. When it is over, you long to relive it. Upon reflection, the amount of time you were in that state of joy seems fleeting.

Beyond desired and undesired events, time has no limits; there is only the never-ending infinity of the present moment. When you see that every moment is perfect and has a specific purpose for you, the past and the future will not be your focus. Rather you will be enjoying and submerging yourself more into the here and now. In this state of awareness and discovery, time completely dissolves, leaving nothing but "what is." It no longer takes any time to experience what you desire because it is always happening NOW.

Resistance to truth creates time, and acceptance of the truth dissolves it.

Your reality is a perfect representation of where you are on your journey to understanding You. It is an exact representation of what you believe about your relationship to the universe. By fearing and resisting this truth and the truth that life offers on a moment-to-moment basis, you are working to keep your reality unchanged. Resistance to your own magnificence and perfection is the force that creates time and holds you back from the full measure of your unlimited ability to create and experience a life of peace. Acceptance is the only path that will lead you to the liberating awareness that there is nothing but the infinity of time and peace.

Chapter 11

Why You Have Resistance
and Fear Change

Resistance is behind the persistence of all existence.

Resistance is the force that is at the heart of all the energy of
the universe. Without it there would be no world of relativity and no universe in which to experience life. In order for
anything to exist as matter, some form of resistance is required.
Whether something is a bug, a tree, a mountain, a planet, a solar
system, or a galaxy, there is a certain amount of it that sustains its
unique expression. The force that is resistance says, "I AM something," and this is the will of life. The counterforce called pressure responds, "You are no-thing." Throughout the course of
your life, as in the life of everything else in matter, this pressure
will ultimately prevail to unveil more of what you truly are.

One of the most prevalent ways the message of your transitory nature is revealed is through the observation of the birth
and death of the things around you. The implication is that your
sense of separateness is an illusion. While temporarily you may
feel distinct through whom you have believed and created yourself to be, counterforce will ultimately show you differently.

The experience of your individuality and the distinction of yourself from everything else will change as the things you use to create this sense of separateness change. **You may think you are just an individual drop of water, yet you are on a journey to the awareness that you are one with the entire ocean as well.**

Everything in existence is resisting what it *is not* in order to attempt to remain exactly what it has declared itself *to be*. Yet even the minerals that form the stars and the planets will eventually submit to the universe's counterforce and become less than dust. The time this transformation takes is irrelevant when compared to how life can be lived when you fully accept that everything is in a continuous state of change. A new appreciation for life emerges as you see that all of life is heading toward a fuller awareness of the infinite essence from which it emanated.

Everything is on its own unique journey to the awareness of oneness.

Reality is infinitely demonstrating that everything is changing in every moment. To resist this constant state of change is to resist being in harmony with the nature of the universe, which is indefinite and fluid. Mental rigidness and inflexibility are in direct opposition to this nature, and when opposition is demonstrated it can be a cause of negative energy and emotion. This is why at the very core of all things the energy of force or resistance is the root source of all human suffering. It runs counter to acceptance or love, which is the essence of the creative, evolving universe.

Each object in matter is under some level of constant pressure from the truth of its ever-changing nature. Your current physical and spiritual makeup is not permanent, but in a process of infinite and limitless change. The events that trigger you to feel a sense of pressure or heaviness represent a certain degree of resistance you have to the truth of continuous change and what this change may represent for your life.

The only lasting path of freedom from the truth is the acceptance of it.

Once you accept the underlying truth that pressure is begging you to see, mental counterforce dissolves, causing the pressure and heaviness to dissolve with it. You release yourself from the pressure of "time" by the faith-filled act of acceptance, as opposed to the fear-based force of resistance. The irony is that by accepting for the moment what reality says that you *are not*, and freeing yourself from the attachment to this notion, you are offered the gift of awareness, revealing that you are more than you ever imagined yourself to be.

While creative resistance allows for you to be and know yourself as the individual and personality that you are, mental suffering is the signal that something is occurring that you are rejecting as a possibility. Friction is created by the refusal of what is happening and how it is defining you in opposition to what you desire. This resistance is mentally and physically draining and is the root of many different negative states of mind.

Here are a few possible ways friction might show up:

- You thought your significant other could not live without you until that person abruptly ended the relationship.
- You thought you were in control of your indulgences until you found yourself unable to function without them.

- You thought you were physically invincible until you got sick or hurt.
- You thought you were right and had it all figured out until you experienced being wrong.

Counterforce or pressure is a culmination of everything you have not yet included in your self-identity, including everything you do not believe it is possible to experience. As you start to see more of your connection to all of existence, clarity arises about the meaning of the events that happen in life. Resistance to many things begins to wane and the pressure that resulted from these things subsides. In general you become more open to possibility and therefore less thrown off balance when one of these possibilities arises.

As you travel down the path of acceptance, the true spirit of who you are is seen to be defined more by your attitude and general state of energy (consciousness) than by your changing physical body and possessions. You become more adaptable and enter more fully into the flow of life.

You cannot ultimately avoid the truth of your essence.

To become free from any resistance and any suffering you feel in your current reality, one of two things has to change. Either your circumstance must change or your beliefs about your circumstance and what it means to you must change. Only one of these ways of change is entirely under your control: your beliefs. By mustering the will to face the worst of your fears and get to the root of what they are trying to protect, you are putting yourself on a transformational path. Your ability to let go of any resistance to "what is" and accept any new possibility before you is a key to your eternal happiness.

The opportunity for understanding and transformation is available to you in every moment. The perfection of the reality before you, which includes the reality of your perfection, can be accepted at will. When you do not see yourself as perfect, it's a clue that you are in a form of resistance. You are denying a truth about who you were or a truth about some component of who you are. This denial arises when you believe this truth to mean personal failure or unworthiness. The full capacity to love yourself and your world is then withheld to some degree because you have yet to believe in your perfection.

Seeing yourself as flawed in any way automatically restricts the amount of love and acceptance you allow yourself to feel on the inside. In turn you become destined to a certain need from the world and in particular from the people around you to compensate for your own condemnation. A good portion of your time in life is then spent trying to attain a feeling of acceptance and love from the outer world to neutralize the lack of love you give to yourself.

A major misconception here is that you think you can get something from the outside world that will make up for what you believe is missing on the inside. In truth, your experience of reality works from the inside out. In order to experience your perfection and love, first you have to believe yourself worthy of it. **You must realize that perfection and love are who and what you already are.**

When you resist a certain situation in your life, you are many times resisting the answers to your questions about life and a great opportunity to evolve. If you have asked to find true love and find yourself in a bad relationship, there is perfection for you in this experience. This is exactly what needed to occur. Either you are learning the steps necessary to improve the current relationship or you are becoming more aware of what to look for before entering into another relationship. How could you know unless you experienced a bad relationship first? You have brought yourself this relationship to help you more clearly define your intended experience of a loving and fulfilling one.

If you resist the truth of an unfulfilling relationship, denial will only draw out your suffering and create anxiety and pressure in you. Reality cannot change in the manner you desire when you are in an illusion about the circumstances; you must work from the truth. When this is finally done there is an immediate lift in pressure that energizes your entire being. Now back in harmony with the perfection of the moment, you can take the proper action that moves you speedily toward your intended reality. An amazing thing happens when you finally embrace what reality has to offer: Reality changes.

Your story will *be* your story until it *was* your story.

The key cause of your resistance to the awareness and answers that have the power to change your reality and end your suffering of mind is *fear*. Fear prevents the acceptance of the truth that could allow for your reality to change. The reason for this fear and resistance can be boiled down to one question:

"Who will I be if I AM not who I AM right now?"

Your I AMs declare the story of who you are, a story that is ferociously protected by your ego. The character or role you take in the story of your life could be the victim, villain, saint, or sinner. It makes no difference. You will play the role and create the experience that you believe validates your existence the most. The story is designed to get you the validation you need to feel alive. Therefore to drop the story means you would have to let go of the attention you perceived you gained from it. The core of fear is not knowing who you will be if you change the story.

- "If I AM not married, how will I survive?"
- "If I AM not making this particular amount of money, who will love me?"
- "If I don't have these physical attributes, who will notice me?"

The question is: What does it cost you in terms of personal suffering to keep your story going? When confronted with the unknown, the ego often uses fear to prevent change. It projects the idea of being "worse off" or "less loved" in the future. This is why a physically abused wife might feel that it is better to stay in her marriage than face the unknown of being alone. This is why a worker who feels he has great talent and can make more money working for a different employer stays in an unsatisfactory job. This is why a guy who meets a girl he is really attracted to never asks her out. He is eliminating an entirely new reality full of possibilities all to avoid the feeling of rejection if she says no. Fear and resistance thwart the new action that could create a new reality. Each outcome is looked at from the perspective of the worst outcome, and then no action is taken—thus destining reality to stay the same. Shut off by experiencing the false, learned concepts of guilt, regret, shame, and failure, these negative concepts stymie the creative power of life, draining energy and producing a frustrated mind-set.

The origin of all fear is the idea of not being able to exist. Therefore, fear will arise anytime there is a threat of losing a significant piece of what gives one a sense of being alive.

For example, if you feel validated by the car you drive, but because of a financial change you can no longer drive it, you will feel fear and pain to the degree that the car defined you. The same is true of a breakup with a significant other, the loss of a job, a change in looks due to age, the death of a loved one, or any other change in something that is a big part of who you have defined yourself to be.

Many people suffer because the memory of suffering in the past and the fear of suffering more in the future prevent the faithful action that would bring love, acceptance, and healing to them now.

Fear prevents millions of people from taking conscious control of the creation of their lives. It prevents them from the acceptance, love, and faith needed to experience the fully creative beings that they are. This is what leads to an unchanged reality and a life of quiet desperation. *But at any moment this can all change.*

Fear not only prevents you from having new experiences, it also increases the potential to experience the exact reality that you fear. When you focus your thoughts on what you don't want to happen, your attention and energy is not focused on what you want to happen, which means that you are not present in the moment to act toward its creation. Rather you are stuck in the experience of time, reliving a painful past or projecting an unpleasant future.

Because your focus of thought is not on the desired result, you have no chance to creatively manifest it.

The great irony of fear is that it contributes to the conditions necessary to experience what is feared.

When you were a child, at one time or another you may have had a fear of monsters. You imagined they were under your bed, in your closet, or outside the bedroom window. As you matured, you realized the false nature of this fear. However, as a child you believed it to be real. Because you believed it to be real, you *experienced* it as real. Waking up from a bad dream or a loud noise in the middle of the night may have left you wide-eyed and paralyzed. Frozen and afraid to move even the tiniest muscle, you lay there barely able to breathe. Your heart pounded in your chest, as fear held you captive. All you wished in that moment was for your mom or dad to turn the light on, for it to be morning, or for the courage to run into your parents' bed.

Looking back on it now, you can easily see how the belief in monsters gave you what seemed like a real experience of it. Your physiology and emotions changed during that deep moment of fear. Today if you woke up in the middle of the night, you most likely would have a much different experience. Being woken by a loud noise in your home today might direct your thoughts to more of an adult fear, such as an intruder.

When you heard noise as a child, your mind confirmed it as your worst fear. When you hear a noise as an adult, your mind may also connect it to your worst fear. To the degree that you define yourself with fear, you will use your experience to confirm the necessity of fear, and keep it alive and real. Your experience is just as dependent upon your beliefs today as when you were a child.

Like all beliefs you seek to experience, when you focus on your fears as a real possibility you will seek to know it by selectively using the sensory information around you to confirm it. Consider the following examples.

You have a fear of flying. In the middle of a flight, you encounter turbulence. Immediately you connect the turbulence, which is perfectly normal, to the idea of the plane crashing. Your heart beats faster, your palms sweat, and your breathing gets shallow and quickens. As luggage shifts in the overhead compartments, your perception again shapes this into the sound of the plane cracking or breaking. You look at the flight attendants and imagine you see panic in their faces where none exists. You are looking for information to support your fear and using every second of your experience to do so. Therefore, until you are safely on the ground, you will not relax.

You have a fear that you will not be truly loved. Because of this fear you are overcompensating to the point of smothering your partner in your current relationship. You call him or her several times a day to check in and you are all over your partner when you're together. You get emotional and volatile when you don't get the attention you need that would keep your fear suppressed, all in the effort to manipulate your partner to give you the constant validation and love that you need. The paradox is that this behavior actually works against you as it causes your partner to withdraw from the relationship. Your fear single-handedly creates the exact outcome you fear.

The ego is not selective. It uses anything at its disposal to convince you that the fear is real. Whether it is the noise in a plane or the tone of your significant other's voice, all sensory input will be manipulated and used by the ego for the purpose of fulfilling what you believe about yourself to be true ("I AM afraid of flying" or "I AM unlovable").

For example, the fear of being alone and not finding someone to marry creates a situation where you may rush into a marriage with the first person who offers to marry you. Over the years, you may realize that the two of you are completely different people with different interests. This truth always existed but you ignored it because of your fear of being alone. Later on, these differences could cause friction and distance that leads to either a divorce or a soulless marriage. At that moment, the fear is realized.

At the other extreme of this belief is someone who is so scared of divorce or failing at marriage that the person never puts himself or herself in a position for it to happen. The person never marries, hence experiencing the realization of the ultimate fear of being alone and unloved.

Another example is when a parent has a fear that their kids will not be "good" kids (however they define this). This causes them to be overprotective, conservative, unrelenting, and repressive. The potential counterforce from the kids is that they are rebellious, angry, sneaky, and out of control, taking advantage of every opportunity to explore the world that they have been protected from experiencing. What gets repressed in the world ultimately is expressed. The children's behaviors are created out of the fear of communicating with their parents about things they feel will disappoint them. The degree to which they do not follow the parental restrictions is the degree to which the parents' fears will be realized.

At the other extreme behavior from this fear is a set of parents who have no rules and completely ignore any behavior that needs correction. This can lead children to test the furthest extremes of the parents' boundaries in a desperate cry to be given some structure. Because the parents fear having "bad" kids, they choose to ignore any behaviors that would cause them to have to take action and interpret the behavior as bad, which leads to experiencing the exact behavior they fear most.

The fear of being sick can cause increased anxiety over every ailment and pimple on your body. This could lead to dominant thoughts of sickness and death that cause depression and stress. This stress then weakens the immune system in your body, which causes you to feel "sick" on a constant basis. Hence, the fear has been realized.

At the other extreme, warning signs that the body gives that something needs attention are ignored out of fear that they might indicate something serious. No doctor visits are scheduled. This is comparable to turning the radio up louder on your car when you hear an unfamiliar engine noise. Whatever is ignored then turns into something incapacitating and worse in the body's effort to get conscious attention from the mind. The fear has been realized.

The fear of being poor causes some people to live lives where they work very hard and have a meager existence. Every penny is socked away in the bank and no financial risk is ever taken. There is stress regarding any amount of money that is spent. Not wanting to be financially strapped has produced the experience of it. Whether a person has enough money or not is irrelevant, for the experience is one of being financially restrained. The fear has been realized.

At the other end of the spectrum, an individual spends without care in an effort not to feel the constraints of his or her financial situation. The ignorance involved in careless spending creates a karmic cycle of debt and repayment that eventually catches up with the spender. The original fear is realized when credit and the means to pay it off run out.

In each of the preceding examples, fear works counter to the desired experience by producing more of the conditions necessary to experience what is feared than what is desired. Because the belief of what is possible from a positive standpoint does not exist when fear is overwhelmingly present, it cannot be realized. The experience of this feared reality is then used by the ego to confirm the belief in rationalizations, such as:

- "I'll never marry the right one."
- "My kids are just rotten; they'll never listen."
- "I always have to worry about money."

Each of these statements is false. They are rationalizations designed to help ease the suffering that comes from the idea of failure. They are signs of resignation. There is no shame in failure; there is only opportunity after opportunity to learn what you need to know to get you where you asked to go. A fear-driven experience begs you to see how you let your worries about your future dominate your current creative ability.

> The moment you realize that you create it all, you will realize that you can change it all.

You hold all the creative power in your life. One of the keys to understanding this fact is realizing the impact that fear has in preventing what you desire. Now, imagine what kind of an impact an equal amount of faith could have in creating what you desire! Your reality can only produce what you believe yourself worthy of being, doing, and having. When you demonstrate fear you are displaying what you believe is probable for you. Fear is a self-fulfilling prophecy. On the other hand, faith is also a self-fulfilling prophecy. It is the demonstration of the belief in what is desired as the probable outcome. That is why faith is the key that leads to the creation of your desires.

A major understanding that much of mankind has yet to realize is that who you were in a past moment is not who you are in this moment—unless you allow it to be so.

The choices you make that lay the conditions for your experiences are only limited by your fears. Ultimately there is nothing to fear, not even death. If you wonder how this could be, ask yourself, *Have I ever experienced death?* "No, but I've seen other people die," you'd say. While you may have seen a body die; you cannot know what happened to the energy or essence that once filled that physical body. Their spirit is no longer even remotely apparent, as anyone who has ever seen a dead body can testify. But until your body dies, you can't know if the fear of your death is valid or not. Many people who have had near-death experiences describe almost the exact same recollection of being separated from their bodies. They describe death not as an end, but as a release and transformation.

Those who choose to hold on to the fear of death keep ignoring or rationalizing what numerous others have described since the beginning of the written word, including all of the most well-known, loved, and respected saints, sages, and spiritual leaders from history who have offered something beautifully different.

Can you imagine what it would be like if you arrived at a
point where you overcame all of your fears? The answer is you
would be unlimited in your love and what you choose to create
for yourself from this love.

Resistance and the fear of change stem from one of the ego's
main intents, which is to keep you existing in what is known. It
does this by using concepts such as shame and regret to prevent
new action. Until you have crossed the threshold of intolerability and finally choose a new way of living life, the self-image
that has driven your life up to this point will remain the dominant factor over how your reality gets created.

For many people fear and a poor self-image embed themselves in the mind beginning in childhood through the learned
concept of conditional love. When love is used as a tool to manipulate a child into certain expectations by the parent or guardian, it often leads to a high level of insecurity. Running in the
street or throwing a temper tantrum certainly needs attention
and teaching, however, the damage is done when the manner
in which the parent teaches or disciplines is one that causes the
child to question his or her self-identity, or to experience a lack
in the feeling of being loved. During this highly impressionable
age of identity formation (I AM), what children are told about
who they are has a huge impact.

In one example, if a child breaks something and is told that
he or she is dumb or stupid for doing so or made to feel "less
than" for the act, the child is likely to believe this and then build
it into who he or she believes himself or herself to be. If, on the
other hand, children are taught that the act of breaking something is wrong or incorrect, rather than that they are wrong or
incorrect, the critical core sense of self-love and self-acceptance

remains undamaged. When children feel unaccepted and un-loved because of what they are told, interpret, and believe, they become starved for acceptance and love and search for it end-lessly in the world.

This is a critical understanding in life. The more you build an idea of yourself as loved and accepted, the more you will offer this *love and acceptance* to yourself and others throughout your life. On the other hand, the more you develop a poor, unloved, and unaccepted sense of self, the more you will continually project the feeling of *hate, fear, need,* and *resistance* to your world.

You can only offer as much love and acceptance to your world as you offer to yourself.

The feeling of not being good enough or not worthy enough to be loved is completely false, no matter under what circumstance you thought this to be true. This can include never being treated as if you were loved, feeling other siblings were favored over you, experiencing the unexpected death of your parent or par-ents, being abandoned at any age, and being repeatedly abused mentally or physically. None of these events has anything to do with your ability to be loved or your worthiness to be loved. Every one of these circumstances had to do with the personal issues and lack of understanding of those who you perceived withheld their love from you in some way. It never had anything to do with you! Only the way you have perceived these experi-ences has made it so. You are as worthy of love as you believe yourself to be. You will only see yourself worthy when you have accepted and loved yourself for the perfection of who and what you were and of who and what you are.

To get to the personal realization of perfection, the concepts of guilt, shame, and regret must be eradicated from the mind. These are highly destructive notions that cause an incredible amount of mental pain for much of mankind. Because we tend to believe in these concepts, the ego has devised four main ways to attempt to avoid experiencing them and the painful self-reflection they bring.

- **Denial**: nonrecognition of an event in order to avoid its message.
- **Delusion**: the reshaping of an experience to avoid the message it is offering.
- **Contempt**: holding someone else responsible for an event to avoid its message.
- **Judgment:** declaring someone wrong to avoid the message of an event.

Each of these reactions is used to avoid having to feel regretful, shameful, or guilty. For example, when a child is caught stealing and doesn't want to acknowledge responsibility, the child's reactions could be:

Denial	"I didn't do it."
Delusion	"I was going to pay for it."
Contempt	"My friend made me do it."
Judgment	"This store charges too much."

When an adult doesn't want to take responsibility and feel regret for a divorce or a breakup, the adult's reactions could be:

Denial	"She'll never go through with it."
Delusion	"He loves me and he will be back."

Contempt   "This whole thing is her fault."
Judgment   "He's a rotten person for doing this."

The ego's resistance will continue in these ways until each person realizes the purpose and perfection for the creation of the experience.

The damaging issue with regret, guilt, and shame is when these feelings are incorporated into your identity, thereby producing an effect on who you are. This has huge implications on why you have resistance and the fear of change in your life as you desperately try to avoid feeling the emotional pain from these concepts.

The truth is that unless you allow them to, these concepts cannot and will not define you. They are simply the immediate form of feedback you receive based on the actions you have taken in life. They are only useful in making new choices in the future that are more aligned with the intent you have about who you'd like to be.

Shame is feeling bad for who you were. It does not have to be who you are. If you carry the shame of the past into your present, you are burdening your future (I AM shameful). You will do things that cause you to reexperience it. You will also feel all the negative energy surrounding this idea of a shameful person. You will be your own judge and jury until you accept who you were and realize you have the power to choose in every moment who you will be. Then you will be free to act in a way that defines you positively and therefore experience shame no more. Carrying the idea of shame past the initial feeling it gave you will only serve to chain you to its experience.

Guilt is a negative sense of responsibility about having done something that made you feel bad or "less than." It is acknowledgment of something you did or for a way you acted that doesn't please you. If you continue to focus on what you did, you won't be in the best state of mind to act differently now. You will walk around in a negative state of mind, which will affect your self-definition and self-esteem. Because you define yourself as guilty (I AM guilty), it serves to increase the probability that you will act in a way that again creates the feeling of being guilty. The most beneficial purpose of past guilt is the awareness it offers you of how your past actions align or don't align with your beliefs about who you are now. This provides you with a clearer sense of what choices to make now.

Regret is the feeling that you should have made a better decision or acted differently in a past moment. Regret is the complete denial of who you were, and many people often feel some form of it their whole lives (I AM regretful). Regret is an illusion that only serves to keep one stuck in time. This leads to a negative state of mind and ultimately to the choices that foster more regret. Other than an initial feeling that serves to offer you information about a way you may not want to act in the future, regret, when held on to, is destructive to a fully creative and peaceful life. This is true for two main reasons.

1. **You cannot go back in the past and change anything you did.**
2. **If you could have done better in a past moment, you would have.**

This is a critical point of information in this material. You may want to take a moment to contemplate it again:

If you could have done better in a past moment, you would have.

Throughout your entire life you have acted in each moment to the best of your ability. "Woulda," "coulda," and "shoulda" are lies that your ego has told you to protect your self-definition from truth, liberation, and change. **You are always doing the best you can in each particular moment of life.** The acceptance of this truth has the power to bring an incredible amount of healing and relief.

What keeps most people holding on to regret is the fear that without having some regret for their actions, they are accepting the behavior as "okay," meaning they will be free to do it again in the future. Nothing could be further from the truth. Accepting who you were in the past enables you to choose more effectively who you intend to be. It does not mean you are condoning past behavior. It simply means you are fully acknowledging who you were with open acceptance so that you free yourself to operate from a more truthful, honest, clear, and balanced state of mind.

When you finally see that your acts were the best you could do based on your need to feel alive and attempt to find balance in this world, it produces a major shift in your consciousness and self-love. Accepting that a past action only represents a past self moves you out of protection mode and into creation mode. By embracing the idea that this behavior or action was what you did, what you were, and how you acted in a former time period, you can make peace with the understanding that it was the best you had to offer at the time. There is no longer a need to protect yourself from who you were with denial, delusion, contempt, or judgment. This frees you from living under the pressure of an illusion. Fear and resistance are no longer necessary.

The beauty of the infinitely creative universe is that every moment holds a new opportunity to decide, declare, choose, and act upon who you desire to be.

You can only choose to create what you believe is possible for you. What you believe is possible for you is tied directly to what you feel worthy of in life. When you can see your perfection in the past, you will love and accept yourself fully now. This understanding will be the turning point of your life. You will then be free to choose from the limitless possibilities available to someone worthy of any possibility. When you combine this insight with the understanding that you can't fail, the sky will truly be the limit for you and your life. You will be free to act from the most creative place in the universe: the place of love, acceptance, and faith, and the limitless possibilities this state of mind produces.

> **FAILURE = the condition (or fact) of not achieving the desired end or ends.**
> **Failure does not define who you are unless you allow it to.**

Failure is another concept that we all learned when we were very young. The experience of failure can have negative implications when its purpose is misunderstood. You may have heard the expression, "You have to fail to succeed." This is a very appropriate and true statement. Many who have experienced success in an endeavor only finally achieved their goal after they lived through and learned from failure. Failure itself is not the issue. It is the way that one interprets failure that makes all the difference. Those who go on to succeed take a positive lesson from the failure and treat it as an opportunity for growth and the expansion of awareness. It is not perceived as a personal defect. Failure offers valuable information about what new action to take to arrive at a desired reality and experience. In science, a failure is looked upon with excitement because it offers information on the wrong way to achieve a desired result, which in essence brings the desired answer closer. It becomes easier to see what works when you eliminate the ways that don't work!

Those who languish in sorrow over specific failures are suffering from denial and the inability to accept who they *were*. In essence, they are grieving the loss of a false self-concept. When people believe they understand everything they need for success in a particular area, but are met with the inability to achieve that particular success, this can produce mental conflict. It can be tough to accept the current truth that you are not who you believed, expected, or desired yourself to be; however, the great value of accepting a failure is that it ends resistance and allows you to open your awareness to receive the exact information required to get you where you intend.

Ultimately you can never fail. Even the failure to act will bring you the experience of failing to act and serve exactly what you need to bring you to a level of intolerance that will create an act or an attempt at change.

This is a critical point in this book for you to embrace. Failure is POSITIVE.

Failing is positive because it means you're in the process of developing the necessary awareness related to your ultimate desired experience. The only question is: *Will you choose to persist on your journey long enough to achieve it?*

There are no mistakes in life, only learning experiences. Realizing you are none-the-less for failing in any way, shape, or form is an effective way to attain peace of mind. We are all doing the best we can in each and every moment of existence. We are all on the same journey of understanding, searching for eternal peace, balance, and tranquillity of mind.

You are PERFECT.

The speed of your journey to this awareness is always up to you. The process becomes easier and easier the more you realize your capacity to love, forgive, and accept yourself now. Regret, guilt, and shame—other than initial feelings that are reactions to un-desired acts of self-expression—are meaningless and detrimental to you and to your power to create.

When you realize your perfection you will allow yourself to experience what someone of perfection is worthy of creating and experiencing. You will then act to create the conditions that validate it. When you can't see your perfection, you work to create the conditions that validate something less than perfection while simultaneously attempting to get the missing approval and acceptance from the world around you.

The only approval and acceptance you ever need in your life is your own.

When this liberating truth makes its way into your conscious-ness you become free from any need from your world. You will no longer be at the mercy of anyone or anything in order to be happy and at peace, but in full control of the knowledge of the glory and beauty that is You. You will remove your thoughts of imperfection and see, create, and enjoy your absolute perfection. The realization of your perfection reveals that at your core you are nothing but pure love. You can now choose to create from this love and demonstrate the magnificent creative potential inside of you. A life of loving, deliberate creation awaits You!

Good-bye, Fear

One day I'll break free
From your grip that's on my mind,
Be the limitlessness that I long to be,
Be a creation of any kind.
You are the perceived wall
That keeps my soul from endless joy,
Holding me from the pure love that I AM.
Yours is the cruelest of ploys,
But when faith does cause the strength
Over your spell that seems so strong,
The tide will start to turn,
The time to peace won't seem so long.
Good-bye, fear,
And all the confines that you bring.
Slay you I will.
And my eternal season will be spring.
This world would be better without
All the evil that you make;
Be a place of only love
Nothing sinister, nothing fake.
Know your time is running out,
For I will soon claim victory
Fulfill the dreams that I have dreamed;
Become my true destiny.

PART FOUR

Who You Can Be

Is Based On . . .

Chapter 12

Your AWARENESS of You

*The beauty of life shines forth as you demonstrate
more of the beauty you discover within you.*

The transformation to a new You has already begun. As you become aware of what you are, how you created your past, and why you have held yourself back from receiving the answers that would lead you to experience a new future, you become more aware of the potential of who and what you can be. To love and accept yourself just as you are is the crowning mind-set that makes it possible for you to step toward a number of exciting new possibilities.

In this mind-set you no longer hold yourself back from what you desire. You realize that you are just as worthy as everyone else who has come before you and fulfilled his or her dreams. Every person you admire, respect, or desire to be like, based on the life you see that person living, has been a great messenger of possibility. Anything is possible with earnest desire. The life or experiences you dream about becomes more probable for you the more you continually step toward creating them in your every thought and action.

Which of the infinite possibilities in front of you will you decide to experience?

Who do You choose to be right now?

The following statements summarize some of the main points from the first eleven chapters.

- You are now aware that You, like everything else in existence, are ENERGY.
- You are now aware that You decide who you are in every moment.
- You are now aware that your emotions reveal the state of your energy.
- You are now aware that addiction is only a temporary means to achieve a more tolerable state of mind.
- You are now aware that attempts to get personal validation and approval in place of your own self-approval have karmic repercussions.
- You are now aware that feeling stuck in an undesired reality comes from a false belief you hold about who you really are (I AM).
- You are now aware that it is your fear of being "less than" you are now that keeps you from taking the actions that lead to change.
- You are now aware that you have always done the best you could have in every moment of your life.
- You are now aware that You are already whole, complete, and perfect.
- You are now aware that your acceptance of your worthiness and perfection allows you to tap more of your infinite creative potential.

- You are now aware that You are an infinite expression of love that has been created from an infinite source of love.

- You are now aware that by accepting your unlimited potential to love, you will be able to define yourself and express this love in any way that you choose.

- You are now aware that the past and the future do not exist, and that all you ever have is NOW to decide, declare, and act as you desire to BE: "I AM."

With the expansion of awareness that this knowledge provides, nothing can hold you back from becoming all that you dream of being. Right here, right now you have a never-ending opportunity to accept a simple yet powerful truth about your pure essence. As you come to embrace and know the following two statements, you will immediately begin to release more of the unlimited power you have to transform yourself and thereby begin to transform your entire world. As a result, you will cultivate and experience more lasting moments of peace, love, and happiness in your life.

Please take a few quiet moments to contemplate the following statements.

I AM an infinite source of love for myself and for others.

I AM in control of the creation of my life, and it originates, as it always has, from who I decide that I AM right now.

Now

There is no then.
There was, isn't now.
There is no will be,
Only here and how.
Step outside
This timeless spot.
An imaginary world
Develops that is not.
Dramas unfold,
Dropping clues to a path.
Choose to follow where it leads.
Adding up to perfect math,
Every time it will take you
Right back to the start:
The center of the universe,
The pure love in your heart.
Again in the moment
Is where you will be.
Destined to remember,
It's the only place you're truly free.

Chapter 13

Your DESIRE
to Ask Questions

The answer infinitely awaits the question.

There is a dramatic shift that occurs as you become more aware that the power to determine your journey in life is always within you. Like a rocket ship that breaks through the boundary of Earth's gravitational field, a new freedom from force, pressure, and time emerges. You realize that not only are you free from any force but that you are the force. Now, in this very moment, you can declare who and what you will be from this point forward, and become it. All you have to be willing to do to start the transformation process is ask a question. This is the first step to receiving answers that lead to the creation of a new you.

In a mind that resonates at a complete state of peace there are no questions. In this state of harmony all is seen as perfect, there are no desires or needs, only a complete sense of fulfillment. Your questions therefore all originate from a certain level of either creative need or discontent with your current reality. Some of the more prominent questions of life are: "Why am I always unsettled and discontented?" "How can I find my real purpose in life?" "When will I experience true love?" "What does it take to be consistently happy?" Human curiosity is the way each of us expands our understanding of the world. It is the demonstration of the intention to know and survive in a new way and this is what attracts the information and answers that increase our awareness. When we come to understand something new we feel a certain degree of contentment and peace as this new knowledge allows us to feel that much more in control of the world around us.

> Any new understanding is an expansion in awareness that results in a temporary state of balance with the universe.

Balance and peace occur when we are in harmony with our world. Whenever something is happening in our lives that we do not understand, we feel a sense of turmoil or conflict. Our sense of identity as defined by our beliefs is not getting the confirmation it needs. At these times our need to know and to be answered becomes more intense.

In every social paradigm, whether religious, scientific, philosophical, or spiritual, the awareness that comes from receiving answers is expressed differently. In science, an "aha" moment of new understanding about the universe brings the receiver a moment of great joy. In spirituality, a moment of enlightenment about the self and the world comes with an overwhelming sense of peace. In religion, a moment of grace and light is accompanied by the full feeling of love. These amazing feelings of joy, peace, and love all emerge from new and more expansive realizations about the universe and the life that inhabits it.

The expansion of awareness that occurs through the experience of new answers is the essence of evolution, which allows for the continual creation and survival of life. For those individuals who have had to face very challenging circumstances in life, it is the understanding of why these things have occurred in a particular manner that often gives them the strength to carry on. Finding purpose in what seems to be chaos is what allows many people to overcome what seem to be insurmountable difficulties in life.

> Ask and it will be given to you; seek and you will find; knock and the door will be opened to you.
>
> —*Matthew* 7:7

The core intent of life is to live. From nature we have learned that species that become aware of change and adapt to it the fastest have the greatest chance of survival. From life we have learned that the only constant in the universe is change. Put these two elements together and you come away with the instruction, "Adapt or cease to exist." This core intent also represents the heart of curiosity and questioning for humans. The awareness that results from asking questions drives our adaptation and the actions that lead us to the ongoing expression and experience of life.

Ignorance has a price to pay, which often includes pain. Pain is one of the more extreme ways that the universe attempts to give us the information we need for survival. This is exactly why a traffic jam occurs whenever there is even a small accident on the side of the road. "Rubbernecking" is really the deep sense of curiosity that humans have for anything unknown or unfamiliar. It is not the accident that is unfamiliar, but how it happened—along with the potential for injury or death—that draws us to become onlookers. Death is such an unknown and deeply feared event that people take advantage of any opportunity to gather more information about it. "Did they die?" "How did they die?" "Were they wearing seat belts?" "Could that have been me?" We are in a constant search for information that will quell our fears about death or help us to avoid life's painful learning experiences.

Since the universe is constantly changing, in order to stay in harmony with it our awareness must expand. If a species's desire is to survive, yet it ignores the changing environment around it, the species eventually will no longer have the knowledge to react in a way that will ensure its survival. The probability for extinction then rises. The desire to know is therefore an expression of the will to live and experience life. As such, it is one of the core reasons for prayer, meditation, and self-reflection.

The most important thing is to never stop questioning.

—*Albert Einstein*

The power of your creation starts with a question. What is it that you desire to know, as it relates to how you want to create and experience yourself? It is highly improbable that you would be curious about something from which you saw no perceived benefit. The more you realize this, the more revealing it becomes to look at your current interests: Why are you so interested in who wins an election, how many calories are in a certain kind of ice cream, what your neighbors just did to their house, what your favorite movie star is wearing, or what someone thinks of you?

All of your curiosity relates to who you want to be and what you desire to experience. Information that you believe will help in this quest opens your awareness so that you hang on every word you hear and absorb every bit of information like a sponge. Information that you don't believe will help you often has a very hard time holding your interest. For a new answer to enter your awareness you have to exhibit a desire and readiness to understand. As the Buddhist proverb goes: "When the student is ready, the teacher will appear." Throughout the course of your life, the teacher will continue to show up in many different people and experiences.

Your ability to be at peace is based on receiving consistent validation that you are who you believe you are. You, like everyone else on earth, are constantly seeking this validation by creating the experiences that bring it to you and allow you to feel alive. If who you believe yourself to be is someone who experiences X, then you need knowledge of how best to manifest X in your reality so it can become real. Questions arise in your mind the moment you have the intention to experience something new. No matter how, when, and why you desire this new experience to happen, you will need to undergo a learning process to gain the required knowledge.

- If you desire to experience a loving and lasting relationship, you will have to ask what it takes to create and experience one. This will include the information you will gain from going through unsatisfactory relationships.
- If you desire to live with more health and vitality, you'll need to question what has kept you from it thus far, and then work to create the conditions that will allow this idea to become a reality for you.
- If you desire to build a successful business, you will have to

go through the process of building one and inquire about what works and what doesn't on the way to fulfilling your dream of having a successful one.

"Where there's a will there's a way" is the old adage. The "will" part is nothing more than your level of desire for whatever you intend to create. The level of your true desire always reveals itself through the effort and persistence you put into your questioning to find the "way." Your questioning will need to continue even during experiences that apparently run counter to your desire. The consistent desire to achieve your intention is the power that keeps you constantly asking new questions to get you past attempts that haven't worked. Persistence is the powerful demonstration of faith, and it is a key attribute in life because it dramatically increases the probability that you will overcome any obstacles you confront and ultimately prevail.

Fall seven times; stand up eight.

—*Japanese proverb*

Those who have achieved their dreams in life at some point all asked, "How?" Then they opened their minds and fearlessly allowed themselves to receive the answers no matter how overwhelming or how self-revealing they were. These answers provided a pathway to what they wanted to experience. Through the consistent attempt to create the experience they desired, they were able to learn more of what was necessary ultimately to achieve it. To those who succeed, even in the face of enormous setbacks, giving up was not seen as an option. They understood that the best way to achieve what they desired was to choose continually to act and experience, learning from what happened along the way.

People often look at others who achieve what they desire and remark, "I wish I had the courage to do that." But for the person whose life they admire, it was more a matter of desire than courage that led to the actions taken. Most men and women who have been honored for demonstrating courage in life weren't thinking of the courage it would take to do what they did while they were doing it. Instead, they were focused on acting and expressing the true self that they believed they were. Courage is an idea reserved for onlookers who have yet to muster the sufficient personal will or desire required to head down a path that will lead them to have a similar experience.

When people say that they don't have courage, they mean, "That's not who I AM." Either there is no desire to act in the same way or, if there is a desire, the belief does not exist yet that tells them they are capable of a particular experience. However, since they now see that the act itself is possible, labeling it as courage is a convenient rationalization to ease the discomfort caused by the self-reflection. "She had a lot of courage to walk up to her future husband and ask him out," some might say. However, the woman who dared to ask a man out didn't just have courage. More important she had a strong desire for companionship and she took conscious control of one of the steps needed to create companionship in her life.

There are endless examples in society of individuals whose desire manifested some of the most amazing questions. Once asked, these questions have led to the answers and realizations of some of mankind's great advancements. The beauty of the world's music, art, and architecture and the amazing understanding and advancements in science and medicine all originated from questions asked by those whose desire for a certain creation and experience brought them to wonder, "How?"

> I do not want the peace that passeth understanding, I want the understanding that bringeth peace.
>
> —*Helen Keller*

Your ability to question and be open to answers is no different from the ability of any of the greatest minds in history or of anyone living today. All you have to do is decide what you would like to experience from this moment forward. What information do you need to know to manifest that experience? What answers are you looking for in your life right now? The more intent you are in your desire to receive answers, the faster answers will enter your space. This is the perfection of the elegant universe.

A question that is asked in earnest is a declaration of the intent to know. The proclamation, "I don't know," is what opens up a space in the mind. This empty space, when combined with the desire for an answer, creates a vacuum that begins to attract new information and answers into it.

Science has concluded that nature abhors a vacuum and immediately seeks to fill it. In religion this is expressed in the New Testament of the Bible as, "Ask and you shall receive." In philosophy or spirituality many teachers in different ways have said, "Not knowing is the opening to knowing." Each statement is a way of expressing how awareness presents itself to us when we have an earnest desire to understand. The result of asking sincere questions is ultimately an expanded consciousness.

There are no unanswered questions, only resisted answers.

The definition of the word "universe" comes from the Latin word *universus*, meaning "whole" or "complete." In a complete or whole universe every question already has an answer. To take this a step further, the concept of "time" can be seen as a measure of where the collective or individual consciousness is in relation to this absolute understanding.

As the questioner, you have the free will to accept or reject the answers that arrive in your daily reality. A quick awareness and acceptance of these answers is actually what collapses your experience of time, where your resistance or rejection of this information adds to, or expands, your sense of time. You will resist new answers about life anytime you are not ready to change your identity and view of the world. The only way you will allow new information into your consciousness is when your will to change is greater than your fear of change. This is when you will begin to see how your current view is limiting you and holding you back.

The moment you make the choice to let go of a belief that is preventing you from accomplishing your intent in life, you create the space for change. New information now has room to enter your mind, allowing you to realize more of your true, unlimited nature. This information always reveals that you are not who you previously thought you were; you are so much more.

Example: If you are wondering why you are having such a difficult time finding a soul mate to spend the rest of your life with, self-examination is the required first step. When you begin an inquiry, you have to look at the previous choices you have made in life that have prevented this particular outcome from occurring. Upon reflection you will discover what your cumulative choices of self-expression have produced for you. Asking, "How do I find this person?" is an acknowledgment that you have not yet been able to find an answer to get to the experience you seek. At some core level of your identity the idea of the experience of having a soul mate has been resisted as a possibility.

To change reality you need a new self-concept ("I AM"). This new belief must contain the truth that having a soul mate is possible and that you are worthy of having the experience. Your new belief will have the effect of changing your identity. As your inner identity changes, your outer choices and reality will change in perfect synchronicity to match it.

> You can only experience what is not resisted as a possibility.

One of the requirements of this process of change is that you achieve harmony with the truth that you are not who you thought you were (in this example, someone capable of attracting a soul mate). Accepting the truth will allow you to look at the thoughts and actions that you need to embrace now to make this idea real. It starts with you focusing on who you really are, why you have been preventing this experience, and what you are exactly looking for in a relationship match. When you finally give up the false and limiting self-definition that keeps you from accomplishing what you desire, you open to the grace and answers offering you who you can be that will allow this experience to happen. It is always who you believe yourself to be that is the real impediment to accomplishing everything you desire.

> Give up a belief that has you as limited and finite and you free yourself to experience more of your true, unlimited, and infinite nature.

The moment a question is asked, the answer presents itself somewhere in the seeker's reality. The issue is always whether or not the asker is ready and willing to allow the answer to come into his or her conscious awareness.

An example of this is when someone is looking for a set of apparently lost keys. The question is: "Where are my keys?" The individual looks everywhere: on the counter, under the couch, in the purse, on the floor, until suddenly someone points out that the keys are in the person's hand! Because the person looking for the keys thought they were lost, the person had eliminated the possibility that he or she was holding them. Because of this belief, the person's senses (sight, sound, taste, touch, and smell) did not allow the information to be perceived. In other words, because the belief is "I AM someone who has lost my keys," the ego had to validate it and make the thought real by denying the obvious. The information that they have their keys in their hand would momentarily invalidate who they believe they are so the contrary information is kept at bay. The belief had become the reality for that short sequence of moments until the truth shattered the illusion. This occurs with every I AM we declare, even down to the simplest and seemingly harmless statements such as "I AM someone who has lost my keys."

Each I AM and element of our self-concept becomes a part of our reality and is protected by every means necessary. Fortunately, the ego is not the enemy holding us back from life experiences. It is our greatest ally. Change the I AM declaration and the ego will work just as hard to manifest a new experience as it did to hold on to the old experience that validated the old self-definition.

In transforming your life, the issue is not whether the answer to any question exists, but only a matter of whether or not you are ready to embrace the new way of looking at and experiencing the world that the answer will bring.

The process of opening your mind to receive the answers you seek is the same for every question you could ever ask. Consider the following examples. As you read the ones that resonate with your personal experience, consider what might be preventing you from allowing the answers to penetrate your awareness.

- Why does my life seem so chaotic?
- Why do I find myself in unfulfilling relationships?
- Why do I often feel depressed, anxious, and fearful?
- Why are my finances such a mess?
- Why am I so unhappy with the way I look?

Every question has an exact answer. If questions have been asked but you have not experienced any answers yet, it may be that you simply aren't ready yet. Many of us do not want to face any truth that may cause a negative self-reflection and state of mind. It can be tough to realize that we played a leading role in creating the conditions for our own unhappiness. This self-protection will persist until we are in so much pain that the conditions are no longer tolerable. This is when we are finally fully humbled and brought to our knees. This is when we intently cry out for answers. Finally the mind is ready to let go of what it thinks it knows that obviously has not worked in the quest for a lasting peaceful state of mind.

An earnest question asked with a fervent and deep desire to understand is usually accompanied by full submission and willingness to receive an answer. At this moment, the questioner no longer guards against the truth of who they have been. The questioner is ready now to accept the raw truth. This process of submission has produced many of the most well-known spiritual, religious, and mystical revelations of history. This can only occur when the questioner finally lets go of all of the false beliefs about themselves and the world they live in.

Information cannot enter a space in your mind that is already being taken up by what you think you know. If you have not experienced the answers to your questions, it is because what you think you know is leaving no room for the real answers to enter your consciousness.

If you knew the answer, you wouldn't be asking.

There is an old story of a Buddhist scholar and a Zen master. The scholar had an extensive background in Buddhist Studies. He came to study with the master and asked him to teach him Zen. Then he began to talk about his extensive doctrinal background and went on and on about the many treatises and philosophies he had studied.

The master listened patiently for a while and then began to brew a pot of tea. When it was ready, the master poured the tea into the scholar's cup. He kept pouring until the tea began to overflow and run all over the floor. The scholar saw what was happening and shouted, "Stop, stop! The cup is full! You can't get any more in!"

The master stopped pouring and said: "You are like this cup. You are full of ideas about Buddha's Way. You come to me and ask for teaching, but your cup is full. I can't put anything more in. Before I can teach you, you'll have to empty your cup."

You, like every other human being, have asked questions about how to experience more peace and joy in your life, and about how to create and experience what you know is contained within you. All your questions have answers that you are capable of realizing.

On this journey of re-creation, you must ask yourself, "Am I ready for my answers?" "Am I tired enough of the way it has been?" As you have learned in reading the preceding chapters, you are always in charge of your life and you are worthy of all the peace and happiness you desire. After a question is asked, it is only a matter of acceptance. Your answers already exist, but a true and heartfelt desire is required for them to be experienced. The answers that are revealed from pursuing this desire are what will shape your destiny and future.

Chapter 14

Your WILL to Accept the Answers

Acceptance is the doorway to transformation.

Every moment of your life holds the answers to your most intense questions. In fact, it is as if they wait for you to allow them into your experience from the second you first ask a question. As irony would have it, these answers often show up most directly in the people, places, and experiences that are resisted or avoided the most. It is the universe's most direct response to whatever you are asking.

The universe does not deny anyone the answer to his or her question but only infinitely provides you with new levels of understanding and support for your continuous journey of expanding awareness. If you ever feel denied an answer to any question in your life, know that you deny yourself by resisting the messages that reality sets before you each day.

Every resisted part of reality is a reflection of a resisted part of You. Who you perceive yourself to be (I AM) determines your relationship and identification with everything in the outer world. You will not and cannot accept anything in your outer reality unless you can first accept how this new view will change You. How you see yourself is the deciding factor in what you embrace and allow. It is also the deciding factor in what you resist and reject.

Imagine you are driving along an interstate highway minding your own business when suddenly the man at the wheel of the car behind you starts repeatedly honking his horn, waving his fist, and cussing at you. If you find you cannot accept or understand the behavior of this irate driver, it is because you are not willing to identify with the driver. To have any sort of compassion for the driver, you have to be compassionate with yourself. You have to be secure enough in yourself to know that unless you were purposefully driving in an irresponsible manner, the reason that the driver behind you is irate actually has nothing to do with you. If you are upset by his anger, it is because you have personalized the irate driver's behavior by thinking it is about you.

For you to stay peaceful in this moment, you would have to realize that you can't know why the driver is upset. You have no idea what he is currently dealing with in his life. In this instance you just happen to be the object of this particular individual's anger, a focal point he is using in order to release negative energy through his emotions. The driver's expressions of anger are merely attempts to restore his inner balance. If you do not feel compassion for the driver, it is because you are not allowing yourself to go to that level of understanding. You are merely trying to defend your self-image as a good driver who isn't doing anything wrong. By responding to the driver's anger by becoming defensive or upset, you are unveiling that you need to protect your pride.

The interesting point about this particular scenario is that it is not really about your driving (unless you were driving irresponsibly). If you engage with a driver venting rage, then the irate driver has accomplished his energetic mission of pulling you into his drama. By reacting in the same manner, you confirm the driver's belief in hostility, competition, and conflict. You have fallen into the trap of validating his illusion and his anger by getting angry and giving his story more energy.

Your part in the event, and the reason a driver like this one would enter your world, is that at some past moment you asked a question that could only be answered by understanding more about who you are and how you respond to life. The experience of an irate driver behind you is an answer, even though you may not recognize it at first. Maybe the question a week ago was, "How can I feel more at peace?" Your recognition of the answer depends on whether or not you accept or resist what is occurring. Your interaction with the driver is an opportunity to react and, thereby, define who you are. Perhaps historically you've been someone who jumps at the chance to engage in conflict with other people. For you, this may be the perfect opportunity to continue the experience or maybe this is your moment of opportunity to choose a new one.

Interestingly, reality will loop through similar occurrences until you tire of the repetition. When you are sufficiently fed up with the drama of engaging with irate people, you will redefine who you are and, hence, alter the energy you send out in the next situation. Your new self-definition may be something on the order of: "I AM someone who is neither affected by, nor engages with, irate people." When you alter your reaction to an experience, you literally change your experience.

When these types of things happen, all the wonder and questioning of "What is the reason for this?" or "Why is this happening to me?" are answered through who you become because of these experiences. The true purpose of life events is revealed in how you choose to react to them and how they define who you are. When you gain control of how you respond to what you are confronted with each day by making a new decision about You, what happens to you starts to change.

Reality is designed to continually offer you answers. This is the sole purpose of the material world. Each moment is an opportunity to understand and become increasingly aware of who you are and the creative possibilities of who you can be. You ask questions and things magically show up (whether or not you have any idea that they are directly linked to your questions). The choice in what to do with what shows up is always yours to decide.

> Each moment offers you free will, the never-ending choice of how to react to your experience, thereby declaring and defining—for a moment—who you are.

Consider this example. You see a homeless man sitting on the side of the street. As you pass him, he asks for a dollar. Based on the beliefs you hold about the world, your response could be one of the following:

- You are afraid, don't look at him, act as if he isn't there, and just keep walking.
- You feel stingy, thinking you don't have enough money to give him any and keep walking.

- You feel disgust and animosity, wondering why he doesn't get a job like everybody else, and you keep walking.
- You stop and give him a dollar.

The first three responses are based on the resistance of what "is." Something has shown up in your reality and you are at odds with it and have made a judgment about it. The truth is, you know absolutely nothing about this man's past or his current state of mind. All you are looking at is how this man is disrupting your current view of the world by presenting you with a reality that you do not want to experience.

What if you knew the following information?

The name of the man asking for a dollar is Brian. He was born to an unwed mother who was an alcoholic. By age four, his mother's boyfriend was molesting him when she was not home. This happened for a period of four years, until Brian was eight years old. At this age his mother was put in jail for selling drugs and Brain then became a ward of the state. He was placed in a foster home at age nine, where an abusive alcoholic foster father repeatedly beat him. This occurred because, as a result of that former abuse, Brian kept his head down and would barely speak. His foster father neither knew nor cared about the reasons for this. To him this was disrespectful and highly insubordinate.

The family that took Brian in were not interested in the child, but took him in for the money they received from the state. At age fourteen, Brian had had enough of the broken bones and bruises and left for the streets. Out on the streets and knowing no way to survive, Brian became involved in drugs and prostitution and the abuse continued. Brian lived like this for another fifteen years, living day to day as the drugs and malnutrition riddled him with sickness and disease. This was the result of a body broken from years of neglect and abuse both physical and mental.

Brian did find some comfort in the people he met on the street and from time to time he lived with some of them. These situations usually lasted until these people no longer had a need for him and what they could use him for. Alone and homeless, with no one, he found himself on the streets again. And this is when you encountered him.

It had been a couple of days since this broken and confused forty-three-year-old man, who looked every bit of sixty-five, had something to eat. Brian asked you for a dollar so he could scrape together what he needed to get some food.

How would you look at him now?

Feeling compassion for other people is not about becoming obligated to them or feeling responsible for their lives. It is about the end of judgment by accepting the fact that there is no way you could possibly know the collective circumstances that have brought them to this point in their lives. You can never truly know why *anyone* does what they do or is the way they currently are, or previously were, until you've walked in their shoes.

If you meet someone like Brain, you are receiving a great gift of reflection. The gift is that you might stop for just one second and be thankful for every moment of your own life. You have presented yourself with this exact circumstance so that you can further declare—through your reaction to it—who and what you are.

Will you judge and ignore the man, or will you accept and honor his request? You were not asked to help him get on his feet. You were not asked to save his life. You were not asked to take him in. All you were asked for was a dollar. Through this man's asking, you were given a wonderful gift: a chance to express for a moment who you are. Maybe understanding that you can't know how or why he is in this position now might even prompt you to offer a compassionate smile along with the dollar. Right now, as you walk by this man, you are blessed beyond words—and you may not even recognize it.

As your perception of what is occurring changes, your experience of reality changes. Before, a homeless man may have been an ugly sight that upset and even frightened you. Now, with the expansion in your awareness coming from understanding more about his life and from realizing that you don't know and therefore cannot judge, your experience could change to an enriched one of understanding, compassion, and maybe even love. The negative energy you formerly sent out into the universe through your contempt for the man may shift to the positive emission of energy defined as compassion.

Change You (I AM) and you change the impact of the matter around You.

Your reality always offers you both an answer and a choice. The only right or wrong about any response you have depends on who you desire to be. Are you happy with who you are right now, or are you ready to act and respond differently, changing your self-definition and your next set of experiences? There are no accidents in what shows up in your life. Every sequence of events is drawn in by you and offers something as it relates to answering a question and learning more about who you truly are.

You are not a victim of circumstance. Circumstance is a victim of You.

As you make declarations and ask questions, the universe responds. Each event you experience is always for you in some way. This is the essence of the perfection of your reality. When a particular experience is resisted, it reveals that you are not ready to see or embrace the message that the event is bringing you.

Desire births questions, questions birth answers, and then answers produce a new, expanded awareness. A new awareness births new choices, new choices birth new actions, and new actions give rise to new realities.

It is possible to ask important questions for years and simultaneously block the answers from reaching your consciousness. You may rationalize that you don't need the answer or that you already have the answer. However, your reality will always reveal the truth. Your circumstances and state of mind demonstrate the truth. The longer you resist the information you need, the longer it will take to experience what you desire. The idea that gaining wisdom and insight takes any specific length of time is an illusion. An answer can be instantaneous or it can take years to penetrate your awareness. The time frame on this process is of your own making.

Two components are necessary to enact the universal principle "Ask and you shall receive." First, you must ask with true desire. This is something millions of people do every day through prayer, meditation, or simple pondering of the facets of their lives. And second, you must have the will to receive. This is the part where many people put up a protective wall.

There are a multitude of reasons why you might resist the answers to your questions about life. Each of these reasons relates to protecting your self-image and fearing change. You just may not be ready yet to let go of a certain way of living, no matter how painful. The primary feelings that create resistance to receiving answers are:

- *Fear* of changing and losing a part of your identity.
- *Anxiety* over who you will "have to be" now with this knowledge.
- *Guilt* for believing something that runs counter to what you learned from those you have loved and trusted.
- *Pride* in being "right," which won't allow you to admit that you have misunderstood reality and therefore might be "wrong."
- *Shame* about how this new information reflects on you.
- *Regret* over not having understood earlier.
- *Anger* at the false rules you were previously operating under.
- *Embarrassment* over past actions.

Feelings like these expose the true nature of unanswered questions. Such reasons are designed to limit your expansion of awareness and keep you as you are. Yet by accepting an answer and letting go of a previous truth, you do not lose a piece of yourself; rather you gain an even deeper sense of your true nature and creative capabilities.

Fortunately, no matter how many times you avoid them, the answers will always keep coming in equal proportion to what you ask. The truth will continue to show up and the more intently and intensively you ask, the more truth makes its way to you through the events in your life. This even includes events that you cannot believe are happening. It is not that you can't believe what is happening, rather it is that you are not ready to accept the reason that it is happening.

The truth will set you free, but first it will piss you off.

—*Gloria Steinem*

Resisting the truth is like trying to hold a ball underwater. For some, it feels like holding down a tennis ball, which is pretty easy. For others, it is like holding down a basketball, which takes a great deal of energy and effort. For the majority of people, the truth is like holding a giant beach ball underwater. All day long, their egos wrestle with refused yet unavoidable information in a vain attempt to keep from seeing the truth that is pushing its way to the surface of their awareness. As a result, at the end of the day, they feel wrecked. Mentally and physically, they are completely drained from resisting what is. Fear prevents them from accepting the truth that their reality is begging them to acknowledge.

This dynamic continues until the day arrives when someone can no longer avoid the overwhelming truth, and the "beach ball" explodes up to the surface of consciousness, where it bobs around in plain view. The charade is finally over and the individual is restored the energy that was put into protecting himself or herself from this truth. Acceptance becomes the only path left, and it leads to an incredible sense of liberation.

Your reality does not have to reach a destructive level for truth and answers to penetrate your consciousness. However, unfortunate events are the *only way* that some people get the message. Any type of undesired experience will keep occurring until you've had enough and finally make a change in who you are. It is absolute perfection.

Here are some examples of ways your desire shifts your creative energy:

- You'll experience job dissatisfaction until **the desire for the right job** outweighs the **need** to take the first one you are offered.
- You'll experience failed relationships until **the desire for a fulfilling relationship** outweighs the **need** to be in any relationship.
- You'll experience physical insecurity until **the desire to love and accept yourself** outweighs the **need** for others to love and accept you.
- You'll experience the frustration of the same circumstances until **the desire for answers and change** outweighs the **need** to avoid change.

The universe operates from an inescapable principle that should become more obvious to you once it has been pointed out. **If you believe you are in need, you create the exact conditions in your life that enable you to experience this need.** This happens because you always seek to experience what you believe about yourself. Experiencing peace in life occurs when you learn to keep the desires you have while releasing any need for them to happen. This is key, because it reveals a state of understanding that you are already whole and complete as you are.

When you see yourself as whole and complete in the present moment, you are without need. You are entirely at peace with the perfection of your experience. You are under no illusions about who you are and answers are neither avoided nor ignored. Your will to know is now no longer blocked by fear but powered by pure faith. The answers then begin to flow to you in a perfect match with your questions. The universe will offer this experience to you exactly when—by understanding, acknowledging, and accepting your perfection *right now*—you offer this experience to yourself.

You will forever be evolving into a new You. You cannot know what you truly need to learn until you go through the necessary, often uncomfortable, experiences that reveal your ignorance. But you can embrace the continual path of seeing life with a more open and faithful mind. A core reason that suffering, wars, disasters, crime, and disease exist is so we, as individuals and as a collective, may experience, reflect, choose, and evolve by our own free will and in our own time.

Most of the time the answers you seek are right in front of you, like the perceived lost keys that you cannot experience as you hold them in your hand. Thinking you know who you are (I AM without keys), you resist considering the obvious. The ability to experience your answers resides in your ability to believe in the moment's truth about You and in your willingness and desire to love and accept this momentary truth. True wisdom comes not in the answer, but in the experience that leads to the realization of the answer.

To perceive new answers to your questions, you must do things in a way that you have never done, including looking at yourself and the world from a fresh perspective. If you are looking for information that you have yet to experience, how can you expect it to reveal itself in a shape and form that you already know? Up to now, has what you "think" you know brought you the answer you seek? If not, it may be time to open up to a whole new set of possibilities. You cannot experience an answer to a perceived problem when you will only accept it in a way that doesn't threaten or change your ideas about life. An answer can only come when you no longer fear the truth it brings with it.

Resistance to any part of your experience is an indication that you have not yet understood that you are the creator of the experience.

If you do not believe you are the creator of your experience, you will be giving this power away to the rest of the universe to create it for you. You will be used and manipulated to the exact degree that you allow it to occur, eventually leading you to a negative state of mind. As discussed in chapter 7, negative imbalance causes disharmony. Not only does imbalance put you in a noncreative state of being, a negative imbalance also clouds your ability to see opportunity. Then the pressure of feeling stuck or trapped without answers produces a level of fear and confusion that blocks the limitless potential in front of you.

In this state, a person is not thinking clearly, but is focusing on the worst outcome. A good analogy of the mind in this state is like trying to see through the water of the ocean during a storm. The tossing and turning waves crash into one another from every angle, making it virtually impossible to see through the turbulence and the debris that gets kicked up. A mind in a chaotic state is the same way. There is a strong lack of clarity until the imbalance works itself off. Afterward, when balance is restored, the ocean of the mind returns to a state of harmony. Everything settles down, clarity is reached, and a person can see perfectly through the crystal clear, calm water.

A balanced mind is capable of providing you with any answer you seek in your life. The ability to shift your focus back in harmony with the truth that anything is possible is vital to creating this state of mind. If you focus only on what you fear, you'll be as blind as if in the center of the storm. Therefore, if you truly desire to receive your answers, you must purposefully intend to see the truth that everything that happens around you, through you, and to you is for you.

You can choose to ignore or eradicate the truth in front of you, or you can choose to understand it. One way stops the pressure temporarily, the other eternally.

Ignorance is often preferred over the truth. In fact, the more something or someone offers a truth that produces fear, the more it is resisted. Every day people ask the questions "How?" and "Why?" and at the same time refuse answers that are right in front of them. History is rife with examples of great teachers who were murdered or imprisoned for delivering their message of truth: Christ, Mahatma Gandhi, Nelson Mandela, Galileo, Dr. Martin Luther King Jr., Abraham Lincoln, and numerous others were persecuted for the reflections that they brought that some in their world were not ready to face.

The attempt to avoid feelings of guilt, shame, and regret cause many to fight the truth they are faced with in their lives. This truth will not be realized until one understands that there is no "fault" and that every choice they made was seen as perfect in the moment they made it. Likewise, in your life, each choice you've made was one you felt was absolutely necessary at that particular time to define who you were and to survive.

Once you are free from protecting yourself from all of the the woulda, coulda, shoulda of the past, there is nothing you will avoid from it. You will now use your memory of an undesired experience as an indication of what you do not want to experience again without deriving a negative sense of self-worth from it. You did the best you could in the past; you are capable of any future you feel worthy of having. In this mind-set you will then open to any and every answer you desire. This is when you will experience true clarity.

After the crippling energy of fear, shame, guilt, and regret has been dissolved, you are free to create your desired life from the only state of mind that remains: LOVE.

When you are operating your life from a loving perspective, there is nothing but answers—and they come into your view in every way imaginable. You will see them more prevalently in books, newspapers, television programs, movies, comments from strangers, tragedies and triumphs you witness, billboards, license plates, your family, spontaneous advice from friends, dreams, and your gut instinct and intuition. You will look back and see the purpose for every experience along your journey. There will no longer be any message that you are afraid of embracing because there is no longer any false identity to protect. You will finally see and acknowledge your beauty and worthiness as a self-creating being. This truth, understood and accepted, will finally end your suffering.

You will know the truth, and the truth will set you free.

—*John 8:32*

This is the point in life when everything powerfully changes. Tired enough from the misunderstandings you have carried for so long and drained from the disharmony they have caused, you are ready to accept your perfection. You are finally willing to welcome a new way of looking at You in the world and loving yourself and creating yourself within it.

You are now open to receiving life-changing information in

the omnipresent way it presents itself in your reality. Each of the numerous "signs" you'll see—including this book—have been drawn into your reality by your own questions. All of it will reveal the amazing grace and power that is available to you in every moment to aid your constant creative expression and support your quest for understanding and peace.

Everything is a coincidence.

LIKE ATTRACTS LIKE

The word "coincidence" can be seen as a combination of the words "coincide," meaning "to occupy the same place in space or time," and "incident," meaning "event, occasion, or happening." Therefore, everything in your life actually fits into this definition, not just "special events." Each object or individual that is part of reality is in an eternal state of coinciding with everything else simultaneously, expressing the perfection of matching intents. This is the elegant nature of the universe.

By embracing this notion you begin to experience more of the gifts that life has to offer. Your intuition strengthens, giving you the power of immediate insight, understanding, and knowing. Your acceptance allows you to begin to go through each day in more of a state of "being" rather than "thinking." You are no longer stuck in time, focusing on a negative memory or a projection of a fearful future. You are simply immersed in the present state of infinite potential. In this state of mind the answers continuously flow into your awareness.

There is nothing you can see that is not perfection, and all of it is for You.

Your will to see and accept the truth in your own life is a reflection of your love for and acceptance of YOU. In this open state you need nothing and fear nothing. You are loved and matter in the world as long as you believe you are loved and you matter. A great liberation occurs as you free yourself from the need for any acceptance other than your own. Self-love flows as you embrace your perfection of your current position on the learning curve of your life.

Intentions cannot manifest if all the right conditions are not met. Your life is about learning the conditions necessary to experience your highest intent from moment to moment. Loving yourself fully is one of the biggest and most powerful conditions you can put in place to achieve this.

The paths to grace and self-love are one.

As you open to your ever-flowing river of answers, you'll experience a new level of peace and serenity that as you walk through life aids in lifting up the love and light in all of those around you. The process to attain any desired experience of life will be unveiled for you, so you can clearly see the path of transformation ahead of you. Intuitive messages and synchronicities will become commonplace.

The next step on the path to who you can be is to begin the creation of a new reality. Armed with a fuller sense of self-awareness, you have a new freedom to declare a new You and expand the limits of possibility for your role in the universe. A new version of You is born as soon as you make a new choice of being. This stems from the most powerful creative declaration in the universe: **I AM.**

Chapter 15

Your POWER to Make
New Choices of Being

It's never too late to be who you might have been.

—George Eliot

The greatest gift we have as human beings is the capacity to self-reflect and then choose how to express who we are. This is an ability that we are graced with in every moment. Each experience we have offers us an opportunity to use this power in our words and actions, thereby declaring and defining for that moment who we are in the universe.

You have been expressing your identity since the moment you were born. In infancy, your unconscious survival actions and reactions, such as eating, sleeping, and developing your motor skills, defined you. In childhood, you declared yourself by the way you explored your boundaries and tested the limits of your world. In your teen years, your identity was likely shaped by the choices of expression you made as you learned how to fit in and find a place of acceptance within your family and culture and among your peers. In your early adult years, your sense of self most likely centered around finding a mate or discovering what means of work would allow you to survive economically.

At every stage of life, you have acted on the basis of who you believed you were—at that time—in order to survive. These actions continue to shape your existence today. The common denominator of your choices is that they all stem from who you believe that you are.

The main issue that stifles so many people's lives is the belief that they are no more capable of change or a more satisfying life than they were twenty years ago, five years ago, or yesterday. Millions operate daily out of the unconscious idea that they are who they were—and this is why their lives don't seem to change. The core I AMs developed in childhood that structure how many view themselves in relationship to the world still have a major influence on their current perceptions, choices, actions, and reactions.

Using the analogy of a computer for a human being, the mind and body would be likened to the operating system of the computer and the personal beliefs (I AMs) are like the software that runs it. Many people are unaware that old software programs are automatically operating in the background of their mind. This software has prevented much of the desired changes in their reality for years. The way they keep interpreting the world and reacting to it does not allow them the type of output that would create something new. It doesn't matter how many books they read or how many motivational seminars they attend, the same issues will keep occurring; regardless of the input, the same problems will keep coming up, and the same questions will get asked without being answered. As long as they continue to operate under the same programming, their lives won't change.

If you desire to produce a different experience than you've had in any area of your life, who you choose to be right now has to be different from who you were up until now. Each belief you have will need to match your intentions, rather than work against them. New choices and actions can only come from a new identity. Otherwise there will be no change, as you will make the same choices in perfect harmony with who you still are.

Many people and experiences have influenced the identity programming that is at the crux of your life. Some experiences have carried more weight and made more of an impact than others, but all of them had an effect. People who may have had significant influence on your self-image include parents, teachers, religious leaders, relatives, friends, and heroes. They helped to shape your idea of the role you are playing in the script that is your life. The question is: Do you want to play a role that's based on your desires or continue to follow a script based on the will and desires of others?

The key to this answer, and consequently to the experience of peace, resides in your capacity for self-love and acceptance. You must come to understand yourself enough so that you will fearlessly declare and live out your own decisions of life, regardless of who else will be affected by those decisions. This is conscious creation, and it is the true nature of being free of mind.

In this eternal moment you are the master programmer of your mind.

As an example of this subconscious programming, earlier in the book we considered how we would react to someone with many tattoos if we felt people with tattoos were threatening. When we see a tattooed man coming toward us, the software related to this belief focuses our senses exclusively on material that validates the belief: information about the man that we interpret as threatening. For example, if he is walking fast toward us, we may construe this to mean he may suddenly harm us. Fear then takes us over as we prepare to defend ourselves. Our subjective experience of reality is "shaped" to serve our beliefs, regardless of the disharmony it creates in us.

This programming reflects what you believe to be true in every aspect of life. Your beliefs will continue to run how you interact with reality and how this affects your state of mind until you decide this type of coding no longer serves you. In order to create change, you will have to evaluate the particular belief that led to what you now desire to change. This requires that you face the "truth" about what you have previously believed. This personal truth is the root of the actions and reactions that have led you to your current experience. Therefore, one of the most important questions to focus on, as it relates to changing your current experience of life, is:

Is my current "truth" about this issue serving me in creating the reality I desire to experience?

For example:

- **Is my current truth about** my abilities at my job creating the position in the company that I desire to have?
- **Is my current truth about** the way I feel about myself creating the love relationship that I long for?
- **Is my current truth about** the way I nurture, discipline, and engage with my children creating the daily relationship with them that I desire?

- **Is my current truth about** my parents, siblings, or extended family creating the peace I would like to experience with all of them?
- **Is my current truth about** what I was taught from well-meaning parents, teachers, and cultural and religious leaders serving me in experiencing daily peace in my life?
- **Is my current truth about** who I AM giving me the life I desire to live?

It is critical to evaluate whether the current way you are looking at a particular area in your life is serving your intended desires. What you will eventually discover is that your current belief or truth is the key component that provides the reality you experience in any moment. What should be of great hope and comfort is that You are always the one who chooses the beliefs and truths that end up creating your life! The question is: Are you ready to evaluate and question what you currently believe so that you might open up and create something new?

> **Your life does not get better by chance, it gets better by change.**
>
> —*Jim Rohn*

Becoming more aware of the unlimited power you have to create can have a transformational effect on your life. This path leads you to realize how much you may have been unconsciously operating and making decisions out of past programming that was "installed" in you by others. This is why self-awareness is the path to complete autonomy and peace. The awareness that you are in control and that everything in your life originates from your power to choose who you are (I AM) enables you to live a life that harmonizes more with your true will, desire, and purpose.

Having this power does not mean you are always exercising this power. Surely there have been times in your adult life when you gave away your power to others. This inevitably creates some suffering because when your life is driven by the influence of others' desires, you are out of harmony with your own true will. There are not many human beings on the planet who enjoy the feeling of their life going in a direction counter to their true wishes. Nonetheless many adults still allow their parents to hold power and manipulative influence over them. Many allow their significant other to control their choices. Many are at the mercy of their children's desires. Others defer their choices to the influences of or pressure from friends or colleagues, bosses, or social, cultural, and religious dictates. These choices usually create feelings of being confined and repressed, rather than peaceful and fulfilled. We all have to do what we feel is necessary to survive each day with the people around us, but by failing to eventually take more control of your creative expression, you disconnect from your true nature and move further from a place of harmony with your universe.

Regardless of your current set of circumstances, you always hold the power of choice regarding how you interpret the information that determines your state of mind. It does not matter if you are in an unhappy marriage, in an unsatisfying job, in poor physical condition, or even in prison. Your ability to claim more control over the experience of your life is a function of how you choose to define yourself in relation to "what is" in the situation presently before you.

> You can chain me, you can torture me, you can even destroy this body, but you will never imprison my mind.
>
> —*Mahatma Gandhi*

The decision to choose new beliefs and actions is the main factor in how fast an undesired reality changes. Reality transforms when there is a shift or expansion in your consciousness (belief in who you are). This is true both for individuals and for a collective group or organization.

There are endless examples of groups, organizations, and nations that, by declaring and choosing a new way of being, transformed the world. One such famous act of collective power was the signing of the Declaration of Independence. The will of an entire country of people came together in the formulation of this document. The original, collective expression in that one document set the actions and intentions of an entire nation into motion. These ideas have since gone on to impact the entire world.

While you have complete power over your own reality, you only hold control or power over the will of another's personal experience of reality if they agree to it. The effort to manipulate and exert your will and desires at the expense of another's will not provide you the experience of more joy and peace in life. Inevitably, the creative will of others who you are trying to manipulate or repress will resist this force in a drama designed to offer this lesson to you.

Finding peace with the choices of self-expression that others make comes from understanding and accepting that you cannot determine the ultimate will of another. You can only declare your own will and follow your own heart. Peace is best found by accepting others for who they have chosen to be with the same respect you would like for your own choices of being. Love them simply for what they are offering you on your path to an expanded awareness of your own true nature.

Even the untimely death of a loved one, deemed by most cultures one of the most challenging things to embrace, can be looked upon in a different light when we understand that each of us is on our own perfect and purposeful journey through life. Extended periods of grief and pain occur in part due to the unwillingness of the bereaved to move into a state of acceptance or to see any sort of purpose for the death and loss. The understandable mourning is for the part of the self that was defined by the meaning and the experience of the relationship with someone who has now passed away.

However, as with every challenging experience, there is a purpose for those whose reality is affected by the passing. It is the faith to see a greater purpose for the chaos and pain from the passing that produces a powerful positive change in the lives of those who remain. This change can positively affect untold numbers of people in the world, providing the space for the true honor and meaning of the departed's death to surface. The most resisted life events often carry the biggest gifts of awareness. When we embrace these gifts, they empower us with an insight that can change the world.

While others' intentions, choices, and ultimate destinies are their own, who you choose to be and how you choose to express this has a significant impact on those in your life. This is a critical point in the material presented to you in this book. The way you regard or value other people along your journey is part of what influences who they believe they are. If you treat them with understanding, compassion, respect, and love, it will have a positive affect on their energy and the manner in which they treat themselves. Like a pebble dropped in a calm body of water producing ripples in an expanding circular pattern of waves, your energy radiates out to your entire world.

Everyone you come in contact with will be affected in some way by the character and intensity of your energy, and in turn they will then have a certain effect on all the lives around them. There is a multiplier effect. The energy you put out each moment ends up having an incalculable effect on the world. An output of positive energy affects your universe positively, and in turn increases the probability that you will experience more of it on the receiving end as well. An output of negative energy affects your universe negatively, creating the conditions for additional undesired experiences. Balanced, peaceful energy creates more peace. Who you decide to be sets the stage for how the energy of your universe comes back and affects you. In other words, the energy you put out is the energy you will eventually receive, as the universe is revealed to be a karmic mirror that reflects back what is projected out toward it.

> Be the change you want to see in the world.
> —*Mahatma Gandhi*

Not only do you affect your world by the energy you transmit outwardly, but your world also can have an enormous impact on you based on the way you allow it to affect you.

For example, let's say you're watching the news and you see a report of a war somewhere in the world where innocent people are being killed. As this enters your reality, your reactions (based on your power to choose) produce a response that works its way back to the situation you have seen. If you react to the experience with resistance, it will cause your energy to shift to a negative polarity. Resulting emotions in this case could range from frustration to anger, sadness, and depression.

A negative and resistant state of mind does not aid in changing and dissolving the undesired reality that caused it, but only strengthens it by putting more of this type of energy into the world. As you go through your day, if the thought of the war is having a negative effect on you, it robs you of the potential you have in each and every moment to positively affect your world. You become to a certain degree one of the casualties of the war by becoming affected to the point where your power to manifest change is suppressed by the story you keep replaying that puts you in a negative state of mind.

Regardless of your acceptance of or resistance to what is happening, certain conditions have come together perfectly to give rise to this seemingly senseless war. You may wonder, "Why? What can I do? Do I send relief money? Do I hold an antiwar protest rally?" While each of these actions may be helpful—and the choice is always yours to do whatever you believe serves you best—if your intent is to change the reality you perceive, you will have to start by coming to a place of acceptance for what already "is."

Acceptance does not mean you condone what is occurring. Rather it means coming to the true understanding of why something is occurring so you can be in a more effective state of mind to begin to change it.

Will you be consumed and respond with negativity or will you remain at peace? "I AM an individual who refuses to be affected negatively." "I AM going to remain in a place of acceptance and love, and as a result emanate love to every person, place, and thing I come in contact with." When you choose these types of self-creative statements, an entire new world of possibility opens up before you. "As I go through my day I will know that everything is as it should be, and I will release the energy of peace to everyone I pass." These new intents have the power to change everything.

Consider the following hypothetical sequence of events that might result from the decision to stay at peace and emit positive energy to your environment. While at your local store, rather than feeling down about the war and ignoring the cashier, your peaceful and present state of mind prompts you to take a moment to offer her what feels to be a well-needed, compassionate smile and thank-you. She happens to be having one of the worst days of her life. But she smiles back at you and, in an instant, feels a sense of mattering that she hasn't felt in years. This one significant change in thought alters her outlook to such a degree that she decides to put off for one more day the plans she has made to end her life later that night. Because she delays her plan, she is alive the next day to get her mail, which includes a loving letter from her estranged mother. This prompts her to call her mother and reconcile with her after years of separation and pain.

Your energy continues to ripple outward. The cashier's mother is overwhelmed with joy after speaking and reconnecting with her daughter, which prompts her to make a long-distance phone call to her brother, whom she hasn't spoken to in over a year. He happens to be the foreign ambassador to the war-torn country you saw on the news. The ambassador hears his sister's story of reconciliation with her daughter and is so moved by it that instead of giving up on the peace talks, he gets a renewed sense of inspiration and decides to hold one more meeting between the clashing parties. This is the meeting that finally accomplishes a cease-fire agreement.

While this progression of events may seem improbable, ask yourself, "How do I know?" **Your thought that this sequence is improbable or even impossible is the exact reality-creating belief that keeps you from experiencing it as possible!** You can never know what chain of events will take place due to the energy you send out to your world on a daily basis. The only evidence you will ever have that you've effected change is your reality and your resulting state of mind. How does it feel to be at peace, offer a smile, and see it shift someone else's state of mind, if only for a moment? A moment is all it takes.

The only control you ever truly have is over yourself. When you come to this understanding, you will realize the power you hold to transform your world.

The classic Frank Capra movie *It's a Wonderful Life* beautifully portrays the significant effect that one person's presence, attitude, and love have on the entire world. The main character, George Bailey (played by James Stewart), doesn't think he matters to his family, friends, and community until he is given a glimpse of what his world would look like if he had never been born. The importance and significance of every single person in relation to the whole universe is dramatically exemplified in this movie classic.

The scenario of how your energy can impact a war on the other side of the globe can just as easily be an example of how your presence, attitude, and love determine your fate in getting a certain desired job, meeting an ideal mate, or changing your financial situation. In every moment you are adding to or detracting from the conditions that result in your self-creation and the creation of the collective experience of all things in the universe.

It is really incredible to see that by making the decision to choose to be a more powerful light in the world and heal your own suffering, you help to heal the suffering of others, too. Every human being seeks the same validation from their reality: to be accepted and loved for who they are so they can experience themselves as they have believed and declared (I AM). When you make the choice to see your own perfection and the purpose of your being, it allows you to see the perfection in everyone else. By offering compassion and love to those in your world, you have the effect of helping to raise the self-love in all those around you. You help them by telling them through your energy, actions, and words that who they are right now is good enough. They don't have to be anybody else but who they are being for you to accept their presence in the world. The result is that a change for them is a change for you.

Who you choose to be in each moment, and the energy you send out that demonstrates this, works in very powerful and subtle ways. Many times we don't even realize how much of a difference this can make in what possibilities manifest for us. The following are some examples. The energy you put out could be the difference between:

- Getting a speeding ticket and getting a warning from a police officer.
- Being introduced by a friend to a quality man or woman for a date and never being thought of or mentioned.
- Being respected, admired, and treated well by your significant other and being ignored, disrespected, and unappreciated.

- Signing the client or closing the deal and being told, "No thanks."

Many doors that you never see are opening and closing for you based on the energy that is generated from your true will to be (I AM). Like a magnet, this power draws from the field of infinite possibilities and condenses it into what you experience. This has been called accessing the quantum field, and you do it continuously.

It is important to realize that you cannot fool the universe. Who you demonstrate yourself to be has to be authentic or else you will eventually have to face the result of building your life on an illusion. Life by its nature of revealing possibility is designed to continually dissolve any illusions and limits you hold in your mind. These powerful revelations generally occur in your most challenging moments of accepting truth. As much as you may fear having one of these moments, they are actually great gifts because they offer you the self-awareness that leads to a more fulfilling life.

> If you make choices of being from an illusion of who you are, you are only creating a bigger illusion of yourself that will ultimately be dismantled by truth.

How you respond to each situation you encounter and who you choose to be each day is forever up to you. The question is if you are looking for change, will you repeat yesterday's undesired reality by acting from the same fears and a sense of limits (an idea that always leads to another illusion), or will you follow your heart and travel the narrow road of fearless truth and self-acceptance? If you desire more peace and fulfillment, move through the journey of life confidently choosing to be who you *desire* to be, not who you think you *need* to be in order for others to love you. Eternal peace is found in your truest and most powerful choices of being, the choices that allow you to love yourself.

There are thousands of extraordinary examples from history and pop culture of individuals who have made powerful creative choices of being. Many of the choices they made, which have produced an array of different outcomes, were verbalized publicly as I AM statements. The reality of what each of these individuals accomplished demonstrates how much they believed in the declarations they made about themselves. Below are a few examples.

I AM a firm believer in the people.—Abraham Lincoln

I AM going to be an artist.—Georgia O'Keeffe

I AM my own experiment. I AM my own work of art.
    —Madonna

I AM the toughest golfer mentally.—Tiger Woods

I AM enough of an artist to draw freely upon my imagination.
    —Albert Einstein

I AM always trying that which I cannot do, in order that I may
    learn how to do it.—Pablo Picasso

I AM not ashamed to confess that I AM ignorant of what I do
    not know.—Marcus Tullius Cicero

I AM a little pencil in the hand of a writing God who is sending
    a love letter to the world.—Mother Teresa

I AM not a has-been. I AM a will be.—Lauren Bacall

I AM where I AM because I believe in all possibilities.
    —Whoopi Goldberg

I AM an opera singer. This is how people will remember me.
   —Luciano Pavarotti

I AM prepared to die, but there is no cause for which I AM
   prepared to kill.—Mahatma Gandhi

I AM the way, the truth, and the light.—Jesus of Nazareth

I AM still learning.—Michelangelo Buonarroti

I AM awake.—Gautama Buddha

I AM the greatest.—Muhammad Ali

Just like the I AM statements you make, all the preceding statements represent a certain piece of who each of the individuals above believed himself or herself to be. Every I AM statement gives an instruction to the ego. The deeper you believe in your I AM statements, the more intensely and fearlessly your ego will act to create the sensory experience of it for you in your reality.

The last quote in the list, one that is well known, gives a glimpse into the magic and power of self-creative statements. Muhammad Ali stated that he was the greatest boxer before he experienced being the greatest boxer. Because he stated and believed "I AM the greatest," his ego enabled him to fearlessly manifest the exact conditions necessary to achieve and experience it.

Your life at this moment is the sum total of the collective choices you have made throughout your journey. These choices have always been based on who you believed you were in the moment you made them. You will forever be the reflection of your thoughts about what is possible for you right now.

The thought "I AM" is creation itself.

Who you decide to be from the unlimited possibilities of expression in front of you is limited only by you. Your past was once your future. Today you can make different choices of being from the ones you made yesterday, and tomorrow you can make different ones from today. However, NOW is the only moment you ever have in which to decide and declare who you are and, thus, how you will experience this reality called life.

The power of choice is the power of the universe that exists within you. If you claim this power through understanding the infinite love and perfection that you are, eternal peace and tranquillity will be yours.

Chapter 16

Your FAITH
to Take Action

Without action the dream will only remain a dream.

The truest testament of your will to create the life you imagine for yourself will be in your actions. Your actions are always a direct revelation of who you believe that you are. Anytime you choose new actions it demonstrates that you believe something new is possible for you. The reality you experience can only change when you put new thought into action or as it has been said, "when the talk becomes the walk."

Up until this moment your life has been the sum of all of your past I AM statements and actions. These thoughts and actions have led to every experience that has created who you are today. Although many try to convince themselves that they are someone or something that they are not, the universe cannot be fooled. You can deny, delude, and attempt to manipulate the truth for a while, but who you are will continue to be presented to you through the circumstances of your life. You cannot escape the truth of who you are unless you decide to accept and change who you are.

> Acknowledging and accepting a particular truth is the only path out of the constant undesired experience of this truth.

Your thoughts and actions will begin to change and evolve in a more positive way as your faith in yourself deepens. When you uncover the real thoughts you have about yourself that limit you in some way, you will be able to uncover the creative source of your actions, and this awareness will free you to declare and create a new version of you. Once again, in the next moment, your actions will reveal the true nature of the new thoughts you've just declared.

What is interesting is how we can go on believing things about ourselves even though we aren't taking any of the actions needed to express that what we say is actually true. There is nothing wrong with this until the inability to experience what we believe to be true causes a negative state of mind. This is the point at which our actions will need to validate the belief we hold as true. Any idea in your mind of who you are only works until the time you need to experience it as real. You will find yourself in a peaceful state of mind only when you achieve a state of harmony between your beliefs and your experience of the world.

For example, if you believe you are in good shape or fit, the litmus test is to take off your clothes and stand in front of a full-length mirror and state, "I AM someone with a fit body." If you believe it and the reflection convinces you of it, you will remain at peace and feel nothing but love for your reflection in the mirror. If the image does not match the definition, you will feel some measure of discontent, indicating your true level of desire to be fit. The reason you would feel discontent is that your belief (in this case of having a fit body) does not match feedback from outer reality (in this case, your reflection in the mirror). This inability to validate your self-concept is what creates the friction or internal conflict.

If you have grown tired of the negative energy that is generated each time you have a thought about what kind of physical shape you are in, you have two choices. First, regardless of what culture or the media tries to tell you, there is no absolute idea of what a "fit" body looks like. You could change your idea of what fit is to match exactly how your body looks right now. This choice will put your thought immediately in harmony with the experience of you. Second, if you want to match the current pop culture idea of what fit means, you could take the consistent actions that will change your body to eventually match the public's idea of what a "fit" body is.

The first choice requires no action. It is only a change in your mental perception of the word "fit." Whether or not you truly have changed your perception will be evident in your state of mind upon the thought of your body being fit under your new definition.

The second choice requires creative action to reshape your body to conform to your mental image. A new diet and exercise plan or other means will have to be implemented to achieve this path of change. How much you really desire to be your idea of fit will be represented in how much you act on these choices. If you have really and truly changed your I AMs about who you are and who you desire to be, the results will manifest themselves from these thoughts. This is true for all kinds of less tangible beliefs, such as "I AM a good listener" and "I AM responsible with money." Your beliefs will create your reality only when these beliefs lead to the consistent actions that are necessary to achieve whatever is believed.

Knowing you are capable and worthy of achieving what you desire increases the probability of it manifesting in your life. This will happen in a much faster experience of time if you fully open to the truth of the current circumstances and what it takes to create what you desire along the way. Denial and delusion will only serve to stretch the amount of time it will take to make your intentions real.

For example, if you start your program to become fit and have expectations of losing thirty pounds in two weeks, you may have some more learning to do. Your inability to achieve this result no matter what action you take will provide you with an opportunity to face your false beliefs about what is possible, and then to set a timetable that's in harmony with what is possible for the rate of weight loss for human beings.

Anytime you openly accept the invaluable feedback that comes from failing to achieve your goals, you are actually gaining necessary new insights. This is the critical information that leads you to new, more effective actions that bring you closer to what you desire.

Anything in your life that is causing you disharmony and unease can be handled in this same manner. You can either change your beliefs and perception of how the object of your discontent represents you (so that it no longer affects your self-image) or you can take new actions that will lead you to change.

Here's another example. You are in an unsatisfying job. You are unhappy both with what you do and with how much you are being compensated for it. As in the preceding example, you have two choices. First, you can shift your perception and belief of what is "satisfying work" and what is "enough compensation" to match the satisfaction and compensation levels you are currently experiencing. Or second, you can take the actions necessary to change to a job you believe is worthy of you—in this case, a job that you believe fulfills you and compensates you well.

The second choice requires you to change your I AMs. It is denial to say, "I AM someone who can and will make more money and have a more satisfying job," without taking action to create this outcome in your life. In this particular situation the thought may appear to say, "I can," but the inability to take any action would be the truth of a thought that says, "I can't change jobs," "I don't desire to change jobs," or "I AM afraid of changing jobs."

Your actions always speak louder than your words. If you want to see the beliefs you are truly operating out of in this world, just look at your current actions.

Your level of desire to achieve a new reality is always apparent in the intensity and focus of your actions. In attaining a fit body, if you stay on a strict diet and work out five days a week, you will experience a fit body much sooner than if you don't pay attention to your diet and you work out only once or twice a week. In the example of looking for a new job, if you were to send out five résumés a day and go on three interviews a week, your reality would have the opportunity to change a lot faster than if you were to do nothing. Even if you get turned down for many of these jobs, by simply going through the process you

are receiving the necessary feedback about the conditions you
need to meet in order to be eligible for the type of job you desire. Whether it is more schooling or additional job experience,
with this new information you have the opportunity to make
the needed changes.

The choices you make and the actions you take toward your
dreams and goals are always completely up to you. You determine which ones are right and which ones are wrong for you
based on your true intent. You also determine to a certain degree how much time it will take to accomplish your goals. The
key message is that you are who you are right now, until you
declare and act differently.

Your I AM statements contain the integral instructions that
drive the ongoing creation of your life. These beliefs that form
your personal story are constantly changing and evolving. As
you change your story, your ego follows along perfectly with a
new script of actions that lead to a new reality. If your ego fights
change or hesitates in any way, this is an indication that you do
not yet fully believe in the new you.

You can ask the right questions, you can allow the answers,
and you can believe you have changed who you are; the truth,
however, will be in your actions. Without new actions nothing
will change. The only thing that stops you at this point is fear.
When standing at the forefront of any change, there may be the
fear of leaving the known self and moving to an unknown self.
This is when your thoughts will try to hold you back by telling
you what is not possible, what you are not capable of, and what
you don't deserve. Again it will be reiterated that all of these
limiting self-ideas are false. Your potential to experience more
of your perfection is limited only by you. **No matter what has**

EGO IS YOUR BUDDY & WILL
SUPPORT YOU.

occurred in your life, in this moment you are worthy of any possibility.

When standing at the threshold of a new way of experiencing life, one word that has been used for thousands of years contains all the wisdom and power that is needed to turn your belief in who you are into a living reality:

FAITH

This word has been interpreted in many different ways throughout the history of humanity. Below are two definitions. The first definition of faith pertains to you as the *experiencer* in the present moment of life.

Faith is the unconditional love and acceptance of the self as perfect and complete in each and every moment.

The second definition of faith applies to you as the *creator* when you are faced with any change in life.

Faith is the willingness to enter into the experience of what is unknown with the full acceptance that whatever becomes known will be perfect for you and your journey of life.

One definition is of the faith in who you currently are and the other definition is of the faith in who you will become. Embracing the energy of faith is the tipping point to a new experience of life. When we act upon our faith, we are demonstrating that we understand the perfection of life. We can see how the experiences in life are never wasted.

Those who live in a state of faith know that all experiences are essential for the evolution of their self-awareness. When things happen that at the time seem to have no useful purpose, faith works to bridge them to the moment the purpose of the event becomes clear. It may not be until months or even years later that they are finally able to connect the dots. But they end up saying, "If it had not been for Y, I never would have experienced X." Different people they met and past events they went through suddenly seem crucial to changing their lives for the better.

If you take a moment to reflect on some of your most resisted or undesired experiences of the past, you may see how each of these events shaped who you are today. The seeds for much of your true growth in life often come from your most confusing, disappointing, and challenging experiences. Can you begin to see now how those conditions were necessary to help create who you are today? Now imagine you are your future self, looking back at this time in your life. What will you take from this moment? What seeds of your future are offered to you through this experience?

If we can accept that there is perfection within our uncertain moments, it helps us have the faith to overcome the fear and resistance that are the main obstacles to taking the action that produces real tangible results. The unconditional acceptance of each moment of our lives is the creative path to a peaceful and harmonious way of life.

Faith is taking the first step even when you don't see the whole staircase.

—*Martin Luther King, Jr.*

Faith and fear are at opposite ends of the spectrum of awareness. The following list shows what characteristics each of these states of being can manifest.

Fear is *constricting*.	Faith is *releasing*.
Fear is *imbalance*.	Faith is *balance*.
Fear is *darkness*.	Faith is *light*.
Fear is *repulsion*.	Faith is *attraction*.
Fear is *blindness*.	Faith is *sight*.
Fear is *friction*.	Faith is *harmony*.
Fear is *thinking*.	Faith is *knowing*.
Fear is *judgment*.	Faith is *understanding*.
Fear is *resistance*.	Faith is *acceptance*.
Fear is *need*.	Faith is *completeness*.
Fear is *contemptuous*.	Faith is *compassionate*.
Fear is *boastful*.	Faith is *humble*.
Fear is *self-centered*.	Faith is *selfless*.
Fear is *of time*.	Faith is *timeless*.
Fear is *contraction*.	Faith is *expansion*.
Fear is *illusionary*.	Faith is *real*.
Fear is *lies*.	Faith is *truth*.
Fear is *finite*.	Faith is *infinite*.
Fear is *hateful*.	Faith is *loving*.
Fear is *division*.	Faith is *unity*.
Fear is *chaos*.	Faith is *peace*.

If your desire for a more peaceful and fulfilling life continues, one of the key concepts you will need to understand and embrace is faith. Throughout your life, the ability to achieve what you desire will be either thwarted or achieved depend-

BARRY

ing upon your level of faith in yourself. The more faith you have when deciding on a new version of yourself, the easier it will be for you to demonstrate that new version through your actions.

Remember when you were first learning to drive a car? That was a completely unknown experience. Your first attempt to drive on a freeway or busy street most likely caused you a certain amount of anxiety or fear. However, the more you had the faith to get behind the wheel and drive without incident, the more your faith in driving a car safely grew. You became less fearful about your abilities and more faithful. As an unknown experience became known, your belief in your ability to drive became more secure. The more certain you become about who you are, the more automatic faith you have in taking action on this definition.

Your beliefs are always being tested by your experiences. As any driver who has been in a car accident knows, your faith in your ability to drive may have needed to be restored during those first few days, weeks, or even months back behind the wheel. A tighter grip on the car's steering wheel or perhaps a more timid driving style than usual may have been the result of a shaken faith such as this. However, through the act of continuing to drive and demonstrating a level of faith in the belief that you can safely travel in a car, you are granted the experience.

An alternate experience is to live in fear and never drive again. Because fear constricts the possibilities in your mind to only the worst, it can be one of the biggest obstacles to taking the actions that move you forward in life. This could be your response to every disappointing, unpleasant, or humiliating experience of your life that you fear repeating. You may fear not being loved again after a breakup, never getting a new job after being fired, or getting sick just like the last time. The key point to consider is that what has occurred is only one of an infinite number of possibilities. This possibility, in being manifested, had and has a purpose in your life. Accepting what has occurred and realizing that many other future results are possible is all that's needed to begin making new choices and taking new actions toward your desires.

> Where there is faith there is no fear, only the space for powerful creative action.

Every moment of your life holds the opportunity for endless possibility unless you don't believe this to be the case. If you lock onto a negative experience as being the only one that is possible, you are laying the seeds for a repeat experience. This can lead to tremendous pain and suffering. It stems from a belief that puts your attention and focus on only one possibility in a given area of life. For instance, "My job *never* works out," "I AM *always* feeling sick," "I *never* meet the right one," and "Things will *never* change." Holding limiting ideas about life experiences that haven't happened yet is a sign of a closed and limited mind. These types of beliefs are what cause the actions you take that work toward creating the reality of the negative statements. You become stuck in a self-fulfilling reality loop that can only be broken by having the faith to believe in and take action on a new possibility.

> Don't discard possibilities simply because you haven't experienced them yet. As a matter of fact, that's exactly why you haven't experienced them yet.

Your future will only incorporate as much of your past as you bring into your present identity. Your ability to experience a more fulfilling way of life is based on your willingness to let the past be the past, realizing that this is a brand-new moment to become something new. If you are unhappy with your previous self-definition and actions, you can change them. The amazing power you have to create emerges at the moment you allow yourself to open to a new self-definition that includes more of a belief in what is possible for you.

You always have the choice of listening to fear or faith. When operating according to fear, you are creating from a sense of limits and what is not possible versus creating from the unlimited nature of what is possible. You will only take the actions needed to manifest the life you desire from a state of faith. This faith originates from the realization and acceptance of your worth and ability to experience more of what's possible for you.

Here are a few examples:

Fear says, "If I leave my significant other, I'll never find anyone else who will love me."
Faith says, "If I leave my significant other, I'll finally be open to the opportunity to find a fulfilling relationship. I'll finally allow myself an opportunity to experience true love."

Fear says, "Even if I look for a new job, I won't get hired."
Faith says, "If I look for a new job, I may finally find a job I love and have been waiting for all of my life."

Fear says, "If I AM myself and reveal my true feelings, people won't love me."

Faith says, "If I AM myself and reveal my true feelings, I will love myself for it, because I will be free of feeling that I need to put on a false persona. I will never have to worry about losing love, because I will know with absolute certainty that those who love me love me for my true self."

Fear says, "I AM not."

Faith says, "I AM."

Faith is fear's kryptonite, and it opens up a new world of infinite possibility for you. Whether you want to be the next Steve Jobs or Steven Spielberg, faith is the driving power that puts you on the path to the experience.

To live your dream requires taking consistent fearless action to make it happen. "Driven" is a word that describes a person who puts a desire into action. It takes a certain degree of desire to dare to ask, "How?" It takes another level of desire to face and accept the answer, and it takes even more intensity of desire to achieve the level of faith and belief necessary to relentlessly pursue the actions that manifest your dreams into reality. This is the path that every human being who has ever created anything had to take to experience a dream come true.

The future belongs to those who believe in the beauty of their dreams.

—*Eleanor Roosevelt*

There are endless examples of people who refused to listen to what fear had to say about who they were or what was possible, and acted instead on their faith in who they dreamed they could become.

The story of Daniel "Rudy" Ruettiger is a powerful example from the world of sports of faith against all odds. As a kid, Rudy's dream was to play football for the University of Notre Dame in Indiana. But Rudy did not have the size or athletic ability that would even remotely qualify him for the team, and his grades weren't even good enough to get him into the university.

After a couple of years of bringing up his grades at another university, he applied for the fourth time to Notre Dame and was finally accepted. He then beat ridiculous odds and made it onto the team. However, he was only used as an extra player to play against the starters during practice and was not allowed to dress in his uniform or go on the field with the team on game day. Nonetheless, Rudy stuck it out, holding on to his dream of one day actually playing in a game.

This daily dedication and unwavering faith eventually produced an amazing result. In Rudy's last game as a player at Notre Dame, he was finally allowed to dress with the team. With less than three minutes left in his last game, Rudy's lifelong vision was realized, as the coach sent him onto the field for the final few plays. On the last play of the game Rudy sacked the opposing quarterback and was forever immortalized as his teammates triumphantly carried him off the field. He is one of only two players in Notre Dame football history who has ever been carried off the field. Committed to film in the 1993 motion picture *Rudy*, this inspiring story is an incredibly strong example and testament to the power of faith and taking fearless action in pursuit of a dream.

For untold numbers of people throughout history, faith has been known to produce the miracles necessary to overcome what are seen by others to be insurmountable odds. Life is filled with examples of everyday people who demonstrated incredible will and faith to create a powerful and positive effect on their world. From Helen Keller, who overcame the inability to see, hear, and speak in order to give hope to millions with disability, to Nelson Mandela, who survived twenty-seven years in prison and helped to end apartheid in South Africa, ultimately becoming the country's president. From Susan B. Anthony, who relentlessly spearheaded the movement that gave women the right to vote, to Mahatma Gandhi, who single-handedly galvanized the country of India into nonviolently attaining independence from British rule. From Harriet Tubman, who escaped slavery and abuse to help hundreds of other slaves to freedom, to Elie Wiesel, who survived the horrors of the death camps during the Holocaust to tell about it and earn the Nobel Peace Prize in 1986 for his humanitarian work.

These pages could be filled with many more examples of people all over the world who have demonstrated the awesome power of will and faith and how it changed their world. What is important to remember is that each of these individuals faced the events they were confronted with and used the power of belief and choice to shape their own destiny. This is the same power you have right now to shape your own future.

The only thing more powerful than the word is the act.

Every human being has an endless supply of potential within him or her. This potential can only be made real through faith. Faith enables each of us to believe in ourselves enough to continue to move forward toward our goals and dreams no matter the degree or the amount of setbacks we face along the way. This is the process that changes the world.

The journey of Abraham Lincoln to become the sixteenth president of the United States is another example of unwavering faith. Lincoln was eventually responsible for changing the course of history in the United States with the Emancipation Proclamation and the Thirteenth Amendment to the Constitution, which abolished slavery in America. The following are some of the experiences he had to go through in order to become the man and president that he was:

- At age twenty-two, he failed in business.
- At age twenty-three, he was defeated for a seat in the House of Representatives.
- At age twenty-four, he failed again in business.
- At age twenty-five, he was elected to Congress.
- At age twenty-six, his sweetheart died.
- At age twenty-seven, he had a nervous breakdown.
- At age twenty-nine, he was defeated for Speaker of the House.
- At age thirty-one, he was defeated for Elector in the U.S. Electoral College.
- At age thirty-four, he was defeated for reelection to Congress.
- At age thirty-seven, he was elected to Congress.
- At age thirty-nine, he was defeated for reelection to Congress.
- At age forty-six, he was defeated for a seat in the Senate.

- At age forty-seven, he was defeated for vice president.
- At age forty-nine, he was defeated for a seat in the Senate.

Lincoln was elected president when he was fifty-one. His path of persistence is a demonstration of the truest meaning of faith. The path of his life reveals how faith is expressed and validated only by the continual action that is demonstrated throughout life. These consistent expressions have the power to change everything.

Water continually dropping will wear hard rocks hollow.

—*Plutarch*

Declaring a new version of who you are is not enough to change reality. Only the true belief in the steps you take that follow, which validate these declarations, allows you to experience a new sense of self. Change is always up to you. Will you now:

- ask the questions to which you desire answers?
- allow yourself to receive those answers?
- acknowledge the reality before you?
- accept the truth of who you have been?
- face your fears and illusions?
- embrace your perfection?
- love who you are now?
- choose who you desire to be?
- act out of this new self?
- experience fulfillment in every moment?

There is no right or wrong answer to any of the preceding questions. You can experience your life any way you choose.

Whether or not you have been aware of it, you have been exercising this free will each day. The magical implication is that
at any moment you can choose to change your choices and,
hence, your life. Your life from this moment on is an open book.
You will write the story in your next thought and your next
action.

> **And the time came when the risk to remain tight in a bud
> was more painful than the risk it took to blossom.**
>
> —*Anaïs Nin*

You may at one time or another have heard the saying, "Dream
big." While this is an important idea, it is only one part of the
equation. There is a big difference between dreaming big and
believing in the dream. The distinction is the difference between thinking about what you desire and actually living it.
The way toward the dream is to consistently act in accordance
with what is necessary to create the dream. You have to believe
in your worth as a person enough to allow yourself to experience it. You have to have the faith that you are capable enough
of following through until the very last condition is in place.
You have to love yourself fully. Self-love is what breathes life
into faith, and once you have it you can create at will.

> **What we call the search for happiness is no more of a
> secret than our willingness to choose life.**
>
> —*Leo Buscaglia*

Many people talk about courage and how it is needed to achieve
what they desire. This is only part of the truth. Faith is the real

element behind the strength of the actions that have the appearance of courage. Courage without true faith is destined to yield to fear. Only faith, which is the pure belief in ourselves, holds the power to dissolve any fear and allow for the actions that put us on the path to our dreams.

The Brush

As each day unfolds, it is ours to create.
Our hands hold destiny, producing our fate.
Shape it as we wish—this picture anyway.
Paint this piece unbounded; see what our spirit has to say.

Each stroke of the brush has meaning in its depth,
Bearing memories for a lifetime, in our minds safely kept.
Merge together these images into a story that they tell,
One of unique makeup, like the intricacy of a shell.

As glorious as we make it this painting that is ours
Or as confined as imagined like a window with bars,
The thing to remember is that our hand drives each stroke.
There's always the opportunity to fix what feels broke.

Every moment unveils a piece of spectacular art:
The depth of our soul, the beating of our heart.
So keep your movements your own, no influence on your
vision,
Or else your life's story will be of others' decision.

If the canvas complete does not settle in your mind,
Dive deep inside. See what you find.

What did you make? What purpose did it serve?
Why this color or shade? Why that line or curve?

Know the display that you made and each line that was drawn
Was perfect in time—how could you be wrong?
Before night you should repeat that this journey is long.
A new canvas each day to portray your desired song.

So reflect and consider the next stroke you make.
The only suffering that befalls you is if you paint one
that's fake.
Follow the love that is the center of your core.
Only masterpieces you'll create for now and evermore.

Chapter 17

Your LOVE of You

Everything is self-fulfilling.

Relax and take a big deep breath because right here and right now you are exactly where you are supposed to be. There is no other place or time. This is it. As with every other moment of your life, this moment holds great purpose for you. The perfection of what you are experiencing has emerged from every question you have asked and every circumstance and experience you have gone through and overcome to get to this moment and these words now.

The gift of this eternal moment is what you decide to take from it. What has been offered in many ways throughout these words is the liberating self-awareness that the way you create and experience each moment of life is always in your hands. You determine the quality of life by your willingness to love who you are right now. This love is what leads you to the beautiful state of acceptance of the world around you. It is also what brings you to the recognition that you are always choosing the conditions that create what "will be" in your life.

The journey of self-awareness you are taking is the path of answers that eliminates the disharmony related to the questions that come up in your mind about *who, what, why,* and *how.* Be-coming more conscious of who you really are is the essence of your transformation into a more peaceful, creative, and fulfilled person. This new way of being in the world comes from accept-ing, loving, and honoring your own existence.

True change begins and ends with a change in You.
Everything else is just a distraction that stretches the
experience of time.

Unconditional love is the most powerful force in the universe, which is the reason why the thoughts you have that express love and acceptance for who you are right now—just as you are—are such an important piece of your spiritual evolution. Uncondi-tional love dissolves fear, resistance, separation, and any suffering related to these conditions. What is left when all of these illusions disperse is the experience of peace, harmony, and unity.

When you love yourself completely, because you understand that any reason that holds you back from this type of love is completely false, you allow for the fullest potential of who you are to come alive and shine its light. This light and energy has the power to benefit the whole world. Free from need, and ask-ing nothing, unconditional love is the spirit and energy of being in service to all of life. When you love and accept yourself at this level, your whole experience of life changes.

The evolution of mind to more self-love releases you to see the amazing number of creative possibilities for your life that you never knew existed before. Along with these new possi-bilities comes a sense of appreciation for all that you are and for everything you have experienced that has brought you to this moment. Just as all the people who have come in and out of your life have had an important impact on you in some way, you have also had an extremely important impact and purpose in the lives of others.

The great message that the universe is attempting to bring to you each and every day is that YOU MATTER. Every thought and every action and reaction you have had up until this moment has served a perfect purpose in your life and the lives of every person you have come in contact with. By seeing the truth of the perfection of your past and making peace with it, you step into the only moment you ever have, this one right now. The present moment is the only place where you can harness more of your unlimited power to create who you desire to be and how you decide to matter in the world.

You are not who you think you are, but always so much more.

Who you are right now is not who you were last month, last week, yesterday, or even five minutes ago. You are infinitely changing by expanding your consciousness through the process of experience, interpretation, action, and reaction with each event and moment you have encountered. What has been presented to you through this book has been a part of this transformation. The following statements may reflect recent shifts in your awareness that illustrate a new change in your capacity for self-love.

- You previously held *regret* because you thought you should have done better in the past. Now you have *acceptance* because you know that if you could have done better, you would have.
- You previously held *contempt* for others because you thought they should have done better. Now you have *compassion* for

them knowing if they could have done better, they would have.

- You previously had *pride* because you thought you were "better than" someone else. Now you have *humility* because you know there is no such thing as being better or worse.

- You previously felt *hate* because you resisted something or someone's existence. Now you feel *love* because you understand everything you experience has a greater purpose that is always for you.

- You previously felt *shame* because you thought you didn't matter. Now you have *honor* because you understand that you always matter.

- You previously experienced *chaos* because you resisted change. Now you know *peace* because you embrace the infinite changing existence that you are.

- You previously had *fear* because you thought that you would not be loved. Now you have *faith* because you discovered that the ultimate source of love is within you.

When these ideas are part of who you are, you will know peace. Once you see and believe in the reality of your moment-to-moment perfection, you will experience perfection! You always know where you stand in relation to this awareness because your capacity for self-love and acceptance is always reflected to you in the experiences and energy of your life.

Life is an eternal journey of expanding your awareness to the knowledge of more of what is possible for you. Every day, every minute, and every second your awareness is growing. As your awareness grows, your thoughts and beliefs change. New possibilities emerge as you learn more about yourself and the unlimited nature of what you're capable of knowing and creating. Peace and serenity are the result of the continual creation, acceptance, and expansion of personal possibility.

The rate of this growth to a more fulfilling life is always up to you. You will ask questions and the answers will come in every corner of your reality as no experience in your life is wasted. With mathematical precision the answers to your questions show up in direct relation to the intensity of your desire to experience them. They are right here right now. You are currently on a path where you are becoming more aware of this truth.

One example out of the millions of examples in your reality of how this information at one time or another has been presented to you comes from one of the most well-known movies of all time, *The Wizard of Oz*. Some interesting similarities with your own journey may be found in the allegory of this timeless movie classic.

The story begins as the main character, Dorothy, wonders about a magical place existing "somewhere over the rainbow." She is hopeful and longs for a new experience of a better place than the situation and place that she is in now. Soon after, a storm appears, symbolizing her current state of confusion. After getting caught in a tornado and knocked unconscious, she wakes up to discover she's in a new place where everything looks a little bit different from the way she previously looked at life. This is when the filmmakers poignantly change the movie from black and white to a film with brilliant color. Dorothy is confused and at the same time amazed at this new world she sees before her. This is when she begins her journey home.

The story of Dorothy's journey is filled with just about every metaphor for what is required for each one of our paths through life, as we learn more about who we are and the type of lives we are capable of living. Each of us seeks guidance and help along the way, just as Dorothy does in finding Glinda, the Good Witch of the North, her trusted guide of wisdom. That the Wicked Witch of the West is always trying to stop Dorothy on her quest to go home is symbolic of the fear in life that always tries to stop us from taking the action to get to where we desire to go.

The three prominent characters who accompany Dorothy on her journey are metaphors for three very important qualities that we all already possess that need to emerge for us to experience peace and fulfillment in our lives. The first quality, represented by the Scarecrow, is the ability to think, reason, contemplate, ask questions, and realize the great power within us to understand life. The second quality, represented by the Tin Man, is the ability to offer love, compassion, empathy, and forgiveness for all others and, most important, for ourselves. The third quality, represented by the Cowardly Lion, is courage, the ability to face fear with faith and take the fearless action toward what each of us desires to experience.

The three of them set off with Dorothy to see the great Wizard of Oz, who she believes will help her to get home. Before he agrees to help them, he tells them to get the broomstick of the Wicked Witch of the West and bring it back to him. Dorothy must come face-to-face with her fear before her desire to go home can be fulfilled. Her desire to go home is so intense that she agrees to take on the challenge. Interestingly, in facing her fear of the Witch, she literally and figuratively dissolves the fear forever. As irony would have it, all it took was a simple bucket of water that she tosses on the Scarecrow, whom the Witch has lit on fire. In protecting him, she accidentally splashes the Witch, who simply melts away.

Now in possession of the Witch's broomstick, Dorothy heads

off to see the Wizard and unmask another great illusion. When Dorothy, Scarecrow, Tin Man, and Lion arrive to give the broomstick to the Wizard, Dorothy's dog, Toto, who is not under any illusion about the Wizard, pulls a curtain back, revealing a simple elderly man pushing buttons and pulling levers. The illusion of the great and powerful Oz has been unmasked. Relenting, the man behind the curtain does offer to help them. He tells them that they really aren't missing the things they think they are, but merely the recognition that they already have these things within them. So he gives a diploma to the Scarecrow, a medal of courage to the Cowardly Lion, and a ticking heart to the Tin Man, telling him, "A heart is not judged by how much you love, but by how much you are loved."

The "Wizard" offers Dorothy a ride home in his hot-air balloon. But his plan goes awry as he takes off without her and knows no way of controlling the balloon to bring it back. Dorothy is left to face the final truth: The great and powerful Wizard she believed in so strongly and who she thought could get her home has no power at all. Finally, Dorothy must turn to see where the real power is. Through the help of her guide, Glinda, she realizes that the whole time this great power was already within her. The Scarecrow seems annoyed when he asks, "Then why didn't you tell her before?" to which Glinda responds, "Because she wouldn't have believed me. She had to learn it for herself."

As the final act, Dorothy repeats a sentence, "There's no place like home, there's no place like home, there's no place like home," demonstrating the most powerful thought in the universe: the thought of love and gratitude by accepting and being thankful for everything you have right where you are now. As she embraces this truth, the journey is complete.

You are on your own unique journey down the Yellow Brick Road. The experience of life is your great school of awareness, in which you come to realize more of who and what you really are. As you learn this you become more and more peaceful right where you are now. You were born with the great capacity to think for yourself, to ask questions and receive answers, to love and be loved, and to overcome any obstacle or fear. The great power of the creation and the control over your experience of life lies within you. Peace, harmony, and a fulfilling life are no further away from you than your own two feet.

The journey of consciously creating life is a repeating cycle of the following five steps:

1. **ASK** your questions.   *Desire*
2. **ACCEPT** the truth of your answers.   *Will*
3. **CHOOSE** who you are (I AM).   *Power*
4. **ACT** on this belief in yourself.   *Faith*
5. **EXPERIENCE** the perfection of the results.   *Love*

The universe can only respond to the identity you truly believe you embody. If you believe you are in need of the right person, a better job, more money, a different body or look, or a more enriching relationship with your children or your spouse, then the universe will surely grant you that experience through the continued creation of need. You will thirst and need as you do until you realize that you are your own unlimited source of fulfillment. When you love yourself enough, and see your true unlimited worth and perfection, you will no longer declare yourself lacking or incomplete in any way. Instead you will have the faith to say, "I AM worthy of my dreams," and, by doing so, grant yourself permission to take the new actions that create them.

You are never who you were or who you will be, only who you choose to be now.

As it is said in different religions, "God helps those who help themselves." Which simply means that you can't just say that you believe you are worthy, not act on the belief, and then expect what you desire from the universe to just magically appear. You must display your true love and belief in yourself by taking faith-filled action. This is what the universe directly responds to. As you display your faith and love, you become a well of strength and inspiration for others to drink from in their times of thirst, as they meet their own challenges on the path of self-discovery and peace of mind.

Since your beliefs in who you are (I AM) represent the key to what you create in your world, several powerful thoughts have been listed below to consider for your life.

Before this moment, if you had guilt, shame, or regret about certain experiences in your life, the burden of these thoughts may have created many moments of suffering for you. To be free from the suffering, choose to replace them with the following loving thought:

"I know that for each and every moment of my life I AM doing the best that I can. While I may not condone some of the actions that I have taken previously, I will draw upon the wisdom gained from those experiences to choose

differently right now. I will choose new actions because I
have declared that I AM not who I was, but rather I AM
who I decide to be right now."

If you had judgment and contempt for people you thought were
responsible for the current conditions of your life, the burden of
these thoughts may have made you feel angry, hurt, and physically drained. Let these thoughts rule you no more. Choose to
replace them with the following thought:

"I take full responsibility for the decisions in my life that
have led me to this moment. If I have previously given my
power of choice away, as the conscious director of my life I
choose to reclaim this power of choice now. I understand
that everything I experience has a purpose related to my
highest intent. At any given moment the universe is always
showing me what I need to learn and accept to get exactly
where I have asked to go. I choose to accept everyone and
everything in my experience that allows me to learn the
lessons I have brought myself. I understand that everyone is
doing the best he or she can in his or her own way for
daily survival, just as I AM."

If you have not believed yourself good enough or worthy enough
to have the experiences you dream about, you may have been
feeling directionless, lost, and trapped in the current experience
of your life. Let these beliefs run your life no more. Choose to
replace them with the following thought:

"I AM worthy of peace, happiness, and every experience I
desire. My future is an open book, where the only

limitations of my experience are the ones I set for myself based on my own self-love. I choose to allow myself the opportunity to achieve my dreams. While I will have new learning experiences along the way, I will succeed because I have learned to fully honor, respect, and have faith in the true love and perfection that I AM."

You cannot lack that which is your essence. However, if you are unaware of what your essence is, you'll act out of this misunderstanding and experience the disharmony that results. Through the odyssey that is your life, you will eventually come to know that at your core you are complete, just as you are. When you've come to this understanding you will realize that you've always had the love you struggled to get from the world because you are this love. At this state of being rather than need this love you will give this love, freely, unconditionally, and endlessly.

Love is all that awaits you.

Beyond the false ideas of self-limitation and lack there is an elegant simplicity and beauty to life. The more you open to see this beauty and simplicity within yourself, the more fluid and peaceful life becomes. In this space of existence time dissolves into an endless moment where there is a connectivity and feeling of oneness with all things in the universe. You realize that in order to experience any thought as real you must first embody and become the creator of the thought.

For example, many people feel they need love and respect and look to "get" it from their world daily. They do not understand that you do not "get" love, you become loving by offering love to yourself and others, and then you are loved for it. You do not "get" respect, you become respectful by showing respect to your-self and others, and then you are respected for it. You do not "get" peace, you become peaceful by offering peace to your world and you remain peaceful because of it. The great paradox of faith is that you must express that you already have what you desire by giving of it first.

The love we give away is the only love we keep.

—*Elbert Hubbard*

The following are some of the most powerful creative state-ments you can make. Accepting and integrating these truths on a daily basis into who you are is a sign that you're well on your way to living the life of your dreams.

- "I AM matter and therefore I matter."
- "I AM worthy and have purpose in every moment of life."
- "I AM love and I AM loved."
- "I AM the creator of my experience of life."
- "I AM who I decide I AM."
- "I AM that I AM."

True peace and contentment in your life occurs when you reach a state of self-acceptance and love that is so complete that you are truly free of anybody's opinions and ideas about who you are except for your own. At this point you are free of anything hav-ing a negative effect on your state of mind. Nothing in your experience is judged or resisted. At this level of love there is no longer any room for fear. Even death is seen merely as a part of a process of transformation of energy and matter that has been occurring forever, with no beginning and no end.

Filled with a new transcendent awareness and understanding, you become a rock of peace and love. You have emerged from the shadow of darkness into light, as your spirit and soul hears the great message that has been coming to you during every waking moment of your experience: Unity and oneness is in all of the creation that surrounds you.

> The great sea has set me in motion
> Set me adrift
> Moving me like a weed in the river.
> The sky and the strong wind have moved the Spirit inside me
> Till I am carried away
> Trembling with joy.
>
> —*Uvavnuk, Inuit shaman*

When you are at peace, you see the truth that the divine nature of everything in existence is leading you to increase your awareness of oneness and love. The movement of this expansion is the inertia of all of the energy in matter. With each passing moment, your consciousness is expanding. You came forth from nothing to become something, and you will return to nothing and become something again. Expand, contract, expand, contract. This is the heartbeat of all of life in the universe.

Your reality is a journey of awareness that will ultimately lead you to an awesome and astonishing conclusion.

The heartbeat of your experience of life is eternally up to you. Go forth now and be more of who and what you truly are. Use your new awareness to live a full and enriching life. Use your understanding of perfection and unity to always choose love.

Use all of it to know peace, as you consciously create yourself anew as a fearless and faithful driver of the life of your dreams. You always have had access to the answers that would bring you peace. Now is always your moment of opportunity to act on these insights and experience a new you. As you claim the grace of awareness, you will experience more of the magnificence of the endless source of love that is you. **You will go forth in the world declaring with full appreciation of being, certitude of purpose, and infinite self-expressed love: "I AM!"**

The Question-and-Answer Process

This free-flow writing exercise can be used anytime you are ready to ask questions and get answers to any aspect of your life. When you follow this exercise with a true and pure intent, you will be astonished at how easily the requested information surfaces in your awareness. If you are in an elevated emotional state (either positive or negative), do not do this exercise. Wait until you are in a more balanced and calm state of mind. Mild emotional states are fine, however, intense emotional states are not conducive to the process.

Here is how the Question-and-Answer Process works.

1. Find a quiet place with no distractions (for example, phone, television, peripheral noise), where you know you won't be disturbed for at least one hour.

2. Set a relaxing mood in the room (for example, by adjusting the lighting, burning a candle, sitting in a comfortable chair at an uncluttered table or desk).

3. In an effort to be in the most contented state of mind possible, take a few minutes to relax, and take some deep breaths.

4. Concentrate on the most important question in your life right now.

5. Write this question as clearly and succinctly as you can at the top of a piece of paper.

6. The moment you finish the question, *immediately* begin writing down every thought that enters your mind. Do not stop writing until you have exhausted all of the possible answers that come into your mind as a result of asking your question.

7. Here's the key to the process. When you finish writing the question down, new thoughts will start to enter your mind. Do not judge them. Do not rationalize them. Do not think about them. Just write them down. No matter what thought pops into your mind, no matter how silly it sounds, how frightening it feels, or how ridiculous, humiliating, or unrelated it seems, write it down.

8. Do not look at what you have written or analyze it in any way until you are finished doing the exercise.

9. Write down every one of your thoughts until no more new thoughts enter your mind. That's when you are done.

If you followed the steps outlined above without blocking or thinking about what you were writing down, you may be amazed at what you learn. You may not like the answers, you may not be happy with what you have written, and you may not be ready to face the information; nonetheless, you will have your answers.

You can use this exercise for your questions any number of times. The more closely you follow the guidelines above, the more effective you will be at allowing the answers to your questions to be written down right in front of your eyes.

I AM Worksheet

This worksheet is designed to allow you to see the truth of whether or not you are "being" the person who will create what you truly desire to experience in your life. The perfection of our universe is that it mirrors back to us through the creative events of our daily lives our true thoughts about who we are.

Here's how to use the I AM Worksheet:

Step 1: Decide exactly what you want to create and experience in your life. For instance, a new job or career, romance, improved finances, physical fitness, enhanced creativity, specific material possessions, a different lifestyle, or finding a purpose. Focus on it until you can visualize the details as specifically as possible. Then write down your intended experience as clearly and concisely as possible in section 1 of the worksheet.

Step 2: Decide who you would have to "be" through your powerful I AM statements in order to attract and manifest this desired experience in your life. Then in section 2 of the worksheet write down the new I AM statements that correspond with your initial written intent. Examples: If you intend to experience meeting a soul mate: "I AM attractive." If you desire a new profession: "I AM capable of that exact job." If you desire to change your financial situation: "I AM disciplined and focused on managing my finances." If you want to acquire something new: "I AM going to have that item by such-and-such date." And if you want to improve your relationship with your kids: "I AM an involved and loving parent."

Step 3: In section 3 of the worksheet, write down at least five actions you could take that would declare, demonstrate, and express the truth of your new self-concept. These are the conditions that need to be created to manifest the desired experience. For example, if in section 1 you wrote down that you would like to be financially free, and in section 2 you wrote down the statement "I AM a disciplined money manager," your action plan will validate this thought with items such as: creating a daily and monthly budget, monitoring your spending, shopping more wisely, and cutting out debt spending.

After preparing this worksheet, if you do not follow your action plan, that is the self-evident truth that you have not embraced one or more of your new I AM statements. An old I AM mindset will produce the same undesired experiences in the future as it did in the past. You cannot fool the universe, as it will only allow you to experience what you believe yourself capable of experiencing. The actions you take or decide not to take will always offer you your true self-image. It is always up to you to initiate change in any moment.

1. Envision and desire it.
2. Declare that you are worthy and capable of it.
3. Become it by acting in accordance with the thought of it.

Use the I AM Worksheet to design as many creative experiences as you choose. Committing your desires to paper strengthens the energy of their manifestation. It also enables you to monitor if you have truly allowed yourself to create what you say you desire.

I AM WORKSHEET

1. Your desired experience (be very concise and specific):

_____

_____

_____

_____

_____

_____

2. I AM statements necessary to manifest the desired reality:

"I AM_____

_____."

"I AM_____

_____."

"I AM_____

_____."

"I AM_____

_____."

"I AM_____

_____."

3. List at least 5 actions that would validate I AM statement #1.

1._____

2._____

3._____

4._____

5._____

4. List at least 5 actions that would validate I AM statement #2.

1._____

2._____

3._____

4._____

5._____

5. List at least 5 actions that would validate I AM statement #3.

1._____

2._____

3._____

4. _____

5. _____

6. List at least 5 actions that would validate I AM statement #4.

1. _____

2. _____

3. _____

4. _____

5. _____

7. List at least 5 actions that would validate I AM statement #5.

1. _____

2. _____

3. _____

4. _____

5. _____

ACKNOWLEDGMENTS

There are so many people who in one way or another had an impact on me that led to this book in its final form, more names than I could put on this page alone. I AM grateful for all of their love and encouragement with this endeavor.

To Mark Douglas for cracking the door for me and for his friendship on the journey; Stephanie Gunning for her great editing and wonderful assistance; my agent, Amy Hughes, for her effort navigating this material to right where it was supposed to be; Sara Carder, my editor at Tarcher/Penguin, for her faith in the manuscript and great support for it, and Andrew Yackira for his adept editorial help.

Others whose help was integral in different ways are Eli Hammer, who offered unwavering belief, support, and friendship; Michael Fine, whose amazing outlook and personal journey continue to inspire me; Darren Weissman, Arielle Ford, Al and Diana Lyons, Karin Meyer, Samuel Arellano, Patrick Reid, Raleigh Pinsky, Scott Coyle, Steve and Susan Boren, Julianne

Wilfert, Betsy Wicklund, Dan Blew, Elese Coit, Tarasa Haase, Benjy Robins, Kenneth Kocialski, and Amy Silverman.

To my mother and father, Maureen and Ed, for their encouragement and love, especially my mother for always telling me as a child, "You can do anything you want when you put your heart and mind to it"; and my sister, Tracy, and brother, Gary, for their love and support and the inspiration they gave me by way of their own amazing faith-filled journeys through life.

And lastly, to the three bright lights of my life: my children, Sydney and Jeffrey, for your pure love and simply for just being exactly who you are, and to my wife, Beth, whose incredible and unconditional love, support, and faith are without end. I love each of you with everything that I AM.

About the Author

Howard Falco is a modern-day teacher and speaker on the nature of consciousness, reality, and the workings of the mind. After going through a sudden and dramatic expansion in awareness in 2002 that left him with a clear understanding of the origin of all human action and inaction, joy and suffering, he set out to honor the experience by sharing what he discovered.

Through his work he guides people to new insights regarding the power of self-awareness as it relates to removing fear, breaking through limits, and achieving a lifetime of peace. The intention is to offer the experience of a more positive and powerfully creative state of mind that leads to a new and more desired personal reality.

His biggest message is that regardless of the current circumstance we find ourselves in, we all have the same access to the understanding and wisdom that brings true inner peace. We only have to realize that each of us is both capable and worthy of experiencing it.

Howard grew up in Chicago, graduated from Arizona State University, and now lives in Arizona with his wife and two children. More information on his work and current schedule can be found on his websites: TruthSerum.net and Howard Falco.com.